Introduction to Computational Genomics

A Case Studies Approach

Nello Cristianini and Matthew W. Hahn

CAMBRIDGE
UNIVERSITY PRESS

CAMBRIDGE UNIVERSITY PRESS
Cambridge, New York, Melbourne, Madrid, Cape Town, Singapore, São Paulo

Cambridge University Press
The Edinburgh Building, Cambridge CB2 2RU, UK

Published in the United States of America by Cambridge University Press, New York

www.cambridge.org
Information on this title: www.cambridge.org/9780521856034

© N. Cristianini and M. W. Hahn

First published 2007

Printed in the United Kingdom at the University Press, Cambridge

A catalog record for this publication is available from the British Library

ISBN-13   978-0-521-85603-4 hardback
ISBN-10   0-521-85603-5 hardback

ISBN-13 978-0-521-67191-0 paperback
ISBN-10 0-521-67191-4 paperback

Contents

Preface   *page* ix
Prologue: In praise of cells   xi

Chapter 1 | The first look at a genome: Sequence statistics   1

1.1   Genomic era, year zero   1
1.2   The anatomy of a genome   3
1.3   Probabilistic models of genome sequences   5
1.4   Annotating a genome: statistical sequence analysis   10
1.5   Finding data: GenBank, EMBL, and DDBJ   18
1.6   Exercises   20
1.7   Reading List   21

Chapter 2 | All the sequence's men: Gene finding   22

2.1   The human genome sweepstakes   22
2.2   An introduction to genes and proteins   23
2.3   Genome annotation: gene finding   29
2.4   Detecting spurious signals: hypothesis testing   31
2.5   Exercises   37
2.6   Reading List   37

Chapter 3 | All in the family: Sequence alignment   38

3.1   Eye of the tiger   38
3.2   On sequence alignment   39
3.3   On sequence similarity   40
3.4   Sequence alignment: global and local   42
3.5   Statistical analysis of alignments   47
3.6   BLAST: fast approximate local alignment   50
3.7   Multiple sequence alignment   53
3.8* Computing the alignments   55
3.9   Exercises   60
3.10 Reading list   60

Chapter 4 | The boulevard of broken genes: Hidden
             Markov models   61

4.1   The nose knows   61
4.2   Hidden Markov models   63
4.3   Profile HMMs   67
4.4   Finding genes with hidden Markov models   69
4.5   Case study: odorant receptors   70
4.6* Algorithms for HMM computations   75
4.7   Exercises   77
4.8   Reading list   77

Chapter 5 Are Neanderthals among us?: Variation within and between species   78

5.1 Variation in DNA sequences   79
5.2 Mitochondrial DNA: a model for the analysis of variation   83
5.3 Variation between species   85
5.4 Estimating genetic distance   87
5.5 Case study: are Neanderthals still among us?   92
5.6 Exercises   94
5.7 Reading list   95

Chapter 6 Fighting HIV: Natural selection at the molecular level   96

6.1 A mysterious disease   96
6.2 Evolution and natural selection   97
6.3 HIV and the human immune system   98
6.4 Quantifying natural selection on DNA sequences   99
6.5 Estimating K_A/K_S 102
6.6 Case study: natural selection and the HIV genome   105
6.7 Exercises   108
6.8 Reading list   109

Chapter 7 SARS – a post-genomic epidemic: Phylogenetic analysis   110

7.1 Outbreak   110
7.2 On trees and evolution   112
7.3 Inferring trees   115
7.4 Case study: phylogenetic analysis of the SARS epidemic   120
7.5 The Newick format   126
7.6 Exercises   127
7.7 Reading list   127

Chapter 8 Welcome to the hotel *Chlamydia*: Whole genome comparisons   128

8.1 Uninvited guests   128
8.2 By leaps and bounds: patterns of genome evolution   129
8.3 Beanbag genomics   130
8.4 Synteny   135
8.5 Exercises   138
8.6 Reading list   139

Chapter 9 The genomics of wine-making: Analysis of gene expression   141

9.1 Chateau Hajji Feruz Tepe   141
9.2 Monitoring cellular communication   143
9.3 Microarray technologies   145
9.4 Case study: the diauxic shift and yeast gene expression   147
9.5 Bonus case study: cell-cycle regulated genes   155

9.6 Exercises   158
9.7 Reading list   158

Chapter 10 | A bed-time story: Identification of
                 regulatory sequences   159

10.1 The circadian clock   159
10.2 Basic mechanisms of gene expression   161
10.3 Motif-finding strategies   162
10.4 Case study: the clock again   167
10.5 Exercises   172
10.6 Reading list   172

Bibliography   173
Index   179

Preface

Nothing in biology makes sense except in the light of evolution.

Theodosius Dobzhansky

Modern biology is undergoing an historical transformation, becoming – among other things – increasingly data driven. A combination of statistical, computational, and biological methods has become the norm in modern genomic research. Of course this is at odds with the standard organization of university curricula, which typically focus on only one of these three subjects. It is hard enough to provide a good synthesis of computer science and statistics, let alone to include molecular biology! Yet, the importance of the algorithms typical of this field can only be appreciated within their biological context, their results can only be interpreted within a statistical framework, and a basic knowledge of all three areas is a necessary condition for any research project.

We believe that users of software should know something about the algorithms behind the results that are presented, and software designers should know something about the problems that will be attacked with their tools. We also believe that scientific ideas need to be understood within their context, and are often best communicated to students by means of examples and case studies.

This book addresses just that need: providing a rigorous yet accessible introduction to this interdisciplinary field, one that can be read by both biologically and computationally minded students, and that is based on case studies. It has evolved from a course taught at UC Davis, where both authors were doing research in computational biology, one coming from computer science (N.C.) and the other from biology (M.W.H.).

The authors had to understand the other's field in order to do research in the hybrid science of computational genomics. The goal of this book is to develop a simple, entertaining, and informative course for advanced undergraduate and graduate students. Based on carefully chosen case studies, the chapters of this book cover ten key topics that we feel are essential to a scientist conducting research in bioinformatics and computational genomics. We will be satisfied if at the end of this first course the reader is able to understand and replicate the main results from the classic papers in this field.

This book benefited from the input of many colleagues and students. In particular, many of the case studies have been based on projects developed by students, post-docs, and research visitors, as well as teaching assistants. In particular we want to thank Elisa Ricci, Tara Thiemann, Margherita Bresco, Chi Nguyen, Khoa Nguyen, and Javannatah Gosh. The authors have benefited from discussions with various outstanding colleagues, and it is difficult to list them all. However in particular we want to thank Linda Bisson, Stacey Harmer, Wolfgang Polonik, Dan Gusfield, Sergey Nuzhdin, Lucio Cetto, Leonie Moyle, Jason Mezey, and Andrew Kern. The first draft has been proof-read by various colleagues: Chris Watkins, John Hancock, Asa Ben Hur, Tom Turner, Quan Le, Tara Thiemann, Vladimir Filkov, and Rich Glor. N. C. acknowledges support from NIH grant R33HG003070-01.

The book's website contains the data, the algorithms and the papers used in the case studies, and much more. It can be found at the URL

www.computational-genomics.net

Bristol, Bloomington

Prologue

In praise of cells

- How cells work
- What is a genome
- The computational future of biology
- A roadmap to this book

The physicist Richard Feynman is credited with jump-starting the field of nanotechnology. In a talk at Caltech in December 1959, Feynman issued a famous challenge: he would pay $1000 to anyone who could write the entire *Encyclopedia Britannica* on the head of a pin. Feynman calculated that the size of the area was approximately 1/16 of an inch across (about 1.6×10^{-3} meters), and that in order to fit all 42 million letters of the *Encyclopedia* one would have to make each letter 1.0×10^{-8} meters across. It took (only) 26 years before the prize was finally claimed by a graduate student at Stanford University.

Now, consider the problem of having to write out the entire set of instructions needed to build and operate a human, and consider having to do so in each of the trillions of cells in the body. The entire human genome is 3.5 billion "letters" long, and each cell is only 2 microns (2×10^{-7} meters) across. (Actually, two complete copies of the genome are present in each cell, so we have to fit a bit more than 7 billion letters.) However all the organisms on earth overcome these packaging problems to live and prosper in a wide range of environments.

In the same 1959 lecture Feynman also imagined being able to look inside a cell in order to read all of the instructions and history contained within a genome. A few decades later the genomic era began – a time when technological advances in biology and computational advances in computer science came together to fulfill Feynman's dream. Bioinformatics and computational genomics make it possible to look inside a cell and read how an organism functions and how it got to be that way. This book endeavors to be a first course in this new field.

Why bioinformatics?

How are all forms of life related? What was the first cell like? How do species adapt to their environments? Which part of our genome is evolving the fastest? Are we descendents of Neanderthals? What genes are responsible for major human diseases? Why do we need new flu vaccines every year?

Modern biology is a goldmine of fascinating questions, and never before have we been so close to the answers. The main reason for this is the new, data-driven approach to biological investigation spawned by the availability of large-scale genomic data. The availability of these data has triggered a revolution in biology that can only be compared to the revolution in physics at the beginning of the twentieth century. The effects of this revolution have been felt in other fields of science, as well. Application of genomic technology to medicine, drug design, forensics, anthropology, and epidemiology holds the promise to improve our life and enlarge our understanding of the world.

Almost as important as this scientific revolution is the cultural revolution that has accompanied it. Many of the questions asked in modern biology can only be answered by computational analysis of large quantities of genomic data. Researchers in computer science and statistics have been recruited to this effort to provide both a conceptual framework and technological support. Biologists, computer scientists, and statisticians now work together to analyze data and model living systems to a level of detail that was unthinkable just a few years ago. The impact of this collaboration on biology has been invaluable and has lead to the new discipline of bioinformatics.

Soon, a new kind of scientist (with knowledge in computer science, statistics, mathematics, biology, and genetics) will arise. Most major universities have already started various types of degrees in bioinformatics and are drawing students with a wide range of backgrounds. The purpose of this book is to provide a first course in the questions and answers to problems in bioinformatics and computational genomics (because many people have preconceived notions of the term "bioinformatics," we use these two phrases interchangeably). We hope to provide the biology necessary to computational researchers – though we obviously cannot cover everything – and the algorithms and statistics necessary to biologists. All of this is in the hope of molding a new type of researcher able to ask and answer all (or almost all) of the questions in modern biology.

A bit of biology

One of the most fundamental questions, the one that underlies many others, is: How do cells work? For both unicellular and multicellular organisms, we want to know how cells react to their environment, how genes affect these reactions, and how organisms adapt to new environments. The general picture is known, but many of the details are missing. Modern biology aims to answer this question in detail, at a molecular level. Here we review some of the most basic ideas in biology to provide the minimum knowledge needed to conduct research in bioinformatics. We stress at the outset that biology is a field of exceptions: all of the generalizations and rules we introduce here will be wrong for some organisms, but covering all of the exceptions would take another book. Throughout the text, we have tried to note when there are important exceptions that bear on the examples given.

Every organism's dream (so to speak) is to become two organisms. An organism reproducing faster, or exploiting its environment more efficiently, rapidly out-competes its rivals for resources. This was the basic point made by Darwin and is vital to understanding the way cells and organisms work. The conceptual framework of evolution is the most fundamental aspect of biological thinking and allows us to organize and interpret all of the data we will be analyzing in this book. No analysis of the genetic differences between individuals in a species, or between different species, makes sense outside of an evolutionary framework. Over the 3.5 billion years life has been on this planet, organisms have become extremely streamlined and efficient, shaped to a large extent by the evolutionary process of natural selection. If we want to understand cells, we have to understand both the power and the limitations of natural selection.

Conversely, in order to understand natural selection, we also must understand much about basic biology.

There are two basic types of cells, those with and without nuclei (called *eukaryotic* and *prokaryotic* cells, respectively). These types of cells largely share the same fundamental molecular machinery, but prokaryotes are simpler, unicellular organisms (such as bacteria), while eukaryotes are often more complex and include both unicellular and multicellular organisms (such as fungi, animals, and plants).

Unicellular organisms are the simplest free-living things; their ability to interact with the environment, derive the energy and materials needed to continually fabricate themselves, and then eventually to reproduce is controlled by a complex network of chemical reactions. Even the individual cells that make up a multicellular organism must each perform thousands of such reactions. These chemical reactions (called metabolism as a whole) are the very essence of cellular life: a cell needs to process various nutrients found in its environment, to produce the components it needs to operate, and then to breakdown components no longer needed. These tasks are carried out via biochemical processes that can be finely controlled by the cell. Each reaction needs to be catalyzed (triggered) by specific proteins – special molecules produced by the cell itself. Many proteins are enzymes, a kind of molecule involved in nearly every activity of the cell. Other proteins are used as structural elements to build cellular parts, as activation or repression agents to control reactions, as sensors to environmental condition, or take part in one of the many other tasks necessary for cellular function. There are thousands of different proteins in each cell, often specialized to control one specific reaction, or to be part of a specific cellular structure. Producing these proteins not only requires the cell to obtain energy and materials, but also requires detailed communication between different parts of a cell or between cells. Much of the cellular machinery is devoted simply to ensuring the production of proteins at the right moment, in the right quantity, in the right place.

A protein is a large molecule formed by a chain of amino acids, which folds into a characteristic shape. The same 20 basic amino acids are used by all known organisms. The exact composition of the chain (which amino acids are in which order) determines its shape, and its shape determines its function – i.e. which reactions it will facilitate, which molecules it will bind to, etc. The need to produce thousands of proteins means that a cell must have a way to remember the recipe for each of them, as well as have a way to produce them at the right time.

A cell's most reliable way to pass on the recipe for making proteins is contained in its genetic material and is passed on to daughter cells at each division. The machinery for reading this information is one of the core components of all living things and is highly similar in all types of cells; the machinery itself is formed by a complex of enzymes, specified by the very instructions it must read! This self-referential, auto-poietic, aspect of life can be mind-boggling.

The genetic material used by cells is formed by molecules of DNA (deoxyribonucleic acid), which have a sequential structure that enables them to act as information storage devices. The way in which they store the recipe for proteins and the information needed to control their production will be discussed in Chapters 1 and 2.

The quest to understand the way in which DNA is used by organisms to pass on genetic instructions has spanned the last two centuries of biology. The initial steps were taken in 1859 by a Moravian monk named Gregor Mendel. Mendel discovered that genetic information is contained in discrete units (what we now call *genes*), passed from generation to generation. The second major step came in 1944, when a group in New York led by Oswald Avery showed that nucleic acids were the molecules used to encode this information. Finally, with the proposal of the structure of DNA by James Watson and Francis Crick in 1953, the mechanism for the replication and retrieval of information stored in a DNA sequence was found. What came in the years following these discoveries has been an incredible series of events, with biologists unraveling the exact way in which proteins are specified by DNA, and revealing how cells use genetic information to synthesize proteins.

The future of biology

Although the big picture came to emerge gradually in the last decades of the twentieth century, it also became increasingly clear that the size and complexity of organisms meant that a detailed understanding of their inner-workings could not be achieved by small-scale experiments. By the end of the century it became possible to automate the acquisition of this knowledge and thus to collect gigabytes of data in a short period of time. The invention of sequencing machines that can read the entire DNA sequence of a bacterium in only a day, and of a larger eukaryote in a month, as well as machines that can identify and quantify all of the genes active in a cell or a tissue, has ensured a steady flood of biological information for the foreseeable future. The analysis of these data promises to be the biggest challenge to biology in the twenty-first century.

The details of the roles played by different proteins in cellular reactions, how these reactions are organized into pathways (whereby the product of one reaction becomes the substrate of another reaction), and how pathways are organized into a complex network that must continually reproduce itself are now the questions that biologists can address. In addition, crucial questions concerning the way in which genes are responsible for differences between species, between individuals of the same species, and the role genes play in evolution can be answered by a large-scale analysis of the entire collection of genetic material contained within each individual.

But there are also many simpler questions that we still cannot answer satisfactorily: How many different proteins do organisms have? How is their production coordinated? How did they arise? What – if not proteins – does the majority of DNA in a cell code for?

It is the aim of this book to provide the tools necessary to answer the above questions by computational analysis of genomic data. The ten chapters of this book cover ten topics that we feel are necessary to a scientist conducting research in bioinformatics and computational genomics. Below we outline these ten topics.

A roadmap to this book

This book is divided into ten chapters, each presenting a major idea or task in computational genomics. On top of this structure, however, the book is divided into three main threads. Chapters 1–4 provide the tools necessary to annotate a genomic sequence – to describe the main features and structures found in a genome, and ideally also their function. In Chapters 5–8 we learn how to go from treating the genome as a static edifice to the dynamic, evolving object that it truly is. Finally, because each of the first eight chapters has looked solely at DNA sequences, we turn to the analysis of gene expression in Chapters 9 and 10, showing how this can be used to identify the function of genes and other structures found in the sequence. We show how the analysis of data produced by DNA microarrays differs from sequence analysis, but we also show how it can be synthesized with sequence data to reveal even more about the inner workings of cells. Below is a short synopsis of each of the ten chapters.

Chapter 1 describes the major features of a genome, by using as a leading example the first genomic sequence of a free-living organism ever obtained: that of the bacterium *Haemophilus influenzae*. We show how to retrieve and handle genomic data, perform some simple statistical analysis, and draw some conclusions. The chapter also introduces probabilistic models of biological sequences and important notation and terminology. After this chapter, the reader will be able to download and manipulate DNA sequences from public databases, and understand their statistical properties.

Chapter 2 explains what genes are and how to find them in a DNA sequence by locating particular regions called open reading frames (ORFs), again in the case of simple bacterial sequences. It also deals with other statistical signals to be found in genome sequences, and discusses a crucial point: how to assess the significance of a pattern and how to report it in terms of p-values. This chapter will enable the reader to find candidate genes and assess the significance of their findings.

Chapter 3 deals with the important algorithmic issue of assessing sequence similarity, the standard way to detect descent from a common ancestor. To this purpose the chapter introduces the technology of sequence alignment as an indispensable tool of bioinformatics, describing in detail the basic pairwise global and local alignment algorithms (based on dynamic programming) as well as briefly discussing multiple alignment and fast pairwise alignment algorithms (such as BLAST). This chapter will enable the reader both to decide if two given DNA sequences are likely to be homologous and to understand how to use common alignment tools.

Chapter 4 uses the example of odorant-receptor proteins to introduce another of the algorithmic workhorses of the field of bioinformatics: hidden Markov models (HMMs). This class of probabilistic models for sequences (and signals therein) underlies many modern gene finding algorithms, but is also used in sequence segmentation, multiple alignment, etc. The chapter demonstrates how to detect change points in the statistical make-up of biological sequences – a task that can help to identify features such as horizontally transferred segments of DNA – and how to summarize all the features of a protein family into a single probabilistic description. The reader should then be able to determine the likelihood that a protein belongs to a certain family, and therefore whether already annotated proteins can be used to assign function.

Chapter 5 introduces the issue of genetic variation among individuals of the same species, by comparing genetic sequences of Neanderthal and *Homo sapiens*. The fascinating question of our relation with these ancient inhabitants of Europe can be entirely answered by analyzing publicly available DNA sequences, and in the process we can learn about single nucleotide polymorphisms (SNPs) and statistical models of sequence evolution. In order to account for the probability of multiple substitutions in DNA sequences, and hence to obtain better assessments of the genetic distance between individuals, the Jukes–Cantor and Kimura 2-parameter models are derived. An analysis of DNA from various apes also hints at fundamental questions about human origins. The reader will be able to assess genetic distance between sequences, understand the mathematics behind the models, and apply this to real data.

Chapter 6 directly addresses the question of sequence evolution under natural selection. A sequence evolves with different rates if it is under selective pressure either to change or to stay constant, and this selective pressure can be quantified by using statistical models and appropriate algorithmic methods. The example of HIV evolution is used in this chapter to illustrate how certain locations of this fast-evolving virus change at a high rate – to keep ahead of the immune system of the host – while others are fairly conserved. Evolution of drug resistance follows similar patterns, and can be similarly detected. The reader will become familiar with the computation and the interpretation of the K_a/K_s ratio on real sequence data.

Chapter 7 takes these ideas one step further, showing how it is possible to reconstruct the evolutionary history of a set of homologous sequences by constructing phylogenetic trees. This is not just important for evolutionary studies, but can have many practical applications, as is demonstrated by the case study of the SARS epidemic. In late 2002 a virus jumped from an animal to a human in China, triggering a violent epidemic that spread to many countries before being identified and isolated. But its time, place, and host of origin, as well as the trajectory followed by the infection, can be reconstructed by an analysis of the viral genetic sequences. Simple algorithms and advanced concepts of phylogenetic analysis are presented, including the basic neighbor-joining algorithm, and more advanced and sophisticated approaches. These methods are also used to answer questions about the origin of HIV, and to address questions about early human evolution. The reader will learn to construct phylogenetic trees from sequence data.

Chapter 8 discusses one of the most recent applications of computational genomics, namely whole-genome analysis of multiple species. This involves large-scale genomic comparisons between different species, and if the species are chosen carefully it can provide a wealth of information, from helping to identify functional regions to reconstructing the evolutionary mechanisms that led to speciation. We take the complete genomes of different species of *Chlamydia*, an internal parasite of eukaryotic cells, and we see how they differ from major large-scale rearrangements of the same genes. We also identify syntenic regions, gene families, and distinguish between orthologous and paralogous genes. The reader will become familiar with the basic concepts and tools of whole-genome analysis.

In Chapter 9 we address another major source of genomic information: gene expression data collected by using DNA microarrays. Exploiting patterns found in this type of data requires using pattern recognition technology, a mix of statistics and computer science. We demonstrate the power of this approach to functionally annotate genomes by studying the case of yeast. A series of landmark papers in the late 1990s introduced the analysis of gene expression data by looking just at yeast genomes, and these studies are repeated in this chapter. The main tools are presented, including data processing, clustering, classification, visualization, and applied to the detection of cell-cycle regulated genes. The reader will be able to perform basic tasks of data mining with gene expression data, and to understand the assumptions underlying the most common algorithmic approaches.

Finally, in Chapter 10 we discuss the integration between expression and sequence information, by studying the circadian clock in plants. Genes regulated by the internal clock (as opposed, for example, to genes responding to external stimulations) can be identified by gene expression analysis, and clustered according to the time phase of their cycle. The upstream sequences of genes of equal phase can reveal common patterns, candidate binding sites for regulatory proteins. This analysis can be performed by the reader, illustrating how sequence and expression information can be synthesized, to annotate not only protein coding but also regulatory regions.

Many more important topics and approaches exist in computational genomics, but in order to make this introduction as gentle as possible, we have selected the above ten themes as representatives of the style of analysis typically found in this exciting scientific domain. More advanced approaches should be more easily accessible to the readers once they have become familiar with the contents presented in this book. Sections marked with a $*$ can be skipped at a first read.

Reading list

A general understanding of molecular biology, genetics, and evolution are all essential for researchers in computational genomics. This can be obtained in many introductory textbooks of biology, as well as in more specialized introductions to the field of genomics. The reader may refer to Brown (1999) and to Gibson and Muse (2004) for a general introduction to genomics and evolution, or follow the links in the book's website to online introductory material about molecular and cell biology. The lecture by Richard Feynman on nanotechnology can be found in the article Feynman (1960). The book's website:

```
www.computational-genomics.net
```

contains links to introductory articles and other online material.

Chapter 1

The first look at a genome
Sequence statistics

- Genomes and genomic sequences
- Probabilistic models of sequences
- Statistical properties of sequences
- Standard data formats and databases

1.1   Genomic era, year zero

In 1995 a group of scientists led by Craig Venter, at The Institute for Genomic Research (TIGR) in Maryland, published a landmark paper in the journal *Science*. This paper reported the complete DNA sequence (the genome) of a free-living organism, the bacterium *Haemophilus influenzae* (or *H. influenzae*, for short). Up until that moment, only small viral genomes or small parts of other genomes had been sequenced. The first viral genome sequence (that of phage *phiX174*) was produced by Fred Sanger's group in 1978, followed a few years later by the sequence of human mitochondrial DNA by the same group. Sanger – working in Cambridge, UK – was awarded two Nobel prizes, the first one in 1958 for developing protein sequencing techniques and the second one in 1980 for developing DNA sequencing techniques. A bacterial sequence, however, is enormously larger than a viral one, making the *H. influenzae* paper a true milestone. Given the order of magnitude increase in genome size that was sequenced by the group at TIGR, the genomic era can be said to have started in 1995.

A few months later the same group at TIGR published an analysis of the full genome of another bacterium, *Mycoplasma genitalium* – a microbe responsible for urethritis – and shortly thereafter the sequence of the first eukaryote, the fungus, *Saccharomyces cerevisiae* (or *S. cerevisiae*, baker's yeast) was published by other groups. The method created by the TIGR group to obtain and assemble genome sequences was itself a watershed; their method relied massively on computer technology, but is beyond the topics discussed here. In the years that followed, the number of complete genomes published grew enormously, and the pace is still increasing. Before the start of the genomic era the collection of publicly available DNA sequence data was distributed among scientists on magnetic tape, then on CD, and finally over the internet. Now whole genomes are available for fast download from a number of public databases.

After completing the sequencing of *H. influenzae*, Venter's group moved to what is the next phase of any genomic project: genome annotation. Annotation

Organism	Completion date	Size	Description
Table 1.1 Some of the genomes discussed in this book, with their size and date of completion			
phage phiX174	1978	5,368 bp	1st viral genome
human mtDNA	1980	16,571 bp	1st organelle genome
lambda phage	1982	48,502 bp	important virus model
HIV	1985	9,193 bp	AIDS retrovirus
H. influenzae	1995	1,830 Kb	1st bacterial genome
M. genitalium	1995	580 Kb	smallest bacterial genome
S. cerevisiae	1996	12.5 Mb	1st eukaryotic genome
E. coli K12	1997	4.6 Mb	bacterial model organism
C. trachomatis	1998	1,042 Kb	internal parasite of eukaryotes
D. melanogaster	2000	180 Mb	fruit fly, model insect
A. thaliana	2000	125 Mb	thale cress, model plant
H. sapiens	2001	3,000 Mb	human
SARS	2003	29,751 bp	coronavirus

involves various phases, and is never really complete. However, most sequencing projects perform at least two steps: a first (usually simpler) analysis, aimed at identifying all of the main structures and characteristics of a genome; then a second (often more complicated) phase, aimed at predicting the biological function of these structures. The first chapters of this book present some of the basic tools that allow us to perform sequence annotation. We leave the more advanced topic of sequence assembly – the initial step of constructing the entire genome sequence that must occur before any analyses begin – to more advanced courses in bioinformatics.

Now that we have the complete genome sequences of various species, and of various individuals of the same species, scientists can begin to make whole-genome comparisons and analyze the differences between organisms. Of course the completion of the draft human genome sequence in 2001 attracted headlines, but this was just one of the many milestones of the genomic era, to be followed soon thereafter by mouse, rat, dog, chimp, mosquito, and others. Table 1.1 lists some important model organisms as well as all of the organisms used in examples throughout this book, with their completion dates and genome length (the units of length will be defined in the next section). We should stress here that there were many challenges in data storage, sharing, and management that had to be solved before many of the new analyses we discuss could even be considered.

In the rest of this chapter we begin our analysis of genomic data by reproducing some of the original analyses of the early genome papers. We continue this aim in the following chapters, providing the reader with the data, tools, and concepts necessary to repeat these landmark analyses. Before we start our first statistical examination of a complete genome; however, we will need to summarize some key biological facts about how DNA is organized in cells and the key statistical issues involved in the analysis of DNA.

It is also worth emphasizing at this point that genomic data include more than just DNA sequence data. In 1995 a group of scientists led by Pat Brown at Stanford University introduced a high-throughput technology that enabled them to measure the level of activity of all the genes in an organism in a single experiment. The analysis of the large datasets generated by these experiments will be addressed in Chapter 9 and, partly, Chapter 10.

1.2 | The anatomy of a genome

As a first definition, we can say that a genome is the set of all DNA contained in a cell; shortly we will explain how some organisms actually have multiple genomes in a single cell. The genome is formed by one or more long stretches of DNA strung together into chromosomes. These chromosomes can be linear or circular, and are faithfully replicated by a cell when it divides. The entire complement of chromosomes in a cell contains the DNA necessary to synthesize the proteins and other molecules needed to survive, as well as much of the information necessary to finely regulate their synthesis. As we mentioned in the Prologue, each protein is coded for by a specific gene – a stretch of DNA containing the information necessary for that purpose.

DNA molecules consist of a chain of smaller molecules called *nucleotides* that are distinct from each other only in a chemical element called a base. For biochemical reasons, DNA sequences have an orientation: it is possible to distinguish a specific direction in which to read each chromosome or gene. The cell's enzymatic machinery reads the DNA from the 5′ to the 3′ end (these are chemical conventions of the nucleic acids that make up DNA), which are often represented as the left and right end of the sequence, respectively.

A DNA sequence can be either single-stranded or double-stranded. The double-stranded nature of DNA is caused by the pairing of bases. When it is double-stranded, the two strands have opposite direction and are complementary to one another. This complementarity means that for each A, C, G, T in one strand, there is a T, G, C, or A, respectively, in the other strand. Chromosomes are double-stranded – hence the "double helix" – and information about a gene can be contained in either strand. Importantly, this pairing introduces a complete redundancy in the encoding, which allows the cell to reconstitute the entire genome from just one strand, which in turn enables faithful replication. For simple convenience, however, we usually just write out the single strand of DNA sequence we are interested in from 5′ to 3′.

Example 1.1

Sequence orientation and complementarity. The sequence 5′ –ATGCATGC – 3′ is complementary to the sequence 3′ – TACGTACG – 5′, which would often be represented in print as simply ATGCATGC if no other directionality is provided.

We have seen that DNA molecules consist of chains of nucleotides, each characterized by the base it contains. As a result, the letters of the DNA alphabet are variously called nucleotides (nt), bases, or base pairs (bp) for double stranded DNA. The length of a DNA sequence can be measured in bases, or in kilobases (1000 bp or Kb) or megabases (1 000 000 bp or Mb). The genomes present in different organisms range in size from kilobases to megabases, and often have very different biological attributes. Here we review some of the basic facts about the most common genomes we will come across.

Prokaryotic genomes. As of the writing of this book, the Comprehensive Microbial Resources website hosted at TIGR contains the sequences of 239 completed genomes: 217 from bacteria, and 21 from archaea (including the two bacterial genomes from 1995 discussed above). This number is sure to have risen since then. Eubacteria and archaea are the two major groups of prokaryotes: free-living organisms without nuclei, a structure within cells that is used by eukaryotes to house their genomes. Prokaryotic organisms generally have a single, circular genome between 0.5 and 13 megabases long. *M. genitalium* has the smallest prokaryotic genome known, with only 580 074 bases. In addition to having relatively small genomes, prokaryotes also have rather simple genes and genetic control sequences; in the next chapter we will explore these issues in depth and see how they affect the identification of genes. Because of this simplicity and their fundamental similarities to more complex genomes, we will use many prokaryotic genomes as first examples for the analyses performed in the book. We will focus in particular on *H. influenzae*, *M. genitalium*, and *Chlamydia trachomatis*.

Viral genomes. Although viruses are not free-living organisms, an examination of viral genomes can be very informative. At least a thousand viral genomes have been sequenced, starting from what is considered the "pre-genomic" era, dating back to the late 1970s. Although these genomes are usually very short – between 5 and 50 kilobases (Kb) – and contain very few genes, their sequencing was a milestone for biology, and they enabled scientists to develop conceptual tools that would become essential for the analysis of the genomes of larger, free-living organisms. As they are an excellent model for practicing many of the methods to be deployed later on larger genomes, we will use them to illustrate basic principles. Their analysis is also highly relevant for epidemiological and clinical applications, as has been demonstrated in cases involving HIV and SARS (see Chapters 6 and 7). Peculiarly, viral genomes can be either single- or double-stranded, and either DNA- or RNA-based (we will learn more about the molecule RNA in the next chapter). Because of their small size, we can analyze a large number of viral genomes simultaneously on a laptop, a task that would require a large cluster of machines in the case of longer genomic sequences.

Eukaryotic genomes. The nuclear genome of eukaryotes is usually considered *the* genome of such an organism (see the next paragraph for a description of the organellar genomes contained in many eukaryotes). These nuclear genomes can be much larger than prokaryotic genomes, ranging in size from 8 Mb for some fungi to 670 gigabases (billions of bases or Gb) for some species of the single-celled amoeba; humans come in at a middling 3.5 Gb. Because of the large size of eukaryotic genomes, their sequencing is still a large effort usually

undertaken by consortia of labs; these labs may divide the work up by each sequencing different linear chromosomes of the same genome. Currently we have
sequences representing more than 50 different eukaryotic organisms, including
various branches of the evolutionary tree: the fungus, *S. cerevisiae* (baker's
yeast); the round worm, *Caenorhabditis elegans*; the zebrafish, *Danio rerio*;
important insects like the fruitfly, *Drosophila melanogaster*, and mosquito,
Anopheles gambiae; mammals such as humans, *Homo sapiens*, and mouse,
Mus musculus; and plants such as rice, *Oryza sativa*. The large size of such
genomes is generally due not to a larger number of genes, but rather to a
huge amount of repetitive "junk" DNA. It is estimated that only 5% of the
human genome is functional (e.g. codes for proteins), while at least 50% of
the genome is known to be formed by repetitive elements and parasitic DNA.
Added to the packaging problems associated with stuffing these large amounts
of DNA into each cell of a multicellular organism, most eukaryotes carry two
copies of their nuclear genome in each cell: one from each parent. We refer to
the single complement as the *haploid* set, as opposed to the *diploid* set of both
genomes.

Organellar genomes. In addition to these huge nuclear genomes, most eukaryotes also carry one or more smaller genomes in each cell. These are contained
in cellular organelles, the most common of which are the mitochondrion and
the chloroplast. These organellar genomes are likely the remnants of symbiotic prokaryotic organisms that lived within eukaryotic cells. We now have the
genome sequence of the mitochondria and chloroplasts of at least 600 species,
often with multiple whole genomes of different individuals within a species.
These genomes are usually only tens of thousands of bases long, circular, and
contain a few essential genes. There can be hundreds of each of these organelles
in a cell, with more copies resulting in more expressed products. Mitochondrial DNA (*mtDNA*) is particularly important for anthropological analyses,
and we will use it to discuss whole genome comparisons within humans in
Chapter 5.

1.3 Probabilistic models of genome sequences

All models are wrong, but some are useful.
(G. E. P. Box)

When the first whole genome of a free-living organism was sequenced in 1995,
much was already known about the general workings of cellular function, and
many things were also known about DNA sequences. Complete genomes of
small viruses and organelles were available in the early 1980s, as were the
sequences of individual genes from a variety of organisms. Although nothing
done before 1995 compared in scale with the problems that were to be addressed
when analyzing even a simple bacterial genome, earlier experiences provided
the basic statistical techniques that were to evolve into modern whole-genome
analysis.

A large part of the study of computational genomics is comprised of statistical methods. While any undertaking involving millions or billions of data

points necessarily requires statistics, the problem is especially acute in the study of DNA sequences. One reason for this is that we often wish to find structures of interest (such as genes) in sequences of millions of bases, and in many important cases most of those sequences do not contain biologically relevant information. In other words, the signal-to-noise ratio in genome sequences may be very low. As we will see, interesting elements are often immersed in a random background – detecting them requires sophisticated statistical and algorithmic tools.

As a first step, we need to have probabilistic models of DNA sequences. These will set a foundation for all of the analyses that follow in this book. We first define some of the basic concepts in probabilistic models of DNA, and then present a simple statistical framework for the analysis of genome sequence data. To highlight the usefulness of probabilistic models we continue the chapter by carrying out simple analyses of genome sequences. Later chapters will introduce increasingly sophisticated biological questions and the commensurate statistical methods needed to answer them.

Alphabets, sequences, and sequence space. Although we should not forget that DNA is a complex molecule with three-dimensional properties, it is often convenient to model it as a one-dimensional object, a sequence of symbols from the alphabet {A, C, G, T}. This abstraction is extremely powerful, enabling us to deploy a large number of mathematical tools; it is also incorrect, in that it neglects all the information that might be contained in the three-dimensional structure of the molecule. In this book we make this approximation, without any further warning, and will develop statistical and computational methods of analysis based on it.

Definition 1.1
DNA sequences and genomes: formal model. A "DNA sequence," **s**, is a finite string from the alphabet $\mathcal{N} = \{A, C, G, T\}$ of nucleotides. A "genome" is the set of all DNA sequences associated with an organism or organelle.

This representation of genomes as strings from an alphabet is very general, and enables us to develop statistical models of sequence evolution, sequence similarity, and various forms of sequence analysis. Some of them are discussed in this chapter.

Definition 1.2
Elements of a sequence. We denote the elements of a sequence as follows $\mathbf{s} = \mathbf{s}_1 \mathbf{s}_2 \ldots \mathbf{s}_n$, where an individual nucleotide is represented by $\mathbf{s}_i$. Given a set of indices K, we can consider the sequence formed by concatenating together the corresponding elements of **s** in their original order: $\mathbf{s}(K) = \mathbf{s}_i \mathbf{s}_j \mathbf{s}_k$ if $K = \{i, j, k\}$. If the set is a closed interval of integers, $K = [i, j]$, we can denote it also as $K = (i : j)$; the corresponding subsequence is the substring $\mathbf{s}(i : j)$. If it is formed by just one element, $K = \{i\}$, then this indicates a single, specific symbol of the sequence: $\mathbf{s}_i = \mathbf{s}(i)$.

Example 1.2

Elements of a sequence. In the DNA sequence **s** =ATATGTCGTGCA we find
s(3 : 6) =ATGT and **s(8)** = s_8 = G.

Remark 1.1

Strings and sequences. Note that what we call sequences in biology are usually called strings in standard computer science terminology. This distinction
becomes relevant in computer science when defining subsequences and substrings, two very different objects. What we call subsequences in this book –
contiguous, shorter sequences from a longer sequence – are called substrings in
computer science, where subsequences refer to non-contiguous sets of symbols
from a longer sequence.

Nearly all probabilistic sequence analysis methods assume one of two simple models, or variations thereof. They are the *multinomial* model and the
Markov model, and will be described below. As is often the case in modeling,
these do not need to mimic true DNA sequences in every respect. Their main
feature is that they capture enough of the properties of sequences while still being efficiently computable. In other words, they are the result of a compromise
between accuracy and efficiency.

Although in this chapter we deal with DNA sequences, in the rest of the book
we will find various other types of biological sequences; sequences defined on
different alphabets. All the algorithms we present will be valid for any type of
sequence, and we will often define them in terms of a generic alphabet Σ, so as to
preserve generality. The most common other types of biological sequences are
RNA sequences (also defined over a 4 letter alphabet, $\mathcal{N}_{RNA} = \{A, C, G, U\}$),
and amino acid sequences (based on a 20 letter alphabet

$$\mathcal{A} = \{A, R, N, D, C, Q, E, G, H, I, L, K, M, F, P, S, T, W, Y, V\}$$

and discussed further in Chapter 2). It is often also useful to define a sequence
of codons (see Chapter 2), where the alphabet is formed by all triplets from the
nucleotide alphabet $\mathcal{N}$ and will be indicated by $\mathcal{C} = \{AAA, \cdots, TTT\}$.

Multinomial sequence models. The simplest model of DNA sequences assumes that the nucleotides are independent and identically distributed (the
"i.i.d." assumption): the sequence has been generated by a stochastic process
that produces any of the four symbols at each sequence-position i at random,
independently drawing them from the same distribution over the alphabet $\mathcal{N}$.
This is called a *multinomial sequence model*, and is simply specified by choosing a probability distribution over the alphabet, $p = (p_A, p_C, p_G, p_T)$, where
the probability of observing any of the four nucleotides at position i of the
sequence **s** is denoted by $p_x = p(\mathbf{s}(i) = x)$ and does not depend on the position
i. This model can also be used to calculate the probability of observing the
generic symbol $x \in \Sigma$ (i.e. x within any alphabet).

For this model we could assume that all four nucleotides are of equal frequency ($p_A = p_C = p_G = p_T$), or that they are the observed frequencies from some
dataset. Our only requirement is that the distribution needs to satisfy the normalization constraint $p_A + p_C + p_G + p_T = 1$.

The multinomial model allows us to easily calculate the *probability* of a given sequence (denoted P), also called the *likelihood* of the data given the model (denoted $\mathcal{L}$). Given a sequence $\mathbf{s} = \mathbf{s}_1\mathbf{s}_2...\mathbf{s}_n$, its probability is

$$P(\mathbf{s}) = \prod_{i=1}^{n} p(\mathbf{s}(i)).$$

This is equivalent to multiplying together the probabilities of all of the individual nucleotides.

Of course we do not expect DNA sequences to be truly random, but having a model that describes the expectation for a randomly generated sequence can be very helpful. Furthermore, this simple model already captures enough of a sequence's behavior to be useful in certain applications, while remaining very easy to handle mathematically. Even finding violations of this simple model will point us towards interesting regions of the genome. We can easily test if this model is realistic by checking to see whether real data conform to its assumptions. We can do this either by estimating the frequencies of the symbols in various regions of the sequence – to check the assumption of stationarity of the independent and identically distributed (i.i.d.) probability distribution across the sequence – or by testing for violations of the independence assumption by looking for correlations among neighboring nucleotides. Regions that both change in the frequency of A, C, G, and T and where there are strong correlations among nearby symbols can be quite interesting, as we will show later.

Markov sequence models. A more complex model of DNA sequences is provided by the theory of Markov chains. In Markov chains the probability of observing a symbol depends on the symbols preceding it in the sequence. In so doing, Markov chains are able to model local correlations among nucleotides. A Markov chain is said to be of order 1 if the probability of each symbol only depends on the one immediately preceding it, and of increasing order as the dependency on past symbols extends over greater distances. We can think of the multinomial model as a Markov chain of order 0 because there is no dependence on previous symbols. How do we know which model to pick, or what order Markov model to pick? This is a problem of hypothesis testing, a topic we address in Chapter 2. For now, we will simply discuss the basic aspects of Markov models. (Markov chains are central tools in bioinformatics, and we will encounter them again in Sections 5.4.1 and 5.4.2).

Briefly, a Markov chain is a process defined by a set of states (in this case the symbols of an alphabet) and by a transition probability from one state to the next. The transition probabilities are organized in the transition matrix T. The trajectory of the process through the state space defines a sequence. This is represented in Figure 1.1.

The figure shows that, starting at any one of the four nucleotides, the probability of the next nucleotide in the sequence is determined by the current state. If we start at G, the probabilities of any of the four other nucleotides appearing next are given by p_{GA}, p_{GC}, p_{GG}, and p_{GT}. Moving to another nucleotide state means that there are new transition probabilities: if we moved to state A, these would be p_{AA}, p_{AC}, p_{AG}, and p_{AT}. In this manner, a Markov chain defines a DNA sequence. All of the transition probabilities are given by the matrix T,

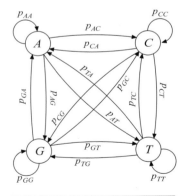

Fig. 1.1 The trajectory of a Markov chain process generates a sequence of symbols. Starting at any one of the four nucleotides, the probability of the next nucleotide in the sequence is determined by the current state.

and the probability for the start state is given by $\pi = (\pi_A, \pi_C, \pi_G, \pi_T)$, again with the obvious normalization constraint:

$$T = \begin{matrix} p_{AA} & p_{AC} & p_{AG} & p_{AT} \\ p_{CA} & p_{CA} & p_{CG} & p_{CT} \\ p_{GA} & p_{GC} & p_{GG} & p_{GT} \\ p_{TA} & p_{TC} & p_{TG} & p_{TT} \end{matrix}$$

$$\pi = \quad \pi_A \quad \pi_C \quad \pi_G \quad \pi_{T.}$$

The Markov model therefore no longer assumes that the symbols are independent, and short-range correlations can be captured (if the transition probabilities are all 0.25, we are again back at a multinomial model).

Example 1.3

Markov DNA sequence. Using the Markov chain defined by uniform starting probabilities (π) and the transition matrix

	to A	to C	to G	to T
from A	0.6	0.2	0.1	0.1
from C	0.1	0.1	0.8	0
from G	0.2	0.2	0.3	0.3
from T	0.1	0.8	0	0.1

$T = $ for the rows above.

we generated the following sequence:

ACGCGTAATCAAAAAATCGGTCGTCGGAAAAAAAAAAATCG

As you can see, many As are followed by As, Ts are followed by Cs, and Cs are followed by Gs, as described by our transition matrix.

The entries in the transition matrix are defined formally as follows:

$$p_{xy} = p(s_{i+1} = y | s_i = x).$$

This says that the probability of going from state x to state y is equivalent to the conditional probability of seeing state y given that it was preceded by state x. We generally define the probability of an entire sequence as a joint probability:

$$P(s) = P(s_1 s_2 \cdots s_n).$$

The computation of this probability can be greatly simplified when we can factorize it. In the case of multinomial models, the factorization is obvious: $P(s) = p(s_1)p(s_2)\dots p(s_n)$; for Markov chains (of order 1) it is only slightly more complicated:

$$P(s) = P(s_n|s_{n-1})P(s_{n-1}|s_{n-2}) \cdots P(s_2|s_1)\pi(s_1)$$

or

$$P(s) = \pi(s_1) \prod_{i=2}^{n} p(s_i|s_{i-1}) = \pi(s_1) \prod_{i=2}^{n} p_{s_{i-1}s_i.}$$

where $\pi(s_1 = x)$ represents the probability of seeing symbol x in position s_1. In other words, we exploit the fact that the probability of a symbol depends only on the previous one to simplify the computation of the joint probability of the entire sequence.

Table 1.2 | Basic statistics of the *H. influenzae* genome: the count of each nucleotide and its relative frequency. The total length of the sequence is 1 830 138 bp.

Base	Number	Frequency
A	567,623	0.3102
C	350,723	0.1916
G	347,436	0.1898
T	564,241	0.3083

1.4 Annotating a genome: statistical sequence analysis

There are various elements of interest in a genome sequence, and many of them will be discussed in various chapters of this book. For example, Chapter 2 will discuss the structure of genes, how we find them, and the way in which they are regulated. Here we examine simpler statistical properties of the DNA sequences such as the frequency of nucleotides, dinucleotides (pairs of bases), and other short DNA words. We will see that this preliminary description is of fundamental importance for genome annotation, as well as a stepping stone for further analysis.

Base composition. One of the most fundamental properties of a genome sequence is its base composition, the proportion of A, G, C, and T nucleotides present. For *H. influenzae*, we can easily count the number of each type of base and divide by the total length of the genome (performing both operations on only one strand of the DNA sequence) to obtain the frequency of each base. Table 1.2 shows the number of times each base appears in the genome, and its relative frequency (the total length, L, of the *H. influenzae* genomes is 1 830 138 bp).

We can see that the four nucleotides are not used at equal frequency across the genome: A and T are much more common than G and C. In fact, it is fairly unusual for all of the bases to be used in equal frequencies in any genome. We should point out that, while we have only counted the bases on one strand of the DNA molecule, we know exactly what the frequency of all the bases are on the other strand because of the complementarity of the double helix. The frequencies in the complementary sequence will be $T = 0.3102$, $G = 0.1916$, $C = 0.1898$, and $A = 0.3083$.

In addition to the global base composition of a genome, it is of interest to consider local fluctuations in the frequencies of nucleotides across the sequence. We can measure local base composition by sliding a window of size k along a chromosome, measuring the frequency of each base in the window, and assigning these values to the central position of the window. This produces a vector of length $L - k + 1$ that can be plotted, as seen in Figures 1.2 and 1.3 (with window sizes 90 000 bp and 20 000 bp, respectively).

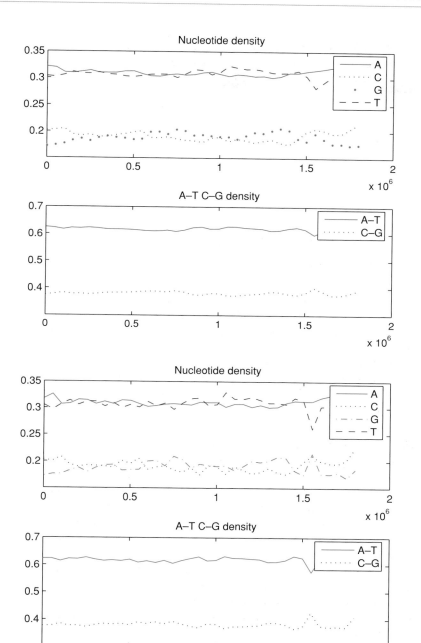

Fig. 1.2 Sliding window plot showing local fluctuations in the frequencies of nucleotides across the sequence of *H. influenzae* (with window size of 90 000 bp)

Fig. 1.3 Sliding window plot showing local fluctuations in the frequencies of nucleotides across the sequence of *H. influenzae* (with window size of 20 000 bp)

Of course, smaller window sizes reveal a higher variance in base composition, and larger windows may miss small regions with different base composition, so a trade-off is inherent in choosing k. Allowing k to vary reveals patterns at different scales, as shown in Figure 1.3. Both extremes may hide interesting patterns, and hence some exploration is necessary when choosing k.

Table 1.3	A comparison of overall GC content in three different organisms (Note that this quantity can vary significantly across species)
Organism	GC content
H. influenzae	38.8
M. tuberculosis	65.8
S. enteritidis	49.5

There is clearly quite a lot of variance in base composition along the genome of *H. influenzae*. This variation highlights a first important violation of the assumption of the multinomial model that nucleotides are drawn from an i.i.d. probability distribution. This distribution clearly changes along the chromosome.

Based on this statistical analysis, various other analyses can be performed: for example we may be interested in identifying positions in the sequence where the base composition changes, or in the variation of the joint frequency of some class of nucleotides ($C + G$ vs. $A + T$), and so on. This is the topic of the next few sections. We will also examine the frequency of dimers (pairs of letters, such as 'AT') and other short DNA words.

GC content. The analysis of frequencies of the four nucleotides performed above seems quite natural, but in fact is overly complex for most biological needs. What most papers report (and is all that is generally necessary) is the aggregate frequencies for C and G (called *GC content*) versus the aggregate frequencies for A and T (AT content). Given that these two quantities are required to always sum to 1, only the GC content is typically reported. The motivation for reporting simply the GC content is that – due to a number of chemical reasons – the content of G and C in a genome is often very similar, as is the content of A and T. In this way, only one value needs to be reported instead of four. Looking back at Table 1.2 we can see that this is exactly the case in the *H. influenzae* genome.

A simple analysis of GC content can reveal significant biological information. For example, in bacteria these frequencies are highly dependent on an organism's replication machinery, and can be very different from species to species (see Table 1.3 for some examples). Because of this, an analysis of GC content can be used to detect foreign genetic material that has been inserted into a genome by identifying locations where this content is different from the genomic average. It is indeed well known that a species may acquire subsequences from other organisms – such as viruses – in a phenomenon known as *horizontal gene transfer*. After completing each bacterial genome sequence, researchers look for horizontally acquired genes, and do so by scanning the sequence for regions of atypical base composition.

As an example, the *H. influenzae* genome contains a 30 Kb region of unusual GC content 1.56 Mb into the genome (positions in circular chromosomes are generally given relative to the site where DNA replication starts during cell division). We can see this region by plotting the GC content landscape of the *H. influenzae* genome, as seen in Figure 1.2, towards the right end of the plot. Examining that plot, we see that there is a short stretch of DNA from approximately 1.56 Mb to 1.59 Mb with a highly different GC content than the rest of the genome. This stretch is attributed to an ancient insertion of viral DNA into the *H. influenzae* genome. Further analysis (using methods developed in Chapters 2 and 3) could reveal the identity of these alien sequences and their most likely origin.

A natural next step for this kind of analysis is to have a method to automatically detect regions with statistical properties that are much different from the average, or that can define the boundaries between very different regions. We call this class of methods *change point analysis*.

Change point analysis. We would like to have a method to identify locations in the sequence where statistical properties, such as GC content, change. These locations, called change points, divide the genome into regions of approximately uniform statistical behavior, and can help to identify important biological signals. Change point analysis can be performed in various ways; one particularly effective approach based on hidden Markov models will be discussed in detail in Chapter 4. For now we limit our treatment to a very elementary approach to carry out change point analysis.

The most simple-minded strategy for finding regions of different statistical behavior involves setting a threshold value that distinguishes two such regions. If we cross this threshold between two windows, we have identified a change point. Of course setting this threshold is a statistical problem, as is the size of the window used. Both have to do with the probability of finding variation in random data, a question of hypothesis testing (which is discussed in the next chapter). For now, we will just give a simple example where the change point in GC content is quite obvious without the need for a statistical analysis.

Example 1.4
Variation in GC content of λ-phage. Bacteriophage lambda (λ) was one of the first viral genomes to be completely sequenced – in 1982 – and is 48 502 bases long. Phages are viruses that infect bacteria, and *bacteriophage lambda* infects the bacterium *E. coli*, a very well-studied model system. An analysis of the phage genome reveals that it is composed of two halves with completely different GC content: the first half $G + C$ rich, the second $A + T$ rich. This is a simple example of a change point in a genome, clearly dividing it into homogeneous regions of base composition (see Figure 1.4).

Remark 1.2
A physical property related to GC-content. An interesting difference between AT- and GC-rich regions is the energy needed to separate (denature) the two DNA strands: AT-rich regions separate at lower temperatures. Given this fact, it should come as no surprise that thermophilic organisms living in the extreme temperatures found in oceanic vents have very GC-biased genomes. It is thought that the difference in GC content in the *Bacteriophage lambda* genome may be due to the need to quickly denature the DNA that is inserted into the bacterial cell being infected.

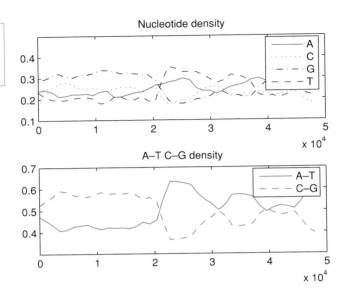

Fig. 1.4 Sliding window plot nucleotide density in lambda phage. Note the peculiar structure of this genome

k-mer frequency and motif bias. Another simple and important property of a genome to be measured is the frequency of all nucleotide words of length 2 (dinucleotides or dimers), or higher (trimers, *k*-mers). (Words of length *k* are often called *k*-grams or *k*-tuples in computer science. We stick to the biological convention of calling them *k*-mers.) We will also consider the algorithmic and statistical problems associated with finding unusual *k*-mers for small to moderate values of *k* (between 1 and 15). We define "unusual" *k*-mers as any words that appear more or less often than is expected. Bias in the number or position of these words can reveal important information about their function.

We count *k*-mers by again looking at only one strand of the genome. For a window of size *k*, we move along the sequence one base at a time – in an overlapping manner – and record every *k*-mer that we observe. This means that there are $L - k + 1$ possible *k*-mers in a sequence of length L (e.g. $L - 1$ dimers in a sequence of length L).

Example 1.5

2-mer frequencies in H. influenzae. The dinucleotide frequencies for *H. influenzae* are shown here:

	*A	*C	*G	*T
A*	0.1202	0.0505	0.0483	0.0912
C*	0.0665	0.0372	0.0396	0.0484
G*	0.0514	0.0522	0.0363	0.0499
T*	0.0721	0.0518	0.0656	0.1189

The left-hand side of the table shows the first nucleotide in the dimer, while the second nucleotide is listed across the top.

We can also plot the frequency of certain 2-mers of interest along a genome, as shown in Figure 1.5 for the dimer AT in *H. influenzae* (note this represents

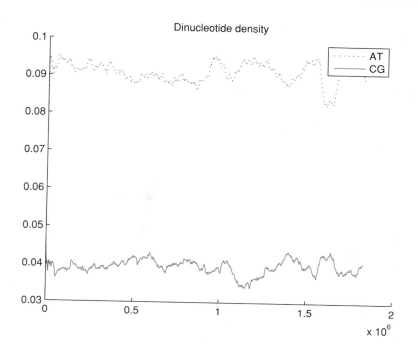

Dinucleotide density

Fig. 1.5 Dimer density for two dimers in *H. influenzae*, Sliding window plot of the frequency of the dimers at AT and CG along the *H. influenzae* genome

the frequency of the word AT, and not the joint A + T frequency; similarly the line CG represents the frequency of the 2-mer CG).

There are many examples of peculiar statistical biases in nucleotide usage, from the universal rarity of the dinucleotide TA to the low frequency of CGs (often called CpGs) in certain organisms such as vertebrates and thermophiles. In order to view these biases more easily, it is convenient to view a simple diagram – called a "chaos game representation" or "genome signature" – that color-codes the observed frequencies of the different *k*-mers. These representations make it easier to see patterns in the frequency of different words as we consider larger and larger values of *k*: for 1-mers there are 4 unique motifs, for 2-mers there are 16, and so on as 4 to the *k*th power. (See the book's website for an explanation of the plotting algorithm behind chaos game representations.)

Example 1.6
Frequent words in H. influenzae. As a further example, we can look for the most frequent 10-mers in the genomic sequence of *H. influenzae*. In this case we would find that the words AAAGTGCGGT and ACCGCACTTT are the two most frequent ones, both appearing more than 500 times. The significance of this finding, however, needs to be established by statistical and biological means.

Finding unusual DNA words. A simple statistical analysis can be used to find under- and over-representation of motifs, and can also help us to decide when an observed bias is significant (we will discuss significance of patterns in Chapter 2). We explain this idea for the case of 2-mers. The main point is to compare the observed frequency N of the given k-mer with the one expected under a background model, typically a multinomial model. The ratio between the two quantities indicates how much a certain word deviates from the background model, and is called the odds ratio:

$$\text{odds ratio} \approx \frac{N(xy)}{N(x)N(y)}.$$

If the sequence had been generated by a multinomial model, then this ratio should be approximately 1. Any significant deviation from 1, therefore, signals some effect of either the mutational process or of natural selection. Of course, deviations from 1 need to be larger than a certain threshold, and this depends on the number of motifs observed in each category, and on the length of the sequence. In Chapter 10 we will use a more realistic background model, given by a set of "reference" sequences, when assessing the significance of 9-mer motifs.

Example 1.7
Finding unusual dimers in H. influenzae. The observed/expected ratio for dinucleotide frequencies in the *H. influenzae* genome are:

	*A	*C	*G	*T
A*	1.2491	0.8496	0.8210	0.9535
C*	1.1182	1.0121	1.0894	0.8190
G*	0.8736	1.4349	1.0076	0.8526
T*	0.7541	0.8763	1.1204	1.2505

Clearly dimers deviating from value 1 are unusually represented, although the amount of deviation needed to consider this as a significant pattern needs to be analyzed with the tools discussed in Chapter 2. Note the difference with the table in Example 1.5, e.g. the dimer CC looks extremely infrequent in that table, but this analysis reveals that this is not likely to be a significant bias because the nucleotide C is low in frequency to begin with.

Biological relevance of unusual motifs. Under- or over-representation of nucleotide motifs may reflect biological constraints, either mutational or selective. Frequent words may be due to repetitive elements (a very common feature of certain genomes), gene regulatory features, or sequences with other biological functions. Rare motifs include binding sites for transcription factors (see Chapter 2), words such as CTAG that have undesirable structural properties (because they lead to "kinking" of the DNA), or words that are not compatible with the internal immune system of a bacterium. Bacterial cells can be infected by viruses, and in response they produce restriction enzymes, proteins that are capable of cutting DNA at specific nucleotide words, known as *restriction sites*. This discovery has immense technological applications, and was rewarded with a Nobel Prize in 1978 (to Werner Arber, Dan Nathans, and Hamilton Smith). The nucleotide motifs recognized by restriction enzymes are underrepresented in many viral genomes, so as to avoid the bacterial hosts' restriction enzymes.

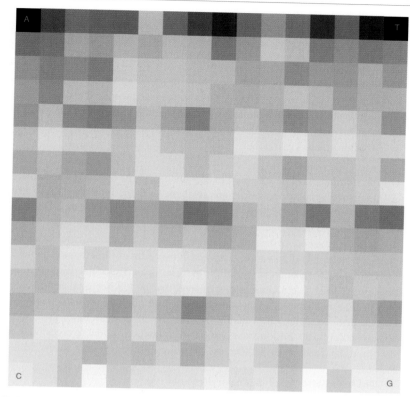

Fig. 1.6 This diagram (called a genome signature) color codes the observed frequencies of the different k-mers found in *H. influenzae*. There are four k-mers each of which is represented by a square in the figure. (Note that k-mers with the same prefix are located in the same quadrant.) This representation can help detect unusual statistical patterns in the sequence

One interesting feature of restriction sites is that they are often formed by palindromes, sequences that can be read the same way from both directions, like ABBA. However, for DNA sequences what we call palindromes are words that are complementary to themselves. For example, the sequence 5′-AACGCGTT-3′ is a palindrome because its complementary sequence, 3′-TTGCGCAA-5′, is read 5′-AACGCGTT-3′ by the cell.

Remark 1.3

Pattern matching versus pattern discovery. Notice that in computer science it is customary to distinguish between the tasks of pattern matching and pattern discovery. In the first case, one is given a specific word (or other pattern) and is requested to find all of its occurrences in the sequence. In the second case, one needs to discover a pattern in the sequence that has certain properties of interest (e.g. the most frequent, or the most surprising word). In bioinformatics the first case would correspond, for example, to finding occurrences of a given DNA motif, as opposed to discovering a new motif that characterizes a certain class of sequences. Algorithmic and statistical issues can be very different for the two tasks.

1.5 | Finding data: GenBank, EMBL, and DDBJ

Throughout this book, we will show how to apply all of our newly gained knowledge by analyzing real DNA (and protein) sequences. This means that we must be able to access, handle, and process genome sequence data. Most of the steps involved are now standardized and are part of the general toolkit of every bioinformatics researcher.

Online databases. The first step in any analysis is to obtain the sequences. All published genome sequences are available over the internet, as it is a requirement of every respectable scientific journal that any published DNA sequence must be deposited in a public database. The main resources for the distribution of sequences are the members of the International Nucleotide Sequence Database Collaboration. This is a consortium of three large databases: the DNA Database of Japan (DDBJ), the European Molecular Biology Laboratories (EMBL), and GenBank, sponsored by the US National Institutes of Health. These databases collect and exchange all publicly available DNA sequence data, and make it available for free. As of August 2005, there were approximately 100 billion bases of DNA sequences collectively stored in the three databases (just a little less than the number of stars in the Milky Way).

The web addresses of the major databases are:

GenBank	www.ncbi.nlm.nih.gov
EMBL	www.ebi.ac.uk
DDBJ	www.ddbj.nig.ac.jp

Sequences in GenBank are each identified by an *accession number*, a number associated with only that single sequence. Each sequence also comes with a certain amount of meta-data (data about data, or annotation) – such as the species name of the organism sequenced – that can be very useful. In Chapter 3 we will see how one can also search some databases by sequence similarity, rather than by using accession numbers. Here are a few examples of accession numbers and the sequences they reference:

AF254446	*Homo sapiens neanderthalensis* mitochondrial D-loop, hypervariable region I
NC_001416	*Bacteriophage lambda*, complete genome
NC_000907	*Haemophilus influenzae* Rd KW20, complete genome
NC_000908	*Mycoplasma genitalium* G-37, complete genome
NC_001807	*Homo sapiens* mitochondrion, complete genome

Data formats and annotation. There are several formats in which a sequence and its annotation can be given. EMBL, GenBank, DDBJ, and other repositories all use their own standard, and a number of formats not associated with any database (but usually associated with a sequence analysis program) are also considered standard. One of these is called *FASTA* (pronounced "fast A"). It is commonly used to encapsulate sequence information along with a very limited amount of information about the sequence.

The format consists of a first line, designated with the ">" symbol, followed by the annotation, which can be in any format so long as it is not interrupted by a line break. Sequence information begins on the next line, and all subsequent lines under that until another ">" symbol is present as the first character.

Example 1.8

A sequence in FASTA format. This is a small DNA sequence in FASTA format. It belongs to the remains of a Neanderthal found in Russia. We will use this sequence in Chapter 5 to study human origins. When more than one sequence need to be represented, they are simply concatenated one under the other, in the same format.

```
>Homo sapiens neanderthalensis mitochondrial D-loop, HVR I
CCAAGTATTGACTCACCCATCAACAACCGCCATGTATTTCGTACATTACTGCCAGCCACCATGAATATTGTACAG
TACCATAATTACTTGACTACCTGTAATACATAAAAACCTAATCCACATCAACCCCCCCCCCCCCATGCTTACAAGC
AAGCACAGCAATCAACCTTCAACTGTCATACATCAACTACAACTCCAAAGACACCCTTACACCCACTAGGATATC
AACAAACCTACCCACCCTTGACAGTACATAGCACATAAAGTCATTTACCGTACATAGCACATTATAGTCAAATCC
CTTCTCGCCCCCATGGATGACCCCCCTCAGATAGGGGTCCCTTGA
```

The FASTA format is accepted by most sequence analysis software, and is provided by most online sequence databases. However, the amount of annotation it allows is limited, and other standards are used when one wants to convey more meta-information.

A GenBank entry contains various sections, the main ones of which are: LOCUS, which identifies that sequence, followed by a short DEFINITION of the sequence and a unique ACCESSION number. The accession number is what really identifies the sequence in a stable way. It is reported in scientific publications dealing with that sequence, and can be used to cross-reference with other databases. The SOURCE and ORGANISM fields identify the biological origin of the sequence. The REFERENCE field contains article references relevant to the sequence; more than one reference can be listed. The FEATURES section contains basic information about the location and definition of various elements of interest in the sequence (such as regulatory sequences). The SEQUENCE section is the main one, and lists all of the nucleotides. The sequences are organized in lines containing six blocks of ten bases each, separated by a space, and numbered for convenience as shown in the following example. The symbols // signal the end of the entry.

Example 1.9

A sequence in GenBank format. The short Neanderthal sequence shown above in FASTA format looks like this in GenBank format:

```
LOCUS AF254446 345 bp DNA linear PRI 11-MAY-2000
DEFINITION Homo sapiens neanderthalensis mitochondrial D-loop,
hypervariable region I.
ACCESSION AF254446
SOURCE mitochondrion Homo sapiens neanderthalensis
```

```
ORGANISM Homo sapiens neanderthalensis
Eukaryota; Metazoa; Chordata; Craniata; Vertebrata; Euteleostomi;
Mammalia; Eutheria; Primates; Catarrhini; Hominidae; Homo.
REFERENCE 1 (bases 1 to 345)
AUTHORS Ovchinnikov,I.V., Gotherstrom, A., Romanova, G.P., Kharitonov, V.M.,
Liden, K. and Goodwin, W.
TITLE Molecular analysis of Neanderthal DNA from the northern Caucasus
JOURNAL Nature 404 (6777), 490-493 (2000)
MEDLINE 20222552
PUBMED 10761915
FEATURES Location/Qualifiers
source 1..345
/organism = "Homo sapiens neanderthalensis"
/organelle = "mitochondrion"
/mol_type = "genomic DNA"
/sub_species = "neanderthalensis"
/db_xref = "taxon:63221"
/country = "Russia: Southern Russia, Mezmaiskaya Cave"
D-loop 1..345
/note = "hypervariable region I"
ORIGIN
1 ccaagtattg actcacccat caacaaccgc catgtatttc gtacattact gccagccacc
61 atgaatattg tacagtacca taattacttg actacctgta atacataaaa acctaatcca
121 catcaacccc ccccccccat gcttacaagc aagcacagca atcaaccttc aactgtcata
181 catcaactac aactccaaag acacccttac acccactagg atatcaacaa acctacccac
241 ccttgacagt acatagcaca taaagtcatt taccgtacat agcacattat agtcaaatcc
301 cttctcgccc ccatggatga ccccccctcag ataggggtcc cttga
//
```

Remark 1.4
Standard nucleotide alphabet. The sequences found in all DNA repositories are
written using a standard nucleotide alphabet. Symbols also exist for ambiguous
nucleotides (positions in the sequence that are not clearly one base or another,
due for example to sequencing uncertainties). The most common symbols are
the following:

A	Adenine	N	aNy base
C	Cytosine	R	A or G (puRine)
G	Guanine	Y	C or T (pYrimidine)
T	Thymine	M	A or C (aMino)

1.6 Exercises

(1) Download from GenBank the complete genomic sequence of *Bacterio-phage lambda*, accession number NC_001416, and analyze its GC content
with various choices of window size.

(2) Compare statistical properties of human and chimp complete mitochondrial DNA (respectively NC_001807 and NC_001643).

(3) Find unusual dimers in rat mitochondrial DNA (NC_001665).

1.7 Reading list

The molecular structure of DNA was elucidated by Watson and Crick and published in 1953 (Watson and Crick, 1953). The first wave of genome sequences appeared in the early 1980s and included small phages and viruses, mostly based on Fred Sanger's work (Sanger *et al.*, 1982), (Sanger *et al.*, 1978), as well as mitochondrial genomes (Anderson *et al.*, 1981; Bibb *et al.*, 1981).

The second wave of genomes included prokaryotes and small eukaryotes, the first free-living organisms ever sequenced, and started in the mid 1990s. The paper (Fleischmann *et al.*, 1995) reports the sequencing and basic statistical analysis of *H. influenzae*'s genome, and is a recommended reading for this course, as is the paper (Fraser *et al.*, 1995) presenting the sequence of *M. genitalium*. Many of the genomic properties discussed in this chapter are addressed in those papers. The article of Blattner *et al.* (1997) reports the sequencing and analysis of *E. coli*'s genome, and that of Goffeau *et al.* (1996) the first eukaryote, the fungus *S. cerevisiae*.

The third wave of genome sequences, starting in the year 1998, includes multicellular organisms. The complete sequence of *C. elegans* was the first to be completed, followed by others including the human genome, published by two competing groups in papers which appeared simultaneously in *Science* and *Nature* (Consortium, 2001; Venter, 2001). The genomes of mouse, rat, chicken, dog, cow, chimp followed at ever-increasing pace.

A general discussion of statistical properties of genomic sequences can be found in Karlin *et al.* (1998), including many of the concepts presented in this chapter. A description of GenBank can be found in the article Benson *et al.* (2004). A discussion of the biological facts needed to understand this chapter can be found in Brown (1999) and Gibson and Muse (2004), including horizontal gene transfer, DNA structure, and general cell biology.

Links to these and many more papers, as well as to data and software for the exercises and all the examples, can be found on the book's website:

www.computational-genomics.net

Chapter 2

All the sequence's men
Gene finding

- Genes and proteins
- Gene finding and sequences
- Statistical hypothesis testing

2.1 | The human genome sweepstakes

In May of 2003 it was announced that Lee Rowen of the Institute for Systems Biology in Seattle, Washington was the winner of GeneSweep, an informal betting pool on the number of genes contained in the human genome. Rowen's guess of 25 947 won her half of the $1200 pool and a signed copy of James Watson's book, *The Double Helix*. GeneSweep had been created in 2000 by Ewan Birney of the European Bioinformatics Institute just as large pieces of the genome were being completed; because of the increasing amount of sequence becoming available, the cost of bets rose from $1 in 2000, to $5 in 2001, to $20 in 2002. One of the most surprising things about Rowen's winning guess was that it was almost certainly 3 000 genes off the mark – above the true number of genes! Researchers had placed wagers on figures as high as 300 000 genes, with only three sub-30 000 guesses. This number of genes put humans below the two plants that have been sequenced and barely above the worm, *C. elegans*.

Though the draft sequence of the human genome was published in 2001, nailing down exactly how many genes it contained turned out to be a tricky proposition. Genes are what make proteins and other biological molecules that are necessary for life, but they are not marked in any physical way in the genome. Rather, they are relatively short stretches of DNA that the cellular machinery must find and read. Because of this lack of obvious signposts marking off genes ("obvious" to us – the cell finds genes very easily), computational methods are needed to find and identify them. Without these methods researchers would be stuck sorting through 3.5 Gb (3.5 billion base pairs) of As, Cs, Gs, and Ts in order to settle the winner of GeneSweep. But even the best gene-finding algorithms have many problems identifying genes in the human genome.

This chapter addresses the computational challenge of finding genes in a genome, a key step in annotation; for simplicity we focus on the much easier problem of finding genes in prokaryotes. Sequenced genomes contain as few as 500 genes – in the bacterium *Mycoplasma genitalium* – to upwards of 30 000 genes in a number of different plant and animal species. Knowing what genes look like, how to find candidate genes in a genome, and how to decide which of these candidates are actual genes will take up the majority of our discussion. While finding complex eukaryotic genes requires commensurately complex methods, finding prokaryotic genes turns out to be a relatively simple task once we learn what to look for (we introduce the computational and statistical methods needed for eukaryotic gene finding in Chapter 4). By the end of this chapter we will be able to identify with high confidence almost all of the genes in a prokaryotic genome.

2.2 | An introduction to genes and proteins

We saw in the Prologue that all cells need to produce the right molecules at the right time to survive. Their life is a continuous balancing act that requires them to maintain relatively constant internal conditions in the face of variation in the external environment. This constancy is achieved by constantly correcting the internal chemical environment to compensate for external change. For multicellular organisms, it is also necessary to orchestrate the growth and development of an individual from a tiny single-celled embryo to an enormous trillion-celled adult. In order to do all of this, each cell directs the production of thousands of specific proteins that each in turn control specific chemical reactions. Here we briefly review how the production of proteins and other necessary molecules is accomplished by a cell. If we understand better how a cell finds genes, it will make our job much easier.

What are proteins? Proteins are perhaps the most crucial piece in the cellular puzzle. They are molecules used for many tasks, from internal communication to the bricks-and-mortar of cells themselves. Some proteins (called degradases) are used to cut apart molecules no longer needed by the cell, while others (called ligases) are used to join molecules together. In humans, a protein called hemoglobin carries oxygen in red blood cells, while hormones such as insulin are proteins used to communicate between organs. For the first half of the twentieth century, many people even thought that proteins would be the carriers of genetic information.

For all their sophistication, it is perhaps surprising that all proteins are formed from chains of simpler molecules called *amino acids* (or AAs for short). Proteins are macromolecules, made by stringing together a chain of amino acids. A typical protein contains 200–300 amino acids, but some are much smaller (30–40 amino acids) and some are much larger (the largest ones reaching tens of thousands of amino acids). Proteins can thus be read as one-dimensional objects, but do not have a linear form in the cell: the amino acids chain rapidly folds itself into the three-dimensional shape that ultimately determines its function. The final shape of a protein is specified by the exact identity and order of the amino acids in the chain, and is largely the result of atomic interactions between amino acids and with the cellular medium (which is mostly water). Even small errors in the amino acid sequence can result in altered protein shape and performance, while major disruptions to their structure are likely to completely abolish function.

| Table 2.1 | The 20 amino acids and their standard symbols |

A	Alanine	L	Leucine
R	Arginine	K	Lysine
N	Asparagine	M	Methionine
D	Aspartic acid	F	Phenylalanine
C	Cysteine	P	Proline
Q	Glutamine	S	Serine
E	Glutamic acid	T	Threonine
G	Glycine	W	Tryptophan
H	Histidine	Y	Tyrosine
I	Isoleucine	V	Valine

Remark 2.1

On protein folding. Protein folding describes the process of producing a three-dimensional protein from a chain of amino acids, and the computational task of predicting this three-dimensional structure based on the AA sequence, called "protein fold prediction," is a challenging one. While the cell seems to fold proteins easily and consistently, it has so far largely eluded our modeling efforts. Though we cannot reliably predict the exact shape of a protein based solely on its sequence, protein fold prediction is a classical topic in bioinformatics; it will not be discussed in this introductory book.

There are only 20 amino acids used to form proteins (Table 2.1). Like the 5′ to 3′ orientation of a string of DNA, amino acid sequences also have an orientation: N-terminus to C-terminus. We will see shortly that the directionality of a gene's DNA sequence maps directly on to the directionality of its resulting protein sequence.

The number of possible proteins is enormous. If we assume that all proteins are just long 400 amino acids long, we can create 20^{400} different proteins. This number is huge (larger than 1 with 520 zeros behind it), and is more than sufficient to account for the total number of existing proteins on earth.

Definition 2.1

Amino acid alphabet. As with DNA sequences, we will model proteins as strings from a finite alphabet. This representation neglects much of the crucial structural information, but also allows for powerful computational and statistical techniques to be employed. The statistical analysis of substrings within amino acid sequences is also as well developed as the one seen in Chapter 1 for DNA strings. For amino acid sequences (also called polypeptides) we use the alphabet

$$\mathcal{A} = \{A, R, N, D, C, Q, E, G, H, I, L, K, M, F, P, S, T, W, Y, V\},$$

which directly represents the 20 molecules listed in in Table 2.1. Each of them also has unique physical properties, but these will not be discussed until Chapter 4.

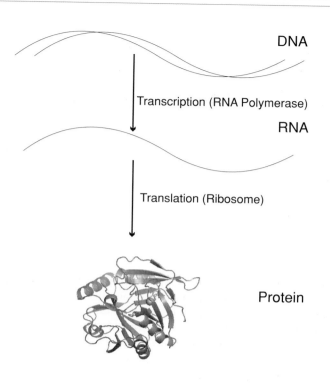

DNA

Transcription (RNA Polymerase)

RNA

Translation (Ribosome)

Protein

Fig. 2.1 An illustration of the central dogma: a gene is first transcribed into an mRNA sequence, then translated into a protein. The amino acid sequence of the protein folds to acquire its three-dimensional structure and hence its functionality

Example 2.1
Sequence of an enzyme in H. influenzae. This is part of the amino acid sequence of the protein manganese-dependent superoxide dismutase in *H. influenzae*:

```
HFDAQTMEIHHSKHHQAYVNNANAALEGLPAELVEMYPGHLISNLDKIPA
EKRGALRNNAGGHTNHSLFWKSLKKGTTLQGALKDAIERDFGSVDAFKAE
FEKAAATRFGSGWAWLVLTAEGKLAVVSTANQDNPLMGKEVAGCEGFPLL
```

From genes to proteins. The simplest way to explain how proteins are made – ignoring many details and condensing complicated cellular reactions – is a simple diagram that shows what is known as the *central dogma*:

DNA → RNA → Protein.

In words, the central dogma states that "DNA makes RNA makes Proteins" (which then helps to make DNA again). While the central dogma is not exactly right, it is right so much of the time that scientists are often rewarded with Nobel Prizes for showing where it is wrong. (*Prions*, the auto-replicating proteins responsible for Mad Cow disease, are one such exception to the dogma that led to a Nobel Prize for their discoverer, Stanley Prusiner of the University of California, San Francisco.) Figure 2.1 illustrates the main phases of the process.

Although the basic method for the production of proteins is the same in all forms of life, the complexity of the process can be quite variable. In this chapter we focus on idealized genes that share characteristics common to all systems, with examples largely taken from prokaryotic organisms. We should also state up-front that not all genes encode proteins – sometimes RNA is the end-product required. We focus for now solely on protein-coding genes.

Transcription and translation. The process of going from a gene encoded in DNA to a protein made up of amino acids is divided conceptually into two steps: *transcription* (DNA→RNA) and *translation* (RNA→Protein).

Let us work backwards for a moment and consider the cellular machine for making proteins, called the *ribosome*. The ribosome can take a sequence of nucleotides (RNA, as we will see) and *translate* this string into a string of amino acids. Since the ribosome cannot work directly from the double-stranded DNA sequence found in chromosomes, the cell must create a workable copy of this DNA that can be delivered to the ribosome. This is where RNA comes in. For physical reasons that we need not dwell upon, the ribosome has a much easier time translating RNA strings into amino acid strings; so the cell *transcribes* the DNA encoding genes into messenger RNA (mRNA), which it then sends on to the ribosome. Hence the two steps of transcription and translation.

The mRNA sequence transcribed is a faithful copy of the DNA sequence: it has a one-to-one correspondence to it and the same $5'$ to $3'$ orientation. (Important exception: RNA uses the nucleotide uracil, U, in place of thymine, T.) This mRNA sequence is then translated by the ribosome to produce a colinear sequence of amino acids. However, things are now a bit more complicated than a simple one-to-one mapping; RNA has four symbols (A, C, G, and U), while there are 20 different amino acids. It is therefore not possible to specify a protein using a one-to-one, nucleotide-to-AA encoding. A more abstract code is needed, and the discovery of how this code works has had important implications for our understanding of gene function, gene failure, and gene finding.

The genetic code. What is the minimum length of a nucleotide string necessary to specify 20 amino acids? We have already seen that a 1-nucleotide code only allows us to specify four amino acids (4^1); likewise a 2-nucleotide code only allows for the specification of 16 amino acids (4^2); but a 3-nucleotide code allows for 64 amino acids (4^3). Every organism on earth uses such a 3-nucleotide code, with each 3-nucleotide unit referred to as a *codon*. By using what is effectively a look-up table, every cell can translate codons into amino acids (or into special punctuation called *stop codons*), and can always succeed in obtaining the amino acid sequence specified by a gene. This look-up table is called the genetic code, and can be seen in Table 2.2.

The genetic code was discovered by the joint efforts of Robert Holley, Gobind Khorana, Marshall Nirenberg, and many others (though the three we have named won the Nobel Prize in 1968 for their work). While we show here what is known as the "universal" genetic code, it is nothing of the sort (another example of our rule that, in biology, every rule has important exceptions). While nearly all organisms use this genetic code, there are a number of instances where slight variants of this code are used; the difference in these codes is generally just the mapping of one or a few codons to different amino acids. The human mitochondria uses one such alternative genetic code, and this will be relevant in the Exercises section at the end of this chapter.

Table 2.2 The standard genetic code

	A		G		C		T	
A	AAA	K	AGA	R	ACA	T	ATA	I
	AAG	K	AGG	R	ACG	T	ATG	M
	AAC	N	AGC	S	ACC	T	ATC	I
	AAT	N	AGT	S	ACT	T	ATT	I
G	GAA	E	GGA	G	GCA	A	GTA	V
	GAG	E	GGG	G	GCG	A	GTG	V
	GAC	D	GGC	G	GCC	A	GTC	V
	GAT	D	GGT	G	GCT	A	GTT	V
C	CAA	Q	CGA	R	CCA	P	CTA	L
	CAG	Q	CGG	R	CCG	P	CTG	L
	CAC	H	CGC	R	CCC	P	CTC	L
	CAT	H	CGT	R	CCT	P	CTT	L
T	TAA	*	TGA	*	TCA	S	TTA	L
	TAG	*	TGG	W	TCG	S	TTG	L
	TAC	Y	TGC	C	TCC	S	TTC	F
	TAT	Y	TGT	C	TCT	S	TTT	F

Because of the many-to-one mapping of codons to amino acids, there is some redundancy built into the genetic code (for example, all four codons starting with AC code for the amino acid threonine). Nevertheless, because we always go from RNA to protein, the specification is unambiguous.

Example 2.2

The genetic code. In this example we see how a DNA sequence can be organized into codons to specify an amino acid sequence. Note that different codons can specify the same amino acid.

DNA	CTT	GTG	CCC	GGC	TGC	GGC	GGT	TGT	ATC	CTG
Protein	L	V	P	G	C	G	G	C	I	L

A wonderful summary of the genetic code was given by Francis Crick in 1962 as part of his own Nobel Prize acceptance speech. It should be noted, however, that the deciphering of the code was far from complete in 1962 – Crick was making educated guesses about many of these points:

At the present time, therefore, the genetic code appears to have the following general properties:

(1) Most if not all codons consist of three (adjacent) bases.

(2) Adjacent codons do not overlap.

(3) The message is read in the correct groups of three by starting at some fixed point.

(4) The code sequence in the gene is colinear with the amino acid sequence, the polypeptide chain being synthesized sequentially from the amino end.

(5) In general more than one triplet codes each amino acid.

(6) It is not certain that some triplets may not code more than one amino acid, i.e. they may be ambiguous.

(7) Triplets which code for the same amino acid are probably rather similar.

(8) It is not known whether there is any general rule which groups such codons together, or whether the grouping is mainly the result of historical accident.

(9) The number of triplets which do not code an amino acid is probably small.

(10) Certain codes proposed earlier, such as comma-less codes, two- or three-letter codes, the combination code, and various transposable codes are all unlikely to be correct.

(11) The code in different organisms is probably similar. It may be the same in all organisms but this is not yet known.

It is impressive to note that nearly all of the above predictions eventually turned out to be true, with the only exception of point 6.

Reading frames and frameshift mutations. Even with the genetic code in hand, there is still a major problem to be overcome by the translation machinery. The ribosome does not simply start reading the mRNA sequence from one end; there are both 5′ and 3′ *untranslated regions* (UTRs) that flank the sequence to be translated into protein. As a result, the translational machinery must know exactly where on the mRNA to start working. And depending on where one starts reading a DNA sequence, there are three different ways to decompose it into codons.

Example 2.3

Reading frames. The sequence: . . . ACGTACGTACGTACGT . . . can be decomposed into codons in the following ways:

```
...ACG-TAC-GTA-CGT-ACG-T...
...A-CGT-ACG-TAC-GTA-CGT...
...AC-GTA-CGT-ACG-TAC-GT...
```

The translation into amino acids, and hence the resulting protein, would be completely different in each of the three cases. The ribosome must therefore know where to start. We call each non-overlapping decomposition of a DNA sequence into codons a *reading frame* (i.e. the succession of codons determined by reading nucleotides in groups of three from a specific starting position).

The way that a gene specifies its reading frame is to begin every protein with the amino acid methionine. Because there is only one codon for methionine – ATG – the ribosome knows that the first ATG in the messenger RNA specifies both the start of translation and the reading frame for the rest of the protein; the next amino acid in the chain is given by the three nucleotides that follow ATG. (Note that we should be writing AUG, since in RNA alphabet T is replaced by U, but for simplicity we use the DNA alphabet, which is the one in which sequences are found in online databases.)

In much the same way, the ribosome does not continue to read the mRNA sequence until it runs out, but instead looks for a stop codon to tell it where to cease translation. There are three stop codons – TGA, TAA, and TAG – and any one of them specifies the end of the growing amino acid chain (unlike start codons, there is no amino acid associated with stop codons). In order to foreshadow the gene-finding algorithms that we introduce later in the chapter, we will merely say here that a stretch of DNA that has a start codon (in any frame), followed by a run of stop-codon-free DNA in the same reading frame, followed by a stop codon, is called an *open reading frame*, or *ORF*. We will return to this concept later.

Mutations in the DNA sequence of a gene occur all the time, due to a number of biotic and abiotic factors. Mutations that change one DNA nucleotide to another within a gene result in a protein that has either one different amino acid or no different amino acids, depending on whether the mutation occurs between codons coding for the same amino acid or not. Often, differences of only a single amino acid have negligible effects on protein function. But if we have a mutation that deletes nucleotides from or inserts nucleotides into a sequence, the consequences can be much more far reaching. Imagine the insertion of just a single new base into a gene: if the cellular machinery does not realize there has been such a mutation, it reads all succeeding codons in the wrong reading frame. We call this a *frame-shift* mutation. Consequently, all the amino acids attached to the growing protein after this mutation will be completely mis-specified. The resulting protein will often be totally ruined, in effect removing an important piece of machinery from the cell.

2.3 | Genome annotation: gene finding

We have seen in Chapter 1 that the first step in genome analysis and annotation involves measuring a number of statistical quantities, such as GC content. Gene finding (or gene prediction) is certainly the second step in this process, and a number of computational techniques have been developed that attempt to find genes without any extra experimental evidence. The methods are divided into two main categories: *ab initio* methods, based on statistical properties of the sequence such as the ones discussed in the previous section; and homology-based methods, based on comparing sequences with known genes or with other un-annotated whole genomes (sequence comparison methods will be discussed later in the book, in Chapters 3, 4, and 8).

For now we will discuss the basic *ab initio* methods, sufficient for prokaryotic gene finding but insufficient for most eukaryotic nuclear genomes. Chapters 3 and 4 will provide some tools needed for comparison-based methods (respectively, alignment and hidden Markov models), and Chapter 4 will also discuss some ideas of the more advanced *ab initio* methods that are needed for eukaryotic gene finding. Chapter 8 will discuss how whole-genome comparisons can also be used to detect genes.

Open reading frames. We have seen that (protein-coding) genes consist of stretches of (non-stop) codons that begin with a start codon and end in a stop codon. A diagram is presented in Figure 2.2, showing the ORF structure of a gene, as well as the transcription signals and the promoter (i.e. regulatory) region. However, only prokaryotic genes consist of single, continuous open-reading frames – eukaryotic genes are interrupted by transcribed, but not translated, sequences called *introns*. The translated portions of the gene are referred to as *exons*. (Actually, and a bit confusingly, not all exons need to be translated: the 5′ and 3′ UTRs mentioned earlier are considered exons. So the

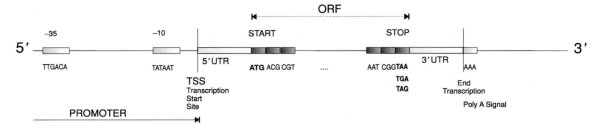

Fig. 2.2 The structure of a eubacterial gene. We can distinguish the promoter (regulatory) region, the start site of transcription, the open reading frame, and the end of transcription signal

true definition of an exon is that part of a gene that is transcribed and eventually specifies the mRNA. Introns are spliced out before the RNA travels to the ribosome for translation.) Because prokaryotic genes do not contain introns, gene finding can be simplified into a search for ORFs.

Definition 2.2

Open reading frame. Given a sequence, **s**, from the alphabet $\mathcal{N} = \{A, C, G, T\}$, we define an open reading frame (ORF) as any subsequence whose length L is a multiple of 3, starting with the start codon ATG, ending in any of the three stop codons {TAA, TAG, TGA}, with no stop codons in the middle. Internal start codons are allowed. For example, the sequence: GTATTATTATGAAGGGCC-CTTCTATAGTATGATTGAAT contains an ORF of length 24 nt:

GTATTATT . ATG . AAG . GGC . CCT . TCT . ATA . GTA . TGA . TTGAAT

Remark 2.2

ORFs on the reverse complement of a sequence. Because chromosomes are double-stranded, genes may be on either strand (but still in a 5′ to 3′ orientation). Given only one strand, we can easily reconstruct the other one by the property of complementarity. We can distinguish three reading frames on each strand for a total of six reading frames. Thus any gene-finding algorithm needs to locate ORFs on both strands, and implicitly requires that we search a second 5′ to 3′ sequence that is complementary to the strand given by GenBank or other DNA databases.

The definition given above just begs the question of how long must an ORF be for us to call it a gene? Ten codons? One hundred? After all, there may be many random stretches of DNA in a genome that will contain start and stop codons in the right order, just by chance. The classic approach to deciding whether an ORF is a good candidate as a gene is to calculate the probability of seeing an ORF of length L in a random sequence (given some specific sequence probability model). We would then make a choice as to how unlikely a given ORF has to be for us to accept it; in general, longer ORFs will be more unlikely to be due to chance. Obviously, the more stringent our conditions, the fewer candidates we will have, and the longer they will be on average.

Here we introduce an algorithm for finding open reading frames. In the next section we present a statistical method for evaluating our confidence that any particular ORF is part of a true gene, based on its length.

Algorithm 2.1

ORF finder. Given a DNA sequence **s**, and a positive integer k, for each reading frame decompose the sequence into triplets, and find all stretches of triplets starting with a start-codon and ending with a stop codon. Repeat also for the reverse complement of the sequence, **ŝ**. Output all ORFs longer than the prefixed threshold k.

Once an ORF has been found, its translation into the corresponding protein sequence is easy, by simply rewriting each triplet from C with the corresponding amino acid from $\mathcal{A}$, using the translation Table 2.2.

Example 2.4

ORFs in the M. genitalium genome. Using the algorithm given above, we can search the *M. genitalium* genome for all open reading frames. For a threshold k of 90 amino acids (i.e. we only accept ORFs as candidate genes if they are longer than 90 amino acids), we find 543 ORFs in the genome. If we fix a threshold of 100 amino acids, we find about 471 ORFs. The original genome paper gave the number of genes as about 470, including non-translated RNA genes that will not be identified by our protein-coding gene-finding algorithm.

Example 2.5

ORFs in H. influenzae genome. For a threshold of 80 amino acids we find 1966 ORFs in the genome of H. influenzae. For a threshold of 90 amino acids, the number is 1814 (the true number is approximately 1750, including RNA genes). Any other choice of a threshold will obviously lead to different results, as well as different false positive and false negative rates.

In the following section we will see how to pick a threshold length that will provide us with believable ORFs as candidate genes.

2.4 Detecting spurious signals: hypothesis testing

The fundamentals of hypothesis testing. When analyzing patterns in a whole genome we need to consider the possibility that they are a result of chance; this will be more of a problem the bigger a genome gets. Hence we must devise methods to help us to distinguish reliable patterns from background noise. Measuring the probability of a pattern (such as seeing an open reading frame of a given length) under a null model is a simple and effective way of doing this, though we will often need to make simplifying assumptions about the statistical nature of the underlying DNA sequence. Calculating this probability and making inferences based on it is a fundamental problem in statistics, and is referred to as *hypothesis testing*.

There are many important, subtle concepts in hypothesis testing, and we cannot cover them all. For the reader unfamiliar with basic hypothesis testing we suggest that you refer to a general book on probability and statistics; for now we cover the topics that will be essential throughout this book. We consider the data (e.g. an ORF of a certain length) to be *significant* when it is highly unlikely under the null model. We can never guarantee that the data are not consistent with the null, but we can make a statement about the probability of the observed result arising by chance (called a *p-value*). For any *test statistic* – the aspect of the data that we are testing the significance of (e.g. ORF length) – we must also choose the statistical threshold at which we decide to call our observation *significant* or *not significant*. This threshold is referred to as α, and defines the probability with which the null hypothesis will be wrongly rejected (an event called a "Type I error" in statistics, and further discussed below). When our p-value is less than α, we consider our data to be significant and unlikely to be due to chance.

Often a threshold value of $\alpha = 0.05$ is used to define significance, a popular (but arbitrary) choice. This value of α means that even if the null hypothesis is true, 5% of the time our data will appear to be significant. Putting it another way, if our data are significant at $\alpha = 0.05$, it means that we would only have seen a test statistic (e.g. ORF length) as extreme or more extreme than our observed value 5% of the time due to chance alone. Finding a low p-value for the data, then, gives support for the rejection of the null hypothesis.

Definition 2.3

Significance level. The *significance level* of a statistical hypothesis test is a fixed probability of wrongly rejecting the null hypothesis H_0, if it is true. The significance level is usually denoted by α:

$$\text{Significance level} = P(\text{Type I error}) = \alpha.$$

Definition 2.4

Test statistic. The *test statistic* is any aspect of the data that we wish to test the null hypothesis against. We wish to know whether observing our test statistic is likely under the null hypothesis, and if not how unlikely it is to appear by chance. A test statistic can be a value that is directly observable from the data (e.g. ORF length, or number of Cs in a sequence of some length) or it may be a function of the data (such as a χ-squared value or other traditional test statistic).

Definition 2.5

p-value. The *probability value* (p-value) of a statistical hypothesis test is the probability of getting a value of the test statistic as extreme as or more extreme than that observed by chance alone, if the null hypothesis, H_0, is true. It is the probability of wrongly rejecting the null hypothesis if the null is in fact true. The p-value is compared with the chosen significance level and, if it is smaller, the result is *significant*.

Remark 2.3

Types of errors in hypothesis testing. Formally, designing a hypothesis test requires us to define a "null" hypothesis, H_0, and an "alternative" hypothesis, H_1 (e.g. the null hypothesis could be that a given ORF is generated by a random process, the alternative that the ORF has been generated by some biologically relevant process). The goal of hypothesis testing is to choose between H_0 and H_1, given some data. Errors in this decision are almost unavoidable, and can be of two types: rejecting a true null hypothesis (a *false positive* or Type I error) or accepting a false null hypothesis (a *false negative* or Type II error). Generally one would like the probability of all errors to be low, but often there is a trade-off between Type I and Type II errors – lowering the risk of one can increase the risk of the other. So typically one fixes the acceptable level of Type I error, α, and calls this the significance level. The numerical value of Type II error is called β, and is sometimes implicitly defined by the choice of α. In our ORF example we decided that we can accept up to 5% false positive ORFs in our list of candidate genes. To define a false negative rate for this type of data we would first have to know the true identity of genes to know how many we have missed.

Computing a p-value for ORFs.   Once an ORF has been found in a sequence, the statistical question is: what is the probability of finding an ORF of the same length (or longer) in a random sequence? This question will help us to better define how long an ORF must be for us to believe that it is a true gene.

Let us formalize the question: What is the probability of an ORF of k or more codons arising by chance? And: What is the threshold value of k such that 95% of random ORFs are shorter than k? This threshold will provide a lower bound on the length of ORFs to be kept by the algorithm given above. It is often the case in bioinformatics that such simple models can provide a first estimate of statistical significance. If we generate random sequences by a simple multinomial model, the answer can be calculated easily.

Imagine a random process generating a sequence of DNA, and let us ask the probability of this process generating an ORF by chance. If all nucleotides are emitted (used) with the same probability – and even if they are not – we can easily estimate the probability of observing a stop codon in a given reading frame. We are really computing the probability of seeing a stop codon, conditioned on seeing a start codon in the same frame, by chance.

What is the probability of picking one of the stop codons? It is the sum of their probabilities: if the distribution of codons is uniform, it will be 3/64, versus a 61/64 probability of picking a non-stop codon (since there are 64 possible codons, three of which are stop codons). So the probability of a run of k (or more) non-stop codons following a start codon is

$$P(\text{run of } k \text{ non-stop codons}) = (61/64)^k.$$

Setting $\alpha=0.05$, we can easily estimate the minimum acceptable ORF length. Since

$$(61/64)^{62} = 0.051,$$

then, by discarding all ORFs of length $k \leq 64$ (62 plus one start codon and one stop codon), we will remove 95% of the spurious ORFs. This provides a first, crude but surprisingly accurate estimate of the threshold to be used for reliable gene finding in prokaryotes.

Do not be mislead by the fact that – in this case – the threshold turns out to be equal to 64 (the same as the number of codons). This is just a coincidence, due to our choice of 95% confidence. If we request a 99% confidence level, ORFs need to be longer. The probability of a stretch of 100 non-stop codons is $(61/64)^{100} = 0.0082$, so with confidence higher than 99% we can conclude that an ORF longer than 102 codons is highly significant. Of course this approach runs the risk of accepting a few spurious ORFs and of rejecting a few valid ORFs that are too short to be noticed. The two types of error give rise to a trade-off between sensitivity and specificity that must be balanced by any gene-finding algorithm.

Non-uniform codon distribution. If we assume that the distribution of codon usage is uniform, then all 64 codons will have the same probability. But if we observe, for instance, nucleotide usage with a strong AT-bias, then AT-rich codons may be more frequent; the more frequent codons would then include both the start and stop codons (ATG; and TAA, TGA, TAG). In fact, almost every organism shows both an unequal usage of amino acids and an unequal usage of synonymous codons that encode the same amino acid (called *codon bias*). Often these biases in codon usage have little to do with underlying nucleotide usage bias and more to do with the requirements of the transcriptional and translational machinery. (This can result in differing GC-contents between coding and non-coding DNA.) Instead of assuming equal codon frequencies, therefore, we can simply estimate the distribution from the genome sequence itself.

Given unequal codon frequencies we can easily repeat the above calculations without even accounting for differences in the frequencies of the non-stop codons. All we need to know is the total frequency of stop codons:

$$P(\text{stop}) = P(\text{TAA}) + P(\text{TAG}) + P(\text{TGA}).$$

So, the probability of a run of more than k non-stop codons following a start codon (again assuming that the DNA sequence has been generated in an i.i.d. fashion) is

$$P(\text{run of } k \text{ non-stop codons}) = [1 - P(\text{stop})]^k,$$

and this can be used to estimate the value of k that corresponds to an α of 0.05 in the same way as above.

Randomization tests. It is often the case that we cannot easily calculate the exact p-value associated with some observation, either for theoretical or computational reasons. In these situations a *randomization* test can be used; randomization tests are a common method in computational genomics, where many of the assumptions of exact methods may be violated. While there are many different types of tests that might fall under the heading *randomized*, all rely upon randomization of the observed data to create a large number of artificial datasets that have many of the same statistical properties as the real data. These replicated datasets are then used to compute a null distribution of a test statistic against which the observed data can be compared. We obtain a p-value by finding the rank of the observed test statistic in our null distribution: if it lies in a percentile less than α, we say it is significant (e.g. for $\alpha = 0.05$ the data must be in the top 5% of the distribution to be considered significant).

A simple way to generate random sequences with the same length and statistical properties as the one being tested is to randomly *permute* the original sequence. There are actually a number of different ways to permute any sequence, with each choice capturing different aspects of the original sequence. For instance, we could generate a new sequence by shuffling the order of individual nucleotides, or by shuffling the order of triplets of nucleotides in some reading frame. Obviously the latter method captures some of the local correlations between nucleotides, but requires some arbitrary choice of reading frame. A second method to generate a random sequence is known as *bootstrapping*: rather than permuting the original data we now sample with a replacement from the data to create a new sequence of the same length. Once again, we must make a choice to sample either individual nucleotides or longer nucleotide strings, although with bootstrapping we do not have to stick to a single reading frame when sampling from the data. There are a number of additional randomization methods that are commonly used, but we do not cover them here.

Example 2.6

ORF length in Mycoplasma genitalium. To test the significance of open reading frames found in the *M. genitalium* genome we use a single-nucleotide permutation test, which is the equivalent of generating a random sequence under a multinomial model using the same symbol probabilities as the original sequence. After permuting the genome sequence, we search for ORFs and record the length of each observed. We find a total of 11 922 ORFs in the original sequence, and 17 367 in the randomized one. This list of ORF lengths in the random sequence becomes our null distribution; we will only keep as candidate genes those ORFs in the real genome sequence that are longer than most (or all) the ORFs in the random sequence. If we use as a threshold the maximum ORF length in the randomized sequence, 402 bp, we find in the original sequence 326 ORFs longer than that. This is a good estimate, since it is known that there are about 470 genes in *M. genitalium*, several of which are not protein coding, and hence would not be found as ORFs. Using this threshold we are of course not able to detect short genes, and we may want to identify these. We could then choose a more tolerant threshold (i.e., a lower one) so that we keep all ORFs of length equal to or greater than the top 5% of random ORFs. Since this choice significantly lowers the length of acceptable candidate ORFs, it is not surprising that such a threshold leads to a list of 1520 ORFs, more than the known number of genes and hence containing many false positives. However we started from more than 10000 candidates, and we have found a highly enriched set of about 1400 that likely contains most of the genes. In Figure 2.3, we see the details of the two ORF-length distributions (gray for the actual sequence and black for its randomized version). It is clear that a threshold of about 150 bp would eliminate nearly all ORFs found in the random sequence.

Example 2.7

ORF length in Haemophilus influenzae. The same analysis can be repeated for *H. influenzae*. If we use as a threshold the length of the longest ORF in the randomized sequence, 573 bp, we find 1182 ORFs in the original sequence that are longer than this. Again, this matches well with the estimated number of

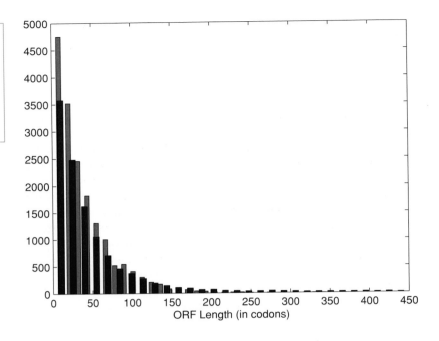

Fig. 2.3 ORF-length distribution for *M. genitalium* (blue) and its randomized genome sequence (red). This figure does not show the long tail of the blue distribution, hiding some of the very long ORFs in the original sequence

genes, although it clearly misses too many valid ORFs. Using a lower threshold, we find 2209 ORFs that are longer than 207 bps, a value greater than or equal to the top 1% of the ORFs in the randomized sequence.

Remark 2.4

Problems with multiple testing. Though we have not addressed them yet, issues of *multiple testing* are found throughout computational genomics, including in the statistics behind gene finding. Briefly, the problem is that when we choose α so as to accept a false positive rate of (say) 5%, this is really a false positive rate on a single test. But if we were to conduct 100 tests – and thousands of tests are routinely carried out across a genome – then we would expect to see five false positives just by chance. In other words, if we found five "significant" genes out of 100 tests with $\alpha = 0.05$, we would have no reason to believe that those significance tests meant anything biologically.

The awesome power (and weakness) of computational genomics. In this chapter we have presented a simple computational method for finding genes. We were able to find a set of about 400 genes in the *M. genitalium* genome and about 1300 genes in *H. influenzae* of which we were highly confident, and the Exercises below will convince you that the method can be applied to other simple genomes.

Finding genes in the laboratory is a long and arduous process; the power of computers coupled with some basic biological knowledge allows us to find candidate genes in just a few minutes. But we should stress that these are just *candidate* genes. We have no evidence at this point that they make translated, functioning proteins. In Chapter 3 we discuss computational tools that may bolster or weaken our candidates by comparison with the sequences of known genes stored in online databases.

2.5   Exercises

(1) Find all ORFs in human, chimp and mouse mtDNA (GenBank accession numbers respectively NC_001807, NC_001643 and NC_005089). Note that the genetic code for mitochondria is slightly different from the standard one. In particular the one for vertebrates has different start and stop codons, resulting in different ORFs: the codon TGA means stop in the universal code, but codes for tryptophan in mtDNA; AGA and AGG code for arginine in the universal code and the stop codon in mtDNA; and ATA represents isoleucine in the universal code and methionine in mtDNA. What fraction of the sequence represents (candidate) protein coding genes?

(2) Repeat the ORF search on randomized mtDNA sequences. How long is the longest ORF that you find in this randomized sequence?

(3) Find ORFs in *H. influenzae* (NC_000907). Try various choices of length threshold. How does this affect the number of ORFs you find?

2.6   Reading list

A modern and stable account of the state of the art of the genetic code, ORFs, and related material can be found in the books Gibson and Muse (2004) and Brown (1999). A discussion of hypothesis testing in a bioinformatics context can be found in Ewens and Grant (2006) and a discussion of bootstrap methods can be found in Efron and Gong (1983).

A nice account of the GeneSweeps story was published in *Science* magazine (Pennisi, 2003). The Nobel lectures of James Watson and Francis Crick can be found in Watson (1964), Crick (1964) and and the one by Marshall Nirenberg Nirenberg (1972). A very early discussion of the genetic code can also be found in Crick *et al.* (1961). At the 1966 Symposium on Quantitative Biology, H. Gobind Khorana and Marshall Nirenberg announced the cracking of the genetic code. This was based on a long series of papers (mostly by Nirenberg and Leder) on various codons (see (Khorana *et al.*, 1966)).

Links to these and many more papers, as well as to data and software for the exercises and all the examples, can be found on the book's website:

www.computational-genomics.net

Chapter 3

All in the family
Sequence alignment

- Sequence similarity and homology
- Global and local alignments
- Statistical significance of alignments
- BLAST and CLUSTAL

3.1 Eye of the tiger

In 1994, at the same time the genomic era was beginning, Walter Gehring and colleagues at the University of Basel carried out a Frankenstein experiment *par excellence*: they were able to turn on a gene called *eyeless* in various places on the body of the fruitfly, *Drosophila melanogaster*. The result was amazing – fruitflies that had whole eyes sprouting up all over their bodies. Scientists refer to genes such as *eyeless* as master regulatory genes (note that genes are often named after the problems they cause when mutated). These master regulatory genes produce proteins that control large cascades of other genes, like those needed to produce complex features such as eyes; *eyeless* controls one such cascade that contains more than 2000 other genes. Turning it on anywhere in the body activates the cascade and produces a fully formed, but non-functioning, eye.

It turns out that all multicellular organisms use master regulatory genes, often for the same purpose in different species. Slightly different versions of the *eyeless* gene are used in humans, mice, sea squirts, squids, and, yes, tigers, to control eye formation. We call these different versions of the same gene *homologs*, to denote their shared ancestry from a common ancestor. This means that at least 600 million years ago there was an organism that itself used some version of *eyeless* in cellular function, and that throughout the evolution of all of these animals this gene continued to be maintained, albeit while accumulating mutations that did not greatly affect its function. The version of this gene found in humans, called *aniridia* (because defects in it cause malformation of irises), is virtually identical to the fruitfly *eyeless* gene in certain key segments. The most important such segment encodes the *PAX* (paired-box) domain, a sequence of 128 amino acids whose function is to bind specific sequences of DNA. This segment has remained essentially unchanged for the past 600 million years. The genes related to *eyeless* also contain another common element: the *HOX* (homeobox) domain. This element, first discovered in Drosophila, encodes a 60-amino acid protein domain that is thought to be part of more than 0.2%

of the total number of vertebrate genes, and is also involved in regulating the activity of other genes. These examples are not exceptional: a relatively large fraction of the genes in any organism are shared even among distantly related species.

But how can we tell that two genes (or their parts), possibly in two different organisms, are actually two versions of the same gene, or at least that they are related? Genes can be passed down for billions of years, slowly changing sequence (and possibly function), but at a pace that often enables us to recognize two homologous genes simply based on sequence similarity.

This chapter covers the computational challenges inherent in comparing gene sequences. Being able to measure the similarity between sequences is probably the single most important calculation in computational genomics, and it has become an everyday task for biologists. The ease with which these comparisons are made is due to methods that pre-date the genomic era by 25 years; we will briefly review the seminal results in this field to bring us to the next stage of genome annotation – assignment of function to genes. All of these methods revolve around the central idea of *sequence alignment*, the task of finding corresponding parts in two related sequences.

Remark 3.1

Multiple levels of homology. Although the different versions of the *eyeless* gene found in animals are all homologous, the actual eyes of these organisms are not. Eyes have evolved independently in insects, vertebrates, and mollusks, and hence are not homologous. Even in organisms without eyes, however, *eyeless* homologs are used in neural development, suggesting that the master regulatory function of this gene has been co-opted each time to control eye formation. Supporting this is the fact that *eyeless* homologs also control tasks such as ear development in vertebrates.

3.2 | On sequence alignment

This chapter deals with the algorithmic and statistical issues of sequence alignment. As we said earlier – and we repeat here for emphasis – sequence alignment is probably the most important task in bioinformatics; it is routinely applied to both amino acid and DNA sequences. The ultimate purpose of sequence alignment is to measure sequence similarity, or how closely sequences resemble each other. It is only by first aligning sequences, however, that we can say whether an amino acid or nucleotide is the same or different between sequences, and hence how similar the sequences are over their entire length. A simple example of alignment between two (artificial) amino acid sequences (VIVALASVEGAS and VIVADAVIS) is shown here to illustrate the notion of alignment before its formal definition is given below:

```
V  I  V  A  L  A  S  V  E  G  A  S
V  I  V  A  D  A  -  V  -  -  I  S
```

This example is discussed in more detail in various parts of this chapter. Note that once such an alignment is available, corresponding parts between two sequences, and a similarity score, can easily be obtained.

Being able to align sequences quickly has many uses in biology. Here we list a few:

- **Prediction of function.** As we saw with the *eyeless* example, organisms share many genes. This fact has important consequences for annotating protein function: if we know the function of a protein in one organism, we can make inferences about the function of similar proteins for which we have no experimental evidence. Assigning protein function is the next step in genome annotation after we have found candidate genes.
- **Database searching.** We can use fast sequence alignment methods to determine whether a gene that we know from one organism (whether or not we know its function) is similar to any known sequence. This extensive comparison will require approximate methods, and is the main function of the algorithm and the program of the same name, BLAST. We cover the uses of BLAST and searchable public databases later in this chapter.
- **Gene finding.** Comparison of whole genome sequences from two or more organisms can reveal the location of previously unknown genes, especially if they are too short to be found by *ab initio* methods. Whole genome comparisons are discussed in Chapter 8.
- **Sequence divergence.** The amount of sequence divergence (or, conversely, similarity) between two sequences can tell us how closely they are related. Whether we are comparing genes from two humans or from a plant and an animal, we need some measure of their similarity; one way to calculate such a metric is to first align the sequences. The application of sequence alignment to variation within populations and between species is the subject of Chapters 5, 6, and 7.
- **Sequence assembly.** Though we will not discuss sequence assembly in this book, it is still important to point out that sequence alignment has uses in this most basic of genomic analyses. Without efficient sequence assembly (genome sequences are normally assembled from a huge number of shorter pieces of DNA), we would not have all the genomes we see today.

3.3 | On sequence similarity

Before we leap into the algorithmics of sequence alignment, there are a few important biological issues that we must first cover.

Homology. After we align genes or proteins, we are able to make objective statements about their similarity: they are 50% similar, or 99% similar, etc. But any two random sequences can be similar to some extent, so similarity does not necessarily imply homology, or relatedness, of the sequences. Homology means that sequences come from a common ancestor and are not simply similar by chance. It is therefore proper to refer to the "similarity" of sequences after alignment, and not to their "homology" (as is found too often in certain corners of biology). There is no such thing as two sequences that are "50% homologous": they either share a common ancestor or they do not, and this is an inference that comes from further analysis. We should say, though, that high similarity between sequences is good evidence for a recent common ancestor and hence homology.

While on the subject of homology, there are a few related issues that would be helpful in understanding the alignment of gene sequences. It so happens that genes can be homologous in a number of different ways – after all, we can be related to people with whom we share an ancestor in a number of different ways (e.g. mother, brother, cousin). The two most common forms of homology are *orthology* and *paralogy*.

Orthologous genes (or the proteins they produce) are ones that are found in separate species and derive from the same parental sequence in a common ancestor. Orthologs reflect the history of splitting (speciation) between species – if an ancestral species carried gene A, then upon splitting into two daughter species both would contain orthologous versions of gene A, even as their sequences evolve. The basic processes of molecular evolution that led to the evolution of sequences include substitution of one nucleotide for another, insertion of nucleotides, and deletion of nucleotides. We collectively call the insertion or deletion of bases *indels*. We will discuss probabilistic models of nucleotide substitution in Chapter 5, and other processes in molecular evolution, including large genome rearrangements, in Chapter 8.

In order to understand *paralogous* genes, we must introduce yet another biological concept: gene duplication. Via cellular mechanisms that we need not discuss in detail, genes are often duplicated to produce multiple copies in one genome. These duplicates often diverge in function very slightly, such that the tasks carried out by a parental copy are now carried out by multiple specialized members of a *gene family*. The *eyeless* gene we discussed earlier is actually a member of the homeodomain gene family, a group of duplicated genes that all fill separate roles as master regulatory genes. The relationship between members of a gene family within a single genome is known as paralogy.

Remark 3.2

Gene duplication and evolutionary novelty. In addition to simply dividing up necessary tasks among members of a gene family, gene duplication is also a great engine of evolutionary novelty. Because an organism initially has exact duplicates of a gene, one of the two copies is free to evolve novel functions; this is often the origin of genes with entirely new roles.

Protein domains. The *eyeless* gene encodes a protein with a specific function – in this case that function is the binding of DNA. Only a short stretch of the protein actually binds to DNA, however; we call these functional stretches of proteins *domains*. The *eyeless* gene has a homeobox domain, a conserved stretch approximately 60 amino acids long and found in a huge number of related regulatory genes. Depending on their function, single proteins can have one or more domains that perform different tasks; as discussed earlier, *eyeless* actually has two domains, the homeobox domain and the paired-box domain (of approximately 128 amino acids). Protein domains are often the most important part of the molecule, and hence evolve very slowly (because very few mutations are allowed in them). This conservation means that protein domains will be much easier to align than other parts of genes – we will see how this manifests itself shortly.

3.4 | Sequence alignment: global and local

In contrast to the frenetic pace of computational genomics in the late 1990s, sequence alignment technology developed glacially. Results came in leaps, often separated by full decades: Saul Needleman and Christian Wunsch introduced the concept of global alignment in 1970; Temple Smith and Michael Waterman the computational advance of local alignment in 1981; and fast heuristic methods, the third panel in alignment's triptych, were introduced by Stephen Altschul, Warren Gish, Webb Miller, Gene Myers, and David Lipman in 1990. All three were published in the *Journal of Molecular Biology*. Of course none of these papers appeared *de novo* – all required important results from other researchers – but they mark important milestones, nonetheless.

We first discuss the algorithms and statistics behind global and local alignment. Only by understanding these basic methods can we come to see the truly daunting computations inherent in modern genomic biology. The basic questions to be answered include: given two sequences, what is the best way to align them against one another? How can we assess the quality of any given alignment? Can an alignment be explained by chance, or should we conclude that it is due to a shared history between the sequences? These are algorithmic and statistical questions.

3.4.1 | Global alignment

A *global* alignment of two sequences (referred to as a *pairwise* alignment) can be thought of as a representation of the correspondence between their respective symbols (i.e. their nucleotides). If two sequences have the same ancestor, we expect them to have many symbols – and indeed entire substrings – in common. For most symbols in a sequence we should be able to identify the corresponding homologous position in the other sequence. This can be represented by an alignment, where mutations between the sequences appear as mismatches, and indels appear as gaps in one of the two sequences.

For example, if we were to align the amino acid sequences $\mathbf{s} = $ VIVALASVEGAS and $\mathbf{t} = $ VIVADAVIS (notice that these are unequal in length), we would obtain something like this:

$$A(\mathbf{s}, \mathbf{t}) = \begin{array}{cccccccccccc} V & I & V & A & L & A & S & V & E & G & A & S \\ V & I & V & A & D & A & - & V & - & - & I & S. \end{array}$$

Notice that the total length of the alignment c, can be larger than both of the input sequences under consideration.

Definition 3.1

Global alignment. A *global alignment* of two sequences, **s** and **t**, is an assignment of gap symbols "−" into those sequences, or at their ends. The two resulting strings are placed one above the other so that every character or gap symbol in either string is opposite a unique character or a unique gap symbol in the other string. It can be represented as a $c \times 2$ matrix, for some value of c, the first row containing the first sequence and (interspersed) gap symbols, the second row containing the second sequence and (interspersed) gap symbols. Note that c – the total length of the alignment – will be either equal to the length of the longest sequence or longer if gaps have been inserted, but cannot be longer than **s** + **t** (since insertion of gap symbols at the same position in both rows is considered meaningless).

We often improve readability by adding an extra row representing matches and mismatches:

$$
A(\mathbf{s}, \mathbf{t}) = \begin{array}{cccccccccccc}
\text{V} & \text{I} & \text{V} & \text{A} & \text{L} & \text{A} & \text{S} & \text{V} & \text{E} & \text{G} & \text{A} & \text{S} \\
| & | & | & | & & | & & | & & & & | \\
\text{V} & \text{I} & \text{V} & \text{A} & \text{D} & \text{A} & - & \text{V} & - & - & \text{I} & \text{S,}
\end{array}
$$

where vertical lines denote an exact match between the two sequences. We can see that there are both individual symbol substitutions between the sequences and several insertion or deletion events. (Because we do not know what the ancestor of these two sequences looked like, we do not know if the length difference is due to insertions in one sequence, deletions in the other, or some combination of the two.)

Alignment scoring functions. Any arrangement of the two sequences in a matrix like the one above is a valid pairwise alignment. We are interested in the best possible arrangement. A crucial aspect of alignments is that we can devise a simple scoring scheme to judge their value, so as to define and find the "best" alignment. Every position in an alignment, which we denote A, specifies a pair of opposing symbols from an expanded alphabet of nucleotides or amino acids that includes the gap symbol, "−." We will call x_i and y_i the symbols appearing at the ith position of the alignment, respectively in the top and bottom row, and a scoring function for position i will be denoted by $\sigma(x_i, y_i)$. Once we define a scoring function for pairs of symbols from that alphabet, the score of the alignment between sequences, M, can be defined as an additive function of the symbol scores. This additive property of alignment scores is a key factor in ensuring their efficient calculation.

So, if we have a function $\sigma(x_i, y_i)$ characterizing the cost of aligning two symbols x_i and y_i, then we can define a function to compute the cost of an entire alignment, as follows:

$$
M = \sum_{i=1}^{c} \sigma(x_i, y_i),
$$

where we sum over all positions of the alignment.

A simple scoring function. An example might be helpful at this point. Consider the simple scoring function assigning a penalty of -1 to indels and mismatches, and an award of $+1$ for matches. This can be written as

$$\sigma(-, a) = \sigma(a, -) = \sigma(a, b) = -1 \quad \forall a \neq b$$
$$\sigma(a, b) = 1 \quad\quad\quad\quad\quad\quad\quad \forall a = b,$$

(where the symbol $\forall$ means "for all," and a and b are any symbols different from "$-$"). If we apply this scoring function to the global alignment given above, we get an alignment score of (7 matches, 2 mismatches, 3 gaps):

$$M(A) = 7 - 2 - 3 = 2.$$

It is clear that the choice of scoring function is crucial in determining the score of the alignment, and we should try to make this function as reflective of biological constraints as possible. It is often the case in constructing scoring functions that positive matches are given a positive value, mismatches are given a negative value, and gaps are given a value intermediate between the two; the score thus reflects the amount of sequence overlap in alignment A.

Substitution matrix. A convenient way of representing many scoring functions is as a matrix, often called a *substitution matrix*. In general, a substitution matrix shows the cost of replacing one letter (of either a nucleotide or amino acid alphabet) with another letter or a gap. (Substitution matrices can be presented without the gap character, but because we are using them for alignments here, we include a column and row for gaps.) For nucleotides, there is a 5×5 substitution matrix, which when given our simple scoring scheme from above would look like this:

	A	C	G	T	−
A	+1	−1	−1	−1	−1
C	−1	+1	−1	−1	−1
G	−1	−1	+1	−1	−1
T	−1	−1	−1	+1	−1
−	−1	−1	−1	−1	N/D

Note that the value $\sigma(-, -)$ is not defined – because we do not need to align gaps with each other – and we indicate this fact by using the notation N/D (not determined).

The notation for the scoring function remains the same, but now $\sigma(x, y)$ can refer to an entry in the substitution matrix. Ideally, the substitution scores should be direct measures of symbol similarity and should reflect as much as possible the underlying evolutionary and biochemical properties of sequences. In practice, heuristic solutions are often adopted to achieve practical scoring functions. Because nucleotides differ very little in biochemical functions, simple scoring functions are often used for DNA alignment. The simplest nucleotide matrix penalizes all changes equally; more complicated matrices can favor certain nucleotide substitutions over others (see Chapter 5).

Amino acids, on the other hand, can be quite different from one another, and mismatches can be of varied effect depending on how similar or dissimilar amino acids are in their biochemical properties. Scores based on inferences about chemical or physical properties of proteins are possible and useful. It is well known that certain pairs of amino acids are much more likely to substitute for each other during evolution than others. This is likely due to certain physicochemical properties that they have in common, such as their hydrophobicity, size, or electrical charge. A good alignment should consider this and incorporate it into the scoring function so that the overall alignment reflects the biological similarity between sequences more closely. The two most common scoring functions that do this are based on observed substitution frequencies in proteins, and are called PAM and BLOSUM matrices (see Chapter 5 for more information). Whichever function we use, remember that the choice of scoring function can have a major impact on the resulting alignment, especially when choosing the "best" alignment, as defined below.

At this point, however, we can give a formal definition of the optimal global alignment between two sequences. An algorithm to find it will be discussed immediately after.

Definition 3.2

Optimal global alignment. The *optimal (global) alignment* of two strings, **s** and **t**, is defined as the alignment $A(\mathbf{s},\mathbf{t})$, that maximizes the total alignment score over all possible alignments. The optimal alignment is often referred to as A^*, $M(A^*)$ its alignment score.

Finding the optimal alignment. It is obvious from these definitions that an alignment of two sequences will have a high score if it only requires a few edit operations – including insertion of gaps, and symbol replacements. If two sequences are closely related, they will have a high alignment score. The more closely two sequences are related – that is, the less time that has elapsed since they shared a common ancestor – the better their alignment should be.

The problem, of course, becomes finding the optimal alignment from all possible alignments. The naïve approach, calculating scores for all possible alignments and ranking them, would have an exponentially high cost. This cost is largely due to the fact that we allow for gaps – finding the optimal un-gapped alignment would be relatively easy. The number of different alignments (with gaps) of two sequences of length n is $\binom{2n}{n}$, a quantity which grows exponentially with n. This means that for two sequences of length 30, there are approximately 10^{17} possible alignments between them!

The computational problem we need to solve is now apparent and can be stated as follows: given two sequences, **s** and **t**, and a symbol-scoring function, σ, find the alignment with the maximum alignment score, A^*. A solution based on enumeration of all possible alignments would have an intractable cost. The problem is efficiently solved by the *Needleman–Wunsch algorithm*. This remarkable algorithm is guaranteed to find the optimal score for any given symbol-scoring function in feasible time.

human		fly
D	—	E
K	—	K
H	—	N
E	—	K
K	—	K
K	—	K
W	—	W
K	—	K
M	—	M
R	—	R
N	—	N
Q	—	Q
W	—	W
H	—	H
V	—	I
Q	—	K
R	—	R
E	—	E
L	—	L
C	—	L
L	—	C
A	—	L
H	—	A
A	—	H
E	—	A
R	—	H
R	—	E
R	—	I
L	—	R
Y	—	R
N	—	R
H	—	L
E	—	T
K	—	F
E	—	H
L	—	F
E	—	E
L	—	E
T	—	K
Q	—	E
Y	—	L
R	—	E
Y	—	L
T	—	T
Q	—	Q
R	—	Y
K	—	R
R	—	Y
	—	T
	—	Q
	—	R
	—	G
	—	K
	—	R

The Needleman–Wunsch algorithm. Without enumerating all alignments, how can we find the best one? Fortunately, this problem is amenable to an efficient solution based on dynamic programming. Dynamic programming (DP) is a general method of computing solutions when a suitable recursive relation can be found; in other words, when the larger problem can be broken down into many smaller, easier problems of the same type. In this case, the optimal alignment of two sequences can be related to the optimal alignment of shorter sequences within them. By exploiting this relation, DP methods – such as the Needleman–Wunsch (NW) algorithm – allow us to start the computation by aligning very short DNA sequences, and growing this alignment efficiently to the full length of the two sequences. When implemented well, this approach has a much lower computational cost than the naïve solution.

There are three elements to DP algorithms in sequence alignment: a recursive relation, a tabular computation, and a trace-back procedure. We discuss all three procedures in Section 3.8, which can be skipped by readers not interested in algorithmic details.

The important feature of this approach is how its computational cost depends on the length of the two sequences: this dependency is proportional to $|s||t|$, the product of the two sequence lengths. This allows us to efficiently align long sequences with modest computers.

Example 3.1
Global alignment of proteins. We demonstrate the use of global alignments on two short subsequences of human and fly Hox proteins (AAD01939, AAQ67266): see adjacent table.

3.4.2 Local alignment

We have discussed the benefits of computing the best global alignment between two sequences, **s** and **t**. A more realistic situation is when we are interested in the best alignment between two *parts* of **s** and **t** (that is, two subsequences). As we have seen in the example of *eyeless* gene, it is often the case that we suspect two different proteins might share a common domain, but it could also be the case that we suspect that two homologous regions of DNA might contain smaller conserved elements within them. The best alignment of subsequences of **s** and **t** is called the *optimal local alignment*. In other words, we are considering the best global alignment over all possible choices of subsequences of **s** and **t**. This can be thought of as removing a prefix and a suffix in each of the two sequences, and testing how well we can align the remaining internal substrings.

For example, we may want to find similar subsequences within the sequences **s** = QUEVIVALASVEGAS and **t** = VIVADAVIS. This could be accomplished by computing the best (global) alignment between all subsequences in **s** and all subsequences in **t**, each subsequence being defined by ignoring a prefix and a suffix in the original sequence. A possible (but not optimal) local alignment is

```
V   I   V   A   L   A   S   V
|   |   |   |       |       |
V   I   V   A   D   A   -   V,
```

where a prefix and suffix have been removed from the original sequences. For clarity we show the subsequences and their prefixes/suffixes in an alignment-like representation:

Q	U	E	V	I	V	A	L	A	S	V	E	G	A	S
R	R	R									R	R	R	R
-	-	-	V	I	V	A	D	A	-	V	-	-	I	S,

where we denote by "R" the removed parts. Note that the optimal local alignment is the one presented in the alignment containing only the subsequences without their prefixes and suffixes above. This can be seen by considering the following formal definition.

Definition 3.3

Local alignment. A *local alignment* of two sequences, $\mathbf{s}$ and $\mathbf{t}$, is a global alignment of the subsequences $\mathbf{s}_{i:j}$ and $\mathbf{t}_{k:l}$, for some choice of (i, j) and (k, l). The *optimal local alignment* is given by the optimal choice of (i, j) and (k, l), so as to maximize the alignment score.

Based on this definition, local alignment appears to be harder than global alignment, since it contains many instances of global alignment within it: we are not only optimizing over all possible alignments, but over all possible choices of starts and ends of each substring. However, a very clever adaptation of the Needleman–Wunsch algorithm, called the *Smith–Waterman (SW) algorithm*, makes it possible to perform local alignment with the same cost as global alignment. The keys to local alignment are to use a slightly more complex scoring function, and to use a different method for reading the desired alignment from the table (the trace-back), as are discussed in Section 3.8. The result is a very efficient procedure that enables us to reveal the presence of common structures in the two input sequences. This has countless applications in genomic analysis.

3.5 Statistical analysis of alignments

Once we determine the highest alignment score for two sequences, we need to decide whether this is due to chance or biology. Over millions of years, sequences accumulate large numbers of substitutions, so that it is sometimes hard to decide if two sequences share a common ancestor. This is made harder by the fact that unrelated sequences can also display some degree of similarity, simply due to chance. Without such a determination of significance, any

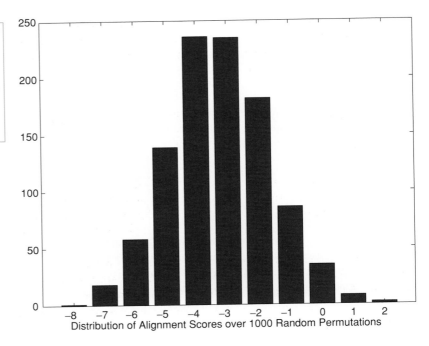

Fig. 3.1 The distribution of global alignment scores for 1000 permutations of the two example sequences. Notice that the score obtained for the original sequences has only been equalled twice in 1000 experiments, and hence is highly significant

inferences that we wish to draw about homology or protein function will be weakened.

As in the case of gene finding, a good way to determine if an alignment score has statistical significance is to compare it with the score generated from the alignment of two random sequences "of the same type." This might mean using randomly generated sequences as a reference (or randomly selected sequences from a database, depending on the application). Although there are various ways to define the random sequences whose alignment scores we want to use as a comparison, the idea is always the same: we use a probability over the set of possible sequences, and we calculate the probability of randomly picking two sequences from that distribution that have an equal or higher alignment score than observed in the real data.

As in Chapter 2, random sequences are produced by permutation of one of the original sequences (so as to respect base composition), or the permutation of the original sequence by blocks (so as to respect local relations such as codons). Alternatively, we could first estimate the parameters of a multinomial or Markov distribution, and then generate random sequences with those parameters. We then align one of the original sequences (the one that has not been permuted) with the random ones, and compare the scores obtained with the original alignment score. This method can be used to estimate the significance of alignments in the form of p-values.

We can use this method to perform hypothesis tests, as discussed in Chapter 2. We rank all the alignment scores, and we see what proportion of the randomly generated sequences have an alignment score equal or greater than the original sequences. We can accept the alignment as significant (possibly indicating homology) if its score is in the top 5% (or another chosen value of α) of the randomly generated scores.

More sophisticated methods are available, based on a theoretical analysis of the distribution of scores for random sequences, but they are too complicated for the purpose of this introductory book. Pointers to literature about advanced methods can be found in Section 3.10.

Example 3.2

Significance of global alignment. Remember that for the global alignment:

$$A(\mathbf{s}, \mathbf{t}) = \begin{array}{ccccccccccc} V & I & V & A & L & A & S & V & E & G & A & S \\ V & I & V & A & D & A & - & V & - & - & I & S, \end{array}$$

we have a score of 2, resulting from seven matches, two mismatches, and three gaps (using our elementary scoring scheme). Now, if we do 1000 random permutations of the second sequence, $\mathbf{t}$, and we find the best global alignment for it with s for every randomization, we get the distribution of alignment scores observed in Figure 3.1.

Only twice out of the 1000 permutations did we find an alignment score equal to or greater than the observed score (in fact, we never see a higher score). This can be interpreted as a p-value of 0.002. We must conclude that our original alignment is highly significant, and would arise by chance much less than 1% of the time.

We can also do the same type of permutation test for local alignments, with little difference in interpretation, as seen in the following example.

Local alignment of PAX genes. We have seen that the *eyeless* protein is one of many factors controlling the development of eyes in many distantly related species. Like *eyeless*, many other PAX and HOX genes are expressed in the developing nervous system and are believed to help regulate neurogenesis. We demonstrate how to use local and global alignment algorithms by discovering conserved domains in PAX and HOX proteins, finding the celebrated paired-box and homeobox domains.

This can readily done by first downloading two sequences from Gen-Bank, one from human and the other from fruitfly, corresponding to the coding regions of the PAX gene discussed in the opening story. Since eukaryotic genes often contain introns, we can get a file from GenBank that contains the sequence of just the mRNA (and the associated protein), where introns have already been removed. The accession numbers are AY707088 and NM_001014694.

We expect these genes to contain two segments in common: a longer segment – the PAX domain – and a shorter segment–the HOX domain. By running Smith–Waterman local alignment, we obtain the segment of 133 amino acids shown in the adjacent table

The score of this alignment (437, with a PAM 50 substitution matrix) is then tested against the score of 1000 alignments between randomized sequences, and is never equaled, indicating a highly significant result (see histogram in Figure 3.2). Indeed, this sequence is found to correspond to the PAX domain, and is in the very beginning of these two sequences (within the first 200 amino acids).

```
human  HSGVNQLGGVFVNGRPLPDSTRQKIVELAHSGARPCDISRILQVSNGCVSKILGRYYETGSIRPRA
fly    HSGVNQLGGVFV-GGRPLPDSTRQKIVELAHSGARPCDISRILQVSNGCVSKILGRYYETGSIRPRA

human  IGGSKPRVATPEVVSKIAQYKRECPSIFAWEIRDRLLSEGVCTNDNIPSVSSINRVLRNLASEK-QQ
fly    IGGSKPRVATAEVVSKISQYKRECPSIFAWEIRDRLLQENVCTNDNIPSVSSINRVLRNLAAQKEQQ
```

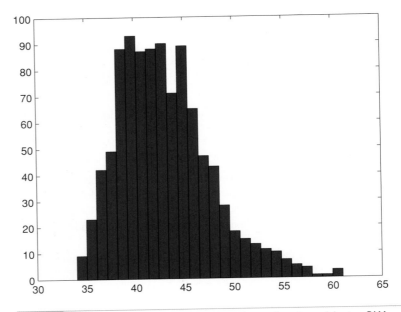

Fig. 3.2 Result of 1000 local alignments with randomized versions of the two PAX genes. The alignment score of the original sequences is 437 and is never reached during statistical testing, indicating a highly significant alignment (the highest random alignment score is 61)

The same two sequences also have a second common element, the homeobox, not found in the previous alignment because it is too short. This element can be seen, for example, by running a global alignment, since these two genes are sufficiently similar to be globally aligned. However, we can also choose to run another local alignment, this time only on the second half of the sequences (hence removing the PAX element, which is longer and therefore preferentially found by the Smith–Waterman algorithm). The result is again clear: a subsequence of length 66 containing the homeobox (featured in Example 3.4), whose score is highly significant; see the adjacent table.

3.6 BLAST: fast approximate local alignment

As the number of DNA sequences deposited in public databases grew during the late 1980s, even the computational cost of the Smith–Waterman algorithm became prohibitive. For large-scale applications such as database searching (the three main genomic databases collectively now contain more than 100 billion bases of DNA sequence), exact methods appeared to be unwieldy. The cost of all dynamic programming algorithms presented above is of the order of $O(nm)$ (meaning that the algorithm takes an amount of time that grows linearly with the product of n and m); although these are amazingly low costs, they are still too high for the scale of applications that are routine in modern computational biology. As a solution, the field turned to heuristic methods – faster methods that are not guaranteed to deliver the optimal solution. The most popular of these is the BLAST algorithm.

Developed at the National Center for Biotechnology Information (the curators of GenBank) by Stephen Altschul and others in 1990, BLAST and the set of sister programs it has spawned are the most used bioinformatics algorithms in the world. They are so commonly used that *to blast* has become an accepted verb (*I blast, you blast, we all blast*). BLAST is considered the third milestone in sequence alignment, after Needleman–Wunsch and Smith–Waterman. The word BLAST is an acronym for Basic Local Alignment Search Tool, and is rumored to be a play on FAST, a predecessor search program by David Lipman and Bill Pearson (now remembered mainly for its widely used file format, FASTA, described in Example 1.8).

BLAST's strategy for increasing speed is mainly accomplished by two shortcuts: don't bother finding the optimal alignment, and don't search all of the sequence space. Effectively, BLAST wants to quickly find the regions of high similarity, regardless of whether it checks every acceptable local alignment. We briefly outline the algorithm it uses below.

An approximate alignment algorithm. BLAST finds local alignments, as described in Definition 3.3; it attempts to find high-scoring local alignments, but does not guarantee finding the maximum scoring ones. The basic version focuses on un-gapped alignments; later versions extended this to gapped alignments as well. However, in many practical applications un-gapped alignments are sufficient. BLAST is used not to infer homology of individual sequence segments, but rather to retrieve similar sequences from a database. Furthermore, BLAST provides a built-in statistical estimate of the significance of its results.

BLAST finds islands of similarity without gaps, called segment pairs. It is of course very easy to locally align two sequences if gaps are not allowed (essentially one needs to just find the optimal choice of prefix and suffix to remove). In practice it can be even easier if the length of the alignment is small, as one could precompute an index of all length l words and their position in the database (the related program BLAT, by Jim Kent and colleagues, does something very similar to this). Together, such short un-gapped alignments can form seeds for regions of high local similarity.

Definition 3.4

Maximal segment pair. Given two strings **s** and **t**, a *segment pair* is a pair of substrings of these two sequences, of equal length, aligned without gaps. A locally optimal segment pair is a segment pair whose alignment score (without spaces) cannot be improved by extending it or shortening it. A maximal segment pair (MSP) in **s** and **t** is a segment pair with the maximum score over all segment pairs between the two.

When comparing all the sequences in the database against the query, BLAST attempts to find all the sequences that when paired with the query contain an MSP whose score is above some threshold, Θ. Θ is chosen based on statistical considerations, such that it is unlikely to find a random sequence in the database that achieves a score higher than Θ when compared with the query sequence. The search starts by identifying a short segment pair, and then by extending it in both directions until the score drops below the specified threshold.

Hence there are two main steps in the BLAST algorithm: first, given a length parameter, l, and a threshold parameter, Θ, BLAST finds all the l-length words of database sequences that align with words from the query with an alignment score higher than Θ. These are called hotspots, or hits. Then, each hit is extended to find whether it is contained within a larger segment pair with a higher score than Θ.

We will not discuss in this book the many crucial algorithmic aspects of BLAST, referring the readers to the references listed in Section 3.10

Remark 3.3
Statistical analysis of BLAST scores. After interrogating a database of sequences, for example by using BLAST, we need to assess the statistical significance of the hits (the sequences retrieved from the database, due to their similarity to the query sequence). An important parameter is the *E*-value: the number of hits we can expect to see just by chance. This is different from the p-value, since this also considers the size of the database itself. The lower the E-value, the more significant the score. For example, an E-value of 1 assigned to a hit means that we might expect to see one match of similar length and percent identity by chance.

Online BLAST tool. Besides being an algorithm to compute local alignments and their significance, BLAST is also a popular online software tool, connected to various NCBI databases, including GenBank. The tool compares nucleotide or protein sequences to sequence databases and calculates the statistical significance of matches. It is regularly used to infer functional and evolutionary relationships between sequences, and to identify gene families. It comes in many flavours: for amino acids, for nucleotides, and many more, but the basic principles are the ones discussed above. Its URL is: `http://www.ncbi.nlm.nih.gov/BLAST/`. Happy Blasting!

Example 3.3
Blasting the homeobox. If we use BLASTP (for proteins) to query GenBank with the Drosophila sequence included in the local alignment on page 49, we find hundreds of hits. The online service reports the first 500, ranging in E-value from 3e-37 to 1e-15. Here is an arbitrary selection, to illustrate the result. Note that the organisms range from flies to plants, from mice to molluscs. Also note that the raw alignment scores have been transformed into a "normalized score" expressed in bits, to ensure comparability between scores of different length sequences. We will not discuss this normalization step here, however pointers to online discussions of this quantity can be found in

Section 3.10.

Sequence	Description	Organism	Score	E-Value
CAA56038.1	transcription factor	*D. melanogaster*	155	3e-37
CAC80518.1	paired box protein	*M. musculus*	139	2e-32
CAA09227.1	DtPax-6 protein	*G. tigrina*	106	3e-22
AAL67846.1	paired-related homeobox	*G. gallus*	90.5	2e-17
AAM33145.1	–	*P. vulgata*	85.5	5e-16

As a comparison, if we BLAST the sequence VIVALASVEGAS we find the following results

ZP_00530569.1	inner-membrane translocator	*C. phaeobacteroides*	26.1	154
AAQ18142.1	poly(A)-binding protein	*C. sativus* (cucumber)	25.2	278
AAM36438.1	conserved hypothetical protein	*X. axonopodis*	25.2	278

none of which is significant (given the very high E-values), as expected.

3.7 Multiple sequence alignment

While pairwise alignment is almost always the first step in assigning biological function to sequences, simultaneously aligning multiple sequences can reveal a wealth of biological information and is necessary for many more advanced analyses in biology. The search for an optimal *multiple* alignment leads to both important conceptual and algorithmic issues, briefly discussed below.

As an example, consider comparing the three sequences, VIVALASVE-GAS, VIVADAVIS, and VIVADALLAS. A multiple alignment (not necessarily an optimal one) would look like

$$
A = \begin{matrix}
V & I & V & A & L & A & S & V & E & G & A & S \\
V & I & V & A & D & A & - & V & I & - & - & S \\
V & I & V & A & D & A & L & L & A & - & - & S.
\end{matrix}
$$

When performed for related sequences, multiple alignment can help researchers identify conserved domains and other regions of interest. We can readily adapt the definition of pairwise alignment to cover this case.

Definition 3.5

Multiple alignment. A *multiple (global) alignment* of k sequences, is an assignment of gap symbols "$-$" into those sequences, or at their ends. The k resulting strings are placed one above the other so that every character or gap symbol in either string is opposite a unique character or a unique gap symbol in the other string. It can be represented as a $c \times k$ matrix, for some value of c, the ith row containing the ith sequence and (interspersed) gap symbols.

The above definition is of course a mathematical one. From a biological perspective, a multiple alignment represents a hypothesis about homology of individual positions within the aligned sequences.

Many algorithmic ideas transfer directly from pairwise to multiple alignment. For example, we can distinguish between global and local multiple alignment, where with local alignment we allow the possibility of dropping prefixes and suffixes from each of the sequences. This problem is related to the problem of motif finding, discussed in Chapter 10, and hence we do not discuss it here. We concentrate here on multiple global alignment.

Two problems arise when extending the concepts of pairwise alignment to multiple alignment. First, we need to be able to score multiple alignments. There are various ways of scoring multiple alignments, as this is a problem that needs to be addressed with an eye towards biology and an eye towards computational convenience. Second, we need to devise an efficient method of finding the optimal alignment. This is a computational question that unfortunately does not have an elegant solution as with pairwise alignment.

The extension of pairwise alignment algorithms such as Needleman–Wunsch or Smith–Waterman to more than two sequences are straightforward, but their cost increases exponentially with k (where k is the number of sequences). This fact means that there is an exponential cost in the number of sequences being aligned, limiting the use of these algorithms to very few sequences.

A number of heuristics have been proposed to find approximate solutions, none of which guarantees finding the optimal multiple alignment. The simplest ones are greedy algorithms, that start with a pairwise alignment and iteratively add the other sequences. Usually they use an initial step of clustering the sequences, so that one first merges the closest sequences, and then gradually adds the ones that are less and less similar. In the next chapter we will address a hidden Markov model approach to multiple alignment .

A very popular and efficient heuristic algorithm for multiple alignment is CLUSTAL, originally developed by Desmond Higgins and Paul Sharp at Trinity College, Dublin in 1988 and extended by Higgins, Julie Thompson, and Toby Gibson into the current version, CLUSTALW. The basic idea behind CLUSTAL is to break down the multiple alignment problem into multiple computationally familiar pairwise alignment problems. First, CLUSTAL clusters the sequences together by rough similarity, and then starts doing pairwise alignments of the most similar sequences, moving out to eventually include all of the sequences.

Example 3.4

Multiple alignment. A multiple alignment of human, sheep, and cow homeodomains (accession numbers: AAH07284, AAX39333, AAP41546). Note that in this case, due to the high level of conservation of these domains, no gaps were needed to align them. In most real applications, gaps would be present in a multiple alignment.

```
KRKLQRNRTSFTQEQIEALEKEFERTHYPDVFARERLAAKIDLPEARIQVWFSNRRAKWRREEKL
KKKHRRNRTTFTTYQLHQLERAFEASHYPDVYSREELAAKVHLPEVRVQVWFQNRRAKWRRQERL
KKKHRRNRTTFTTYQLHQLERAFEASHYPDVYSREELAAKVHLPEVRVQVWFQNRRAKWRRQERL
```

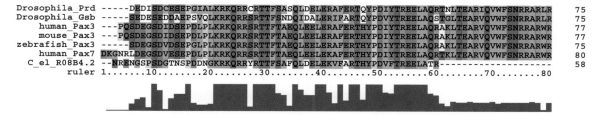

```
Drosophila_Prd   -----DEDISDCESEPGIALKRKQRRCRTTFSASQLDELERAFERTQYPDIYTREELAQRTNLTEARIQVWFSNRRARLR   75
Drosophila_Gsb   -----SEDESEDDAEPSVQLKRKQRRSRTTFSNDQIDALERIFARTQYPDVYTREELAQSTGLTEARVQVWFSNRRARLR   75
     human_Pax3  ---PQSDEGSDIDSEPDLPLKRKQRRSRTTFTAEQLEELERAFERTHYPDIYTREELAQRAKLTEARVQVWFSNRRARWR   77
     mouse_Pax3  ---PQSDEGSDIDSEPDLPLKRKQRRSRTTFTAEQLEELERAFERTHYPDIYTREELAQRAKLTEARVQVWFSNRRARWR   77
 zebrafish_Pax3  -----SDEGSDVDSEPGLPLKRKQRRSRTTFTAEQLEELERAFERTHYPDIYTREELAQRAKLTEARVQVWFSNRRARWR   75
     human_Pax7  DKGNRLDEGSDVESEPDLPLKRKQRRSRTTFTAEQLEELEKAFERTHYPDIYTREELAQRTKLTEARVQVWFSNRRARWR   80
    C_el_R08B4.2  --NRENGSPSDGTNSPDDNGKRKQRRYRTTFSAFQLDELEKVFARTHYPDVFTREELATR-------------------   58
          ruler  1.......10........20........30........40........50........60........70........80
```

Fig. 3.3 A multiple alignment produced by the CLUSTALW package using fragments of various PAX genes

Example 3.5

CLUSTALW. Output of the freely available CLUSTALW package showing a multiple alignment of fragments of various PAX genes as well as the amount of similarity at each position is shown in Figure 3.3. Pointers to the online software packages and relative literature can be found in Section 3.10.

3.8* | Computing the alignments

In this section we describe some of the details behind the Needleman–Wunsch and Smith–Waterman dynamic programming algorithms that were skipped above. Being aware of these details is essential for a computer scientist, but might not be necessary for a biologist or a statistician interested in using these alignment methods to analyze data.

3.8.1 Needleman–Wunsch algorithm

Recursive relations. The idea behind the recursion in the Needleman–Wunsch algorithm is that in order to find the score of an optimal alignment between the first i symbols of sequence $\mathbf{s}$ and the first j symbols symbols of sequence $\mathbf{t}$, all we need to know is the score of the alignment between the two sequences up to the previous position. While this might seem confusing at first – how do we know the score of the alignment up to the previous position to begin with? – it turns out to be easy to perform once you know where to start the calculation.

Consider the first position in an alignment between two sequences. There are only three possibilities for the state of this position: (1) gap in the first sequence, (2) gap in the second sequence, and (3) no gaps, but either a match or mismatch. Given a scoring function (let us continue to use the simple one defined above), we immediately know the score for each of these three possibilities. In either of the first two cases we would pay the gap penalty; in the third case we would not suffer any penalty if $x = y$, but we would if $x \neq y$. Of course any one of the three options might make for a better or worse alignment of the remaining sequence, so it is not yet possible to choose which one is best (otherwise we could use a "greedy" algorithm). However, if we know the possible scores for these three alignments, then we can choose the optimal alignment for the sequences up to *next* position. We write this recursion as follows:

$$M_{i,j} = \max \begin{cases} M_{i-1,j} + \sigma(\mathbf{s}_i, -) \\ M_{i,j-1} + \sigma(-, \mathbf{t}_j) \\ M_{i-1,j-1} + \sigma(\mathbf{s}_i, \mathbf{t}_j). \end{cases}$$

In words, the score of the alignment between $\mathbf{s}_i$ and $\mathbf{t}_j$ is equal to the maximum of the score of the alignment of the three prefixes plus the score for the consequent edit operation. We have effectively reduced the problem of optimally aligning two sequences to that of optimally aligning their prefixes.

Tabular computation. The essential feature of any dynamic programming technique is the tabular computation – we will reduce our computation time by storing the results of calculations we carry out over and over again in a table. For instance, for all the possible alignments between VIVALASVEGAS and VIVADAVIS we would need to perform the same partial computation many times (say, the alignment of VIVA and VIVA). An efficient solution is to cache the partial results that may be reused by maintaining a table filled in by using the recursion in a bottom-up way.

We will maintain partial alignment scores in a rectangular table with $m + 1 \times n + 1$ cells (where m is the length of sequence $\mathbf{s}$, and n is the length of sequence $\mathbf{t}$). The first row and column are associated with the "empty sequence" and, in order to initialize the table, we begin by filling them with multiples of the gap penalty according to the following rules:

$$M_{i,1} = \sum_{k=1}^{i} \sigma(\mathbf{s}_k, -)$$

$$M_{1,j} = \sum_{k=1}^{j} \sigma(-, \mathbf{t}_k).$$

This results in an initialized dynamic programming table whose first row and column are as those of Table 3.1 and depend only on the gap-insertion penalty cost.

After initializing our alignment in this way, we start filling each cell that has its top, left, and top-left neighbor already filled (the first cell to be filled is therefore position $(2, 2)$). To fill in position $(2, 2)$, we choose the best score according to our recursive relationship defined above. Choosing the left neighboring cell, $(i - 1, j)$, is equivalent to putting a gap in the sequence along the side of the table; the resulting score would therefore be -2 (-1 from position $(i - 1), j$ plus -1 for the gap penalty). Choosing the neighboring cell above is equivalent to putting a gap in the sequence across the top of the table; the resulting score is also -2. If we choose the diagonal neighbor, $(i - 1), (j - 1)$, we are not inserting any gaps; the resulting score is therefore $+1$ (0 from the neighbor plus $+1$ for a match). We would therefore put a $+1$ in this position to maximize our alignment score, remembering that we chose the diagonal neighbor (this is for our trace-back procedure, defined below). Moving to position $(3, 2)$, we again evaluate our choices and decide to choose the left neighbor – inserting a gap in the top sequence results in the optimal score (0) given the alignment of V with V in the first position. We can move across the second row in this

Table 3.1 The dynamic programming table resulting from the global alignment of two amino acid sequences. The winning path in emphasized

		V	I	V	A	D	A	V	I	S
	0	-1	-2	-3	-4	-5	-6	-7	-8	-9
V	-1	-1	0	-1	-2	-3	-4	-5	-6	-7
I	-2	0	2	1	0	-1	-2	-3	-4	-5
V	-3	-1	1	3	2	1	0	-1	-2	-3
A	-4	-2	0	2	4	3	2	1	0	-1
L	-5	-3	-1	1	3	3	2	1	0	-1
A	-6	-4	-2	0	2	2	4	3	2	1
S	-7	-5	-3	-1	1	1	3	3	2	3
V	-8	-6	-4	-2	0	0	2	4	3	2
E	-9	-7	-5	-3	-1	-1	1	3	3	2
G	-10	-8	-6	-4	-2	-2	0	2	2	2
A	-11	-9	-7	-5	-3	-3	-1	1	1	1
S	-12	-10	-8	-6	-4	-4	-2	0	0	2

manner, and then across the following rows until we have filled out the entire table.

The alignment score of the global alignment can be read in the bottom-right cell in the table (the score is 2). The alignment itself can be reconstructed from the optimal path with a method called trace-back, described below.

Trace-back. The bottom-right cell of Table 3.1 gives the score of the optimal global alignment between $\mathbf{s}$ and $\mathbf{t}$. However, what we really want is the alignment itself; we obtain this by means of the trace-back procedure. When filling the table in the previous step, we noted the need to keep track of which one of the three recursive rules was used to fill each cell – which one of the three neighboring cells was used to fill in a given cell. The information on the path taken can be stored in each cell in the form of a pointer, and once we reach the bottom-right cell we can trace-back the pointers to the initial top-left cell. This path specifies the optimal alignment.

To translate the trace-back into an alignment we simply remember what each choice in our recursive relation meant when filling out the table. For each diagonal step, there is a corresponding match/mismatch in the alignment; for each vertical step, there is a gap insertion in the top sequence; for each horizontal step, there is a gap insertion in the sequence along the side of the table. Starting with the bottom-right cell, the alignment of this position is determined by the step we took to get there. In this case we took a diagonal step (see Table 3.1) so we align S with S. Tracing back the entire alignment in this way, we end up with the optimal global alignment:

$$A^*(\mathbf{s}, \mathbf{t}) = \begin{matrix} V & I & V & A & L & A & S & V & E & G & A & S \\ | & | & | & | & & | & & | & & & & | \\ V & I & V & A & D & A & - & V & - & - & I & S. \end{matrix}$$

We can see that the score given in the botto... the score if we simply count up the number of ... in the alignment: 7 matches, 2 mismatches, 3 ...

Algorithm 3.1
Needleman–Wunsch global alignment.

- Create a table of size $(m + 1) \times (n + 1)$ fo... and n.
- Fill table entries $(m : 1)$ and $(1 : n)$ with for...

$$M_{i,1} = \sum_{k=1}^{i} \sigma(\mathbf{s}_k, -)$$

$$M_{1,j} = \sum_{k=1}^{j} \sigma(-, \mathbf{t}_k).$$

- Starting from top left, compute each entry using the recursive relation:

$$M_{i,j} = \max \begin{cases} M_{i-1,j} + \sigma(\mathbf{s}_i, -) \\ M_{i,j-1} + \sigma(-, \mathbf{t}_j) \\ M_{i-1,j-1} + \sigma(\mathbf{s}_i, \mathbf{t}_j). \end{cases}$$

- Perform the trace-back procedure.

The computational cost of this algorithm is determined by the size of the table to be filled, and hence is proportional to $|\mathbf{s}||\mathbf{t}|$.

3.8.2 Smith–Waterman algorithm

For local alignment, we again choose a scoring function that gives negative values to mismatches and gaps, positive values to correct matches; the scoring function is again additive. We use the same recursive relation as before, but now we allow a fourth option: whenever a cell would normally take on a negative value, it is instead assigned a value of zero:

$$M_{i,j} = \max \begin{cases} M_{i-1,j-1} + \sigma(\mathbf{s}_i, \mathbf{t}_j) \\ M_{i-1,j} + \sigma(\mathbf{s}_i, -) \\ M_{i,j-1} + \sigma(-, \mathbf{t}_j) \\ 0. \end{cases}$$

One consequence of this recursion is that we now initialize the DP table with zeros. A zero option also guarantees that there are no negative cells. Once the table is filled, finding the best local alignment is simple. First, locate the highest value in the matrix, and trace-back as before until we reach a zero entry. This path constitutes the best local alignment. Any extension of this path to the left or to the right would result in a lower score, as would any restriction (i.e. any subpath that only traversed a part of it). So the score of the local alignment is the highest element in the table, whereas before it was the element found in the bottom-right cell. The option of stopping at the first zero amounts to removing a prefix. That of choosing the start of the trace-back at the highest element of the table amounts to removing a suffix.

Example 3.6
Local alignment DP table. One solution of the local alignment between QUE–
VIVALASVEGAS and VIVADAVIS is given by the subsequences VIVA con-
tained in both sequences (other solutions with the same cost can be found).
That is, the solution is

$$
\begin{array}{cccc}
V & I & V & A \\
| & | & | & | \\
V & I & V & A
\end{array}
$$

For convenience, however, we choose to represent here the entire sequences,
including also the removed prefixes and suffixes that are marked with the symbol
R:

Q	U	E	V	I	V	A	L	A	S	V	E	G	A	S
R	R	R	|	|	|	|	R	R	R	R	R	R	R	R
–	–	–	V	I	V	A	D	A	–	V	–	–	I	S.

The corresponding dynamic programming table is shown below. Every solution
can be found by finding all the cells with maximum value (in this case 4) and
tracing back until a zero entry is found.

		Q	U	E	V	I	V	A	L	A	S	V	E	G	A	S
	0	0	0	0	0	0	0	0	0	0	0	0	0	0	0
V	0	0	0	0	1	0	1	0	0	0	0	1	0	0	0
I	0	0	0	0	0	2	1	0	0	0	0	0	0	0	0
V	0	0	0	0	1	1	3	2	1	0	0	1	0	0	0
A	0	0	0	0	0	0	2	4	3	2	1	0	0	0	1	0
D	0	0	0	0	0	0	1	3	3	2	1	0	0	0	0
A	0	0	0	0	0	0	0	2	2	4	3	2	1	0	1	0
V	0	0	0	0	1	0	1	1	1	3	3	4	3	2	1
I	0	0	0	0	0	2	1	0	0	2	2	3	3	2	1
S	0	0	0	0	0	1	1	0	0	1	3	2	2	2	1	2

Algorithm 3.2
Smith–Waterman local alignment.

- Create table $(n + 1) \times (m + 1)$.
- Fill table entries $(1, 1 : m + 1)$ and $(1 : n + 1, 1)$ with zeros.
- Starting from top left, compute each entry using recursive relation:

$$
M_{i,j} = \max \begin{cases}
M_{i-1,j-1} + \sigma(\mathbf{s}_i, \mathbf{t}_j) \\
M_{i-1,j} + \sigma(\mathbf{s}_i, -) \\
M_{i,j-1} + \sigma(-, \mathbf{t}_j) \\
0.
\end{cases}
$$

- Perform trace-back procedure, from highest element in table to first zero
  element on the trace-back path.

3.9 | Exercises

(1) The genes discussed in the opening story about the Frankenstein experiment can be found in GenBank (*eyeless* at X79493 and human *aniridia* at AY707088). Study their local and global alignments, and discuss their statistical significance.

(2) Use BLAST to verify the biological significance of your findings.

(3) Protein-coding DNA sequences are best aligned after translation into amino acids. Find two homologous ORFs in GenBank, and align them both as nucleotide sequences, and then as amino acid sequences.

(4) Use the links to free software tools found on the book's website, to perform multiple alignment of the sequences presented in this chapter (use CLUSTALW).

3.10 | Reading list

The paper that introduced the Smith–Waterman algorithm is Smith and Waterman (1981), the Needleman–Wunsch algorithm was introduced in Needleman and Wunsch (1970) and BLAST in Altschul *et al.* (1990). The general CLUSTAL algorithm is discussed in Thompson *et al.* (1994), and the CLUSTALW version in Higgins *et al.* (1996). Recommended readings are also the 1986 book by Russell Doolittle on early sequence alignment and bioinformatics methods (Doolittle, 1986), and the discussion by Gribskov and coworkers on the same topic (Gribskov and Eisenberg, 1987). A discussion of advanced statistical testing techniques for sequence alignment can be found in (Ewens and Grant, 2006).

A tutorial on the use of BLAST is also available online, following the links contained on the book's companion website:

www.computational-genomics.net.

In the same website you can find pointers to CLUSTALW and other free alignment software, as well as to all the papers and all protein sequences discussed in this chapter.

Chapter 4

The boulevard of broken genes
Hidden Markov models

4.1 | The nose knows

- Gene families
- Hidden Markov models
- Sequence segmentation
- Multiple alignment

The Nobel Prize in Physiology or Medicine in 2004 went to Richard Axel of Columbia University and Linda Buck of the Fred Hutchinson Cancer Research Center for their elucidation of the olfactory system. The olfactory system is responsible for our sense of smell: it includes a large family of proteins called odorant receptors that in combination make it possible to recognize over 10 000 different odors. These odorant receptors are attached to the surface of cells in our nasal passage, detecting odorant molecules as they are inhaled and passing the information along to the brain.

In order for odorant receptors (ORs) to both sense molecules outside of the cell and to signal the inside of the cell of their discoveries, these proteins must traverse the cell membrane. To do this, odorant receptors contain seven *transmembrane* domains: stretches of highly hydrophobic amino acids that interact with the fatty cell membrane. The seven transmembrane domains result in a highly heterogeneous protein sequence: alternating stretches of hydrophobic and hydrophilic amino acids that mark the function of receptor proteins. Axel and Buck's discovery led to the further description of similar receptors involved in the sense of taste and in the detection of pheromones, chemicals used in signaling between organisms.

The odorant receptors are the largest gene family in the human genome, with approximately 1000 members. However, only 40% of the genes are functional – over 600 human odorant receptors are *pseudogenes*, inactive or defective descendants of functional genes. Mice and rats, for instance, have an almost full complement of functioning odorant receptors, and as a result can distinguish a much fuller palette of smells. When genes are no longer needed for smell – such as when color vision becomes the predominant sense – natural selection no longer maintains their function and they accumulate debilitating mutations. Pseudogenes are often very similar to their functioning relatives, except that they contain stop codons or indels that result in the production of non-functioning proteins.

The analysis of odorant receptors requires more advanced tools than the ones presented so far. The similarity between various OR genes is too remote to be revealed by a simple pairwise alignment, but provides a strong signal when we consider all of them together in a multiple alignment. In addition, we may be interested in modeling the chemical structure of ORs in order to reveal their transmembrane structure.

Probabilistic sequence models: the state of the art. In order to perform the steps outlined above, we will introduce one of the most important tools of computational genomics: hidden Markov models (HMMs). These naturally combine multinomial and Markov sequence models, as well as the algorithmic machinery of dynamic programming discussed in the previous chapter. HMMs are the probabilistic model of choice for biological sequences (both DNA and protein), and allow us more freedom to detect patterns that do not necessarily have rigidly defined structures.

Their uses in computational genomics cover many areas. Here we list some of the most common:

- **Segmentation.** Gene and protein sequences may contain distinct regions whose chemical properties differ widely. HMMs can help us to define the exact boundaries of these regions. Segmentation is also used to define much larger stretches of heterogeneous nucleotide use in genome sequences, and can be used to identify interesting biological features responsible for this heterogeneity (as we saw with change-point analysis in Chapter 1).
- **Multiple alignment.** In the previous chapter we showed that multiple sequence alignment is often efficiently computed by reducing the complexity of an all-versus-all comparison to the relatively easy task of one-versus-all. HMMs make this task even easier by defining a so-called *profile HMM* against which all new sequences can be aligned. These profile HMMs are also what makes it possible to assign protein function quickly, and can be regarded both as a summary of a multiple alignment and as a model for a family of sequences.
- **Prediction of function.** Often, simple alignment of sequences does not allow for firm predictions of protein function; just because we can align sequences does not mean that they are functionally related. HMMs allow us to make probabilistic statements about the function of proteins, or let us assign proteins to families of unknown function. There are now a number of public databases that use HMMs for this step in genome annotation.
- **Gene finding.** So far, our gene-finding algorithms have depended on very rigid definitions of genes: start codon, a run of multiple codons, stop codon. While algorithms of this type work fairly well for prokaryotic genes, they are not at all appropriate for finding eukaryotic genes. In addition, if we wish to find pseudogenes – which may fulfill all of the requirements of functioning genes save for some misplaced stop codons – we require the flexibility of HMMs.

4.2 | Hidden Markov models

In 1989 Gary Churchill, now a scientist at the Jackson Labs in Bar Harbor, Maine, introduced the use of hidden Markov models for DNA sequence segmentation. HMMs had been used in a variety of applications previously – such as in software for speech recognition – but not in sequence analysis. Churchill's use of HMMs allowed him to segment a DNA sequence into alternating regions of similar nucleotide usage. Since then HMMs have been applied to an ever-growing series of analyses in genomics, including gene finding and the prediction of protein function, mostly due to pioneering work by David Haussler at UC Santa Cruz. Now, together with alignment methods, HMMs are among the most representative algorithms of the field of bioinformatics.

The basic need for HMMs arises from the fact that genome data is inherently noisy. Even in regions with a high GC-content, for instance, there may be long stretches of As and Ts; patterns observable in DNA sequences are necessarily a rough facsimile of the underlying state of the genome ("high GC-content" might be one such state). Simple multinomial and Markov sequence models used separately are not flexible enough to capture many properties of DNA sequences. HMMs elegantly put these two models together in a simple and efficient scheme.

A primer on HMMs. The basic idea behind the application of HMMs is to model a sequence as having been *indirectly* generated by a Markov chain. At each position in the sequence the Markov chain has some unknown (hidden) state – but all we are able to observe are symbols generated according to a multinomial distribution that *depends* on that state. In other words, the information that we receive about the hidden Markov chain is indirect, possibly corrupted by noise.

The sequence we are trying to analyze is hence modeled as being the result of a doubly random process: one generating a hidden Markov chain, and one turning this hidden chain into the observable sequence. This second process follows a multinomial distribution: in each hidden state, a different set of parameters is used to produce the observed sequence. One of the keys to HMMs is to take this necessarily noisy observed sequence and infer the underlying hidden states.

Hidden states can represent different types of sequence. The simplest HMMs only have two states – such as "GC-rich" or "AT-rich" – while more complex HMMs can have many states – such as "regulatory DNA," "coding region," or "intron."

HMMs have two important parameters: the *transition probability* and the *emission probability*. The transition parameter describes the probability with which the Markov chain switches among the various hidden states. These switches can happen very often or very rarely; the chain may transition between only two states or among many states. The emission parameter describes the probabilities with which the symbols in the observable sequence are produced in each of the different states. Each of the hidden states should be able to produce the same symbols, just in differing frequencies. The number of emitted

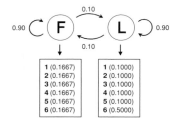

Fig. 4.1 The HMM associated with Example 4.1 : transitions between fair and loaded dice are modeled as a Markov chain, and outcomes of rolls as independent emissions of a multinomial model

symbols can range between two and many; the most common number in sequence analysis is either four (for DNA or RNA) or 20 (for amino acids).

We now give a simple (and classic) example of a 2-state HMM to explore some of the basic ideas.

Example 4.1

Switching between fair and loaded dice. Imagine that we have a pair of dice, one that is fair, but the other is "loaded" (i.e. it does not roll each side with equal probability). A Markov model decides which one of the two dice to roll, and depending on the state of the model either the emission probabilities for the fair or the loaded die is used. In this way we generate a sequence of symbols that is the result of being in two different states.

We will specify our transition parameter so that in either of the two states there is a 90% chance of remaining in that state, and a 10% chance of changing states, as shown in Figure 4.1. For our fair die, the probability of rolling the numbers between 1 and 6 is equal and is given by:

$$0.1667 \quad 0.1667 \quad 0.1667 \quad 0.1667 \quad 0.1667 \quad 0.1667,$$

where each column describes the probability for each of the six numbers; this is our multinomial distribution.

For our loaded die, the emission probabilities are:

$$0.1000 \quad 0.1000 \quad 0.1000 \quad 0.1000 \quad 0.1000 \quad 0.5000.$$

Here the probabilities of rolling 1–5 are still equal, but there is a much higher probability of rolling a 6 (50%).

The visible sequence produced by such an HMM might look like this:

$$s = 4553653163363555133362665132141636651666.$$

If we know the properties of the two dice and of the underlying Markov chain, can we find the most likely sequence of hidden states behind it? In other words, can we guess which die was used at each time point in the sequence? This is a task referred to as *segmentation* (and what we earlier referred to as change point analysis in Chapter 1). Later in this chapter we will describe how to infer these hidden states; here we will simply show you the hidden sequence that generated our visible sequence:

Hidden: **h** = 1111111111111111111122221111111222222222
Visible: **s** = 4553653163363555133362665132141636651666.

Notice that the symbol "6" occurs with high frequency when the sequence is in hidden state 2, corresponding to the loaded die, but this dependency is just probabilistic. Often in biological applications we will train our HMM on one set of data where the hidden states are known, even when we do not know the exact transition and emission probabilities. This allows our model to calculate the most likely transition and emission matrices based on data, and so to better infer the hidden states on novel data. This is especially useful in gene finding where models are often trained on a well-annotated genome and then run on related genomes.

Computing with HMMs. It is an important feature of HMMs that the probability of a sequence (the likelihood of a model) is easily computed, as are all the fundamental quantities necessary to use them. The efficient algorithms that made HMMs popular are based on the same dynamic programming principles behind global and local alignment methods discussed in Chapter 3 and will be discussed in depth separately in Section 4.6. Here we simply review the basics of HMM computations and the parameters used in them.

As a strict generalization of multinomial and Markov models, we have already seen that HMMs need to maintain parameters for both a Markov transition matrix and a number of multinomial models (one for each state of the system). These parameters are generally presented as matrices, one for transitions, T, and one for emissions, E. The transition matrix has dimension $N \times N$ where N is the size of the hidden alphabet, $\mathcal{H}$ (i.e. the number of hidden states). The emission matrix has dimension $N \times M$, where M is the size of the observable alphabet (typically the nucleotide, $\mathcal{N}$, or amino acid, $\mathcal{A}$, alphabet). They are defined as

$$T(k, l) = P(h_i = l | h_{i-1} = k)$$
$$E(k, b) = P(s_i = b | h_i = k).$$

In words: the probability of being in hidden state l, given that the previous position was in state k, is given in the transition matrix by entry $T(k, l)$. And the probability of emitting symbol b is determined by the multinomial model associated with state k, which is given in the emission matrix by entry $E(k, b)$. We denote the sequence of hidden states created by the Markov process by $\mathbf{h}$, and the sequence of symbols generated by the HMM by $\mathbf{s}$. We will assume the sequences have length n. In order for the model to be fully specified, we also need to declare the initial probabilities for the state of the Markov process, denoted $T(0, k) = P(h_1 = k)$.

Basic quantities computable with HMMs. We would now like to make inferences about genome sequences with HMMs. The most common task will be to infer the hidden states of the genome in order to better annotate it, or to better understand its dynamics. Our end goal, therefore, will be to find hidden sequence with the highest likelihood; in order to do this, we must first understand how to calculate probabilities associated with HMMs.

The stochastic process assumed to be generating the sequence is the following: a hidden sequence is generated by the Markov process. Then in each different state, a different multinomial model is used according to the emission parameters associated with that state to produce the observable sequence. This means that, for each position of the hidden sequence, the system emits a visible symbol independently from the appropriate multinomial distribution. The probabilities of these sequences can hence be written as

$$P(\mathbf{h}) = P(h_1) \prod_{i=2}^{n} P(h_i | h_{i-1}) = T(0, h_1) \prod_{i=2}^{n} T(h_{i-1}, h_i)$$
$$P(\mathbf{s}|\mathbf{h}) = \prod_{i=1}^{n} P(s_i | h_i) = \prod_{i=1}^{n} E(h_i, s_i),$$

where we have deliberately used two notations, the second one being more convenient for the description of algorithms in Section 4.6.

This says that the total likelihood of the hidden sequence, $\mathbf{h}$, is simply the product of the individual probabilities of the states at each position in the sequence, with states determined by the transition matrix. The same applies to the likelihood of the observed sequences given the hidden state at each position, with the emission matrix describing the probability of each observed symbol.

If we know the hidden sequence (typically we do not), then we can readily calculate the joint probability of $\mathbf{s}$ and $\mathbf{h}$ under the parameters (T, E):

$$P(\mathbf{s}, \mathbf{h}) = P(\mathbf{s}|\mathbf{h})P(\mathbf{h}).$$

This part is very efficient and not very different from what was done in Chapter 1 for simple multinomial and Markov sequence models.

However when the hidden sequence $\mathbf{h}$ is unknown (as is often the case) we can use the *theorem of total probability* to compute the probability of the observed symbols, $P(\mathbf{s})$:

$$P(\mathbf{s}) = \sum_{\forall \mathbf{h}_j \in \mathcal{H}^n} P(\mathbf{s}, \mathbf{h}_j) = \sum_{\forall \mathbf{h}_j \in \mathcal{H}^n} P(\mathbf{s}|\mathbf{h}_j)P(\mathbf{h}_j),$$

where $\forall \mathbf{h}_j \in \mathcal{H}^n$ means that we must sum over all of the possible hidden chains of length n, a number that grows exponentially with n. Although this calculation requires a large number of summations, it can be efficiently computed by an algorithm called the *forward* algorithm based on dynamic programming.

Given this algorithm we can now compute the most likely hidden sequence, $\mathbf{h}^*$:

$$\mathbf{h}^* = \arg \max_{\forall \mathbf{h} \in \mathcal{H}^n} P(\mathbf{s}, \mathbf{h});$$

note that this is also equivalent to computing $\arg \max_{\forall \mathbf{h}_j \in \mathcal{H}^n} P(\mathbf{h}|\mathbf{s})$. This quantity is also called the "most probable state path," and can be computed with a dynamic programming algorithm called the *Viterbi* algorithm, which is described in Section 4.6.

These two last steps appear to be less trivial to perform algorithmically, as they require us to respectively marginalize and optimize over an exponentially large set in the sequence ($\forall \mathbf{h}_j \in \mathcal{H}^n$). It is remarkable that this can be done in a time that grows only linearly with the length n of the sequence, using a method that is essentially the same method used in Chapter 3 for sequence alignment, and a direct consequence of the Markov assumptions.

We can also estimate the model parameters given some training data where both the hidden and observed states are known, using the maximum likelihood principle and an algorithm called expectation maximization (EM), briefly discussed in Section 4.6.

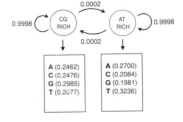

Fig. 4.2 The model of *Lambda phage* sequence obtained by the EM algorithm in Example 4.2

Example 4.2

Segmentation of the lambda phage genome. We saw in Chapter 1 that the lambda phage genome has long stretches of GC- and AT-rich sequence. We can use an HMM to segment this genome into blocks of these two states. Starting with random transition (T) and emission (E) matrices, we can use the EM algorithm to better estimate those parameters (assuming that there are two hidden states and four visible symbols {A, C, G, T }). This yields the model in Figure 4.2 that

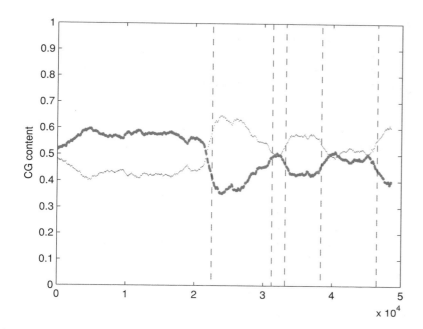

Fig. 4.3 GC content plot for *Lambda phage*, and the segmentation found by a two-state HMM, as described in Example 4.2

essentially describes a sequence with very rare change points; there is a high probability of staying in the same state (99.98%) for both hidden states. (Note that transition probabilities do not necessarily have to be symmetric for the two states.) We also see that state 1 has a high GC-content and state 2 has a high AT-content. Parsing the genome of Lambda phage with the Viterbi algorithm and using the above matrices, we get the results shown in Figure 4.3. Notice that the system did not know what type of segmentation we were looking for (we did not tell it to group G with C and A with T, for example), just that we wanted to divide the sequence into two parts with different statistical properties. We can see from the figure that the segmentation found by the algorithm seems to reflect the GC content of the sequence. The figure shows GC and AT content plots, and the change points found by the algorithm.

4.3 Profile HMMs

In the examples above, we have used HMMs to segment a sequence, detecting boundaries between statistically different regions. In this setting, the hidden states are interpreted as different types of sequence, and typically the hidden alphabet is very small. The Markov chain is characterized by a cyclic graph such as the one in Figure 4.2: a graph that allows the system to alternate among the hidden states, possibly returning many times to the same state. But other interpretations of the hidden states can lead to different uses of this model.

An important problem in computational genomics is to characterize sets of homologous proteins (gene families) based on common patterns in their

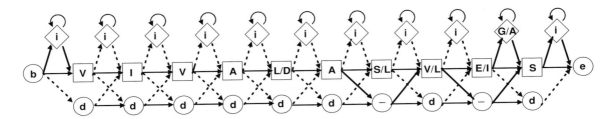

Fig. 4.4 A profile HMM corresponding to the multiple alignment below

sequence. This allows us, for example, to determine if a new protein belongs to a certain family or not. A classic approach to characterizing families is to start from a multiple alignment of all the elements of the family, and look for columns of highly conserved amino acids. The summary of the alignment can be characterized by the frequency with which certain symbols appear in certain positions. Sometimes these can be represented by Position Specific Scoring Matrices (PSSM), specifying the probability of observing a specific symbol at a specific position; these will be discussed in Chapter 10. This method, however, does not work well for cases which include gaps of variable length. HMMs can be used in this situation to provide a more flexible characterization of sequence patterns. This is done by defining a *profile HMM* (pHMM). One way to think of pHMMs is as abstract descriptions of a protein family; another way is as statistical summaries of a multiple sequence alignment.

More formally, profile HMMs encode position-specific information about the frequency of particular amino acids as well as the frequency of insertions and deletions in the alignment. They are constructed from multiple alignments of homologous sequences. They contain match states, which describe the distribution of amino acids at each position, as well as insertion and deletion states that allow for the addition or removal of residues. There is a match state, insertion state, and deletion state for each column of a multiple alignment. In other words, for an alignment 250 amino acids in length, there are 250 match, 250 insertion, and 250 deletion states in the pHMM (not all need to be visited in one path, of course). For each match and insertion state there is a specific probability of emitting each of the 20 amino acids. No amino acids are emitted from deletion states.

An example may clarify how pHMMs can be used to represent sequence alignments. Let us consider again the multiple alignment used in Chapter 3:

```
V   I   V   A   L   A   S   V   E   G   A   S
V   I   V   A   D   A   -   V   I   -   -   S
V   I   V   A   D   A   L   L   -   -   A   S
```

We see that its sequences have many features in common: they all start with the same four amino acids, VIVA, then they have a position where various choices are possible, then they have another conserved position, A. After a variable number of positions, more or less rigidly specified, they all have the symbol S.

All this can be summarized in the pHMM model shown in Figure 4.4, where each path represents a possible sequence. For readability, in each state we write only the dominant symbols of the emission matrix for that state. It should be clear, however, that in general any symbol is possible, with different probabilities. Similarly, transitions with low probability are denoted by dotted lines, and those with high probability by solid lines. At each square node, a symbol can be emitted, according to the emission probability associated with that position. Insertion (diamonds) and deletion (circles) states are present, so certain paths allow us to insert gaps or extra symbols in the profile. The first and last nodes are referred to as the beginning (**b**) and end (**e**), and simply specify the boundaries of the pHMM. Every path between the beginning and end nodes represents a possible instantiation of the profile. Each hidden state can be interpreted as a specific position in the pHMM, and the underlying graph is traversed only in one direction, from left to right (except for insertion symbols, where loops are possible).

The example above is very simplified. In reality, each position of the profile has different emission probabilities associated with each symbol, and each edge of the graph has its own transition probabilities. Any path from the beginning state to the end state can correspond to a valid instance of the pattern. This model allows us to compute the degree to which a given sequence fits the model. Sequences that satisfy this profile will have a certain set of symbols in the correct order, with high probability, but exceptional symbols are easily tolerated.

Profile HMMs allow us to summarize the salient features of a protein alignment into a single model, against which novel sequences can easily be tested for similarity. Also, since pHMMs are an abstract representation of a multiple alignment, they can be used to *produce* pairwise or multiple alignments; sequences are said to be aligned to the model. Aligning a sequence with a pHMM is equivalent to aligning it with the hundreds of sequences used to produce the model. There are free online repositories, like Pfam, that store pHMMs of many protein families. The next section will provide some examples of such alignments related to the family of proteins containing odorant receptors.

4.4 | Finding genes with hidden Markov models

Another important use for HMMs in DNA sequence analysis is to find genes – techniques such as simple ORF finding are not flexible enough to be used for finding many types of genes. Similar methods are limited by a number of problems, including: an inability to detect very short genes that are indistinguishable from background noise; an inability to detect non-translated genes (RNA-coding genes) that have no codon structure; and an inability to deal with eukaryotic genes that have *introns* interrupting the coding sequence. In addition, if we want to find pseudogenes (such as many of the odorant receptors in humans), we must relax our requirements of an intact open reading frame. Gene-finding methods can be significantly improved over simple ORF searches by integrating a number of different sequence signals, each of which is probabilistic in nature. HMMs provide a natural framework for doing this. These signals may include transcription factor binding sites, open reading frames, intron splice sites, and many others.

The state of the art for gene finding is based on quite complex HMM models, most of which are beyond the scope of this introductory book. Although we do not discuss the details here, it should be relatively easy to imagine how an HMM can be used to encode a series of signals associated with genes by combining ideas from profile HMMs and from segmentation HMMs. Section 4.8 provides pointers to relevant articles on this topic. Here and in Chapter 10 we simply discuss in more detail the kind of signals that can be incorporated into a gene model based on HMMs.

Introns and exons. Eukaryotic genes can be very large, upwards of 250 Kb or more. But the proteins they encode generally require only half as many nucleotides to fully specify all the amino acids they contain. The reason for this is that almost all eukaryotic genes are divided up into *introns* and *exons*. While a very long stretch of DNA is transcribed for every gene, some of the resulting RNA will be edited out before the messenger RNA is sent for translation; the parts of the gene that are removed are called introns. The remaining portions of the transcribed gene are the exons. While not all exonic sequences are translated – there will often be 5′ and 3′ untranslated regions at the head and tail of the mRNA – in general exons are coding and introns are non-coding DNA.

One of the major problems in eukaryotic gene finding, then, is to find open reading frames amidst the confusion of intervening non-coding sequences. The manner in which introns divide exons does not make the task easier: rather than always being inserted between codons in-frame (i.e. between the third position of one codon and the first position of the next), introns can break up codons in any frame. While there are often *splice sites* to mark the position of introns, these are not rigidly defined sequences that are always present. In general, splice sites consist of a 5′ AG/GT sequence (i.e. the exon ends in AG and the intron begins with GT) and a 3′ AG/G (i.e. the next exon begins with a G). Other signals in the intron may help to identify splice sites and may also identify *branch sites*, an intronic sequence necessary for splicing. The branch site is usually located 20–50 bases upstream of the 3′ splice site and has the sequence TATAAC. So even though intervening non-coding sequences make ORF finding much more difficult, there are sequence signals that can help us in our search. Using this information together with signal from transcription factor binding sites (Chapter 10) in a complex model like an HMM makes it possible to identify eukaryotic genes.

4.5   Case study: odorant receptors

We are now ready to see HMMs in action by studying the protein family to which odorant receptors belong: 7-transmembrane (7-TM) G-protein coupled receptors. This is an important family containing (in humans) 250 proteins in addition to the 400 ORs. It includes receptors found in the retina to sense light as well as receptors for hormones and neurotransmitters such as melatonin, serotonin, and dopamine. More than half of today's pharmaceuticals target these receptors.

While all of these receptor proteins have the characteristic 7-TM structure discussed above, there is still a large amount of sequence variation between members. This makes it difficult to identify members of the family by pairwise comparison alone. We will use a pHMM representing this important protein family, obtained from the online database Pfam (accession number PF00001) to decide if a given odorant receptor sequence (GenBank number Q8NGD2) belongs to the family or not. As a comparison, we will try to make the same decision based on pairwise global alignment between the same sequence and a typical receptor (GenBank number NP_002368) that was used to create the pHMM (remember that pHMMs are built using the multiple alignment of known homologous sequences). This will illustrate the power of alignment to a pHMM rather than to other sequences. We will also see how a pHMM can be used to obtain a multiple alignment.

Finally, we will use a 2-state HMM to segment the odorant receptor protein, as a way to reveal the alternating hydrophobic and hydrophilic regions characteristic of 7-TM proteins.

As discussed earlier in this chapter, humans have only about 400 odorant receptors. We will use a dataset of 347 well-known human OR protein sequences available from GenBank (the data are available on the book's website). The length of these sequences is mostly between 300 and 330 amino acids, with a mean length of 314 amino acids. The sequence below is a typical example of an OR, of length 312 amino acids:

```
MAMDNVTAVF  QFLLIGISNY  PQWRDTFFTL  VLIIYLSTLL  GNGFMIFLIH  FDPNLHTPIY
FFLSNLSFLD  LCYGTASMPQ  ALVHCFSTHP  YLSYPRCLAQ  TSVSLALATA  ECLLLAAMAY
DRVVAISNPL  RYSVVMNGPV  CVCLVATSWG  TSLVLTAMLI  LSLRLHFCGA  NVINHFACEI
LSLIKLTCSD  TSLNEFMILI  TSIFTLLLPF  GFVLLSYIRI  AMAIIRIRSL  QGRLKAFTTC
GSHLTVVTIF  YGSAISMYMK  TQSKSSPDQD  KFISVFYGAL  TPMLNPLIYS  LRKKDVKRAI
RKVMLKRT
```

4.5.1 Profile HMMs for odorant receptors

We will first address the problem of assigning a given protein sequence to a known family. We will try to perform a pairwise global alignment of an odorant receptor sequence to a typical element of the 7-TM receptor family (a *rhodopsin* protein). Here is the global alignment score of these two proteins. Only the first 50 residues are shown in Table A adjacent.

In order to assess the the significance of this alignment score, we permute the OR sequence many times and realign it with the rhodopsin. One resulting alignment is shown in the adjacent Table B.

Alignment with the randomized OR sequence does produces a slightly lower score, but across 1000 permutations there is not a significantly higher alignment score of the true OR to the rhodopsin. But we can try the same experiment using a pHMM rather than a pairwise alignment, aligning both the real OR sequence and randomized sequence to the pHMM. Only five sequences from the multiple alignment are shown; in actuality, thousands of aligned sequences were used to develop this pHMM.

Table A:

```
OR    MDVG-N-KS-TMSE--FVLLG-LS-I-NS-WELQMFFMVFSLLYVATMV
RHOD  MD-GSNVTSFVVEEPTNISTGRNASVG-NAHRQIPIVHWVIMSISPVG-I-FV
```
Table A: Needleman and Wunsch Global Alignment Score: 54.8

Table B:

```
RND OR  CQG-IIHIFFA-I-TNVQLGAFYFLWKMTV-SPSNALVTVMVLDSVHMYF
RHOD    MDGSNVTSFVVEEPTNISTGRNASVG-NAHRQIP-IVHWVIMSI-S-I-PVGF
```
Table B: Needleman and Wunsch Global Alignment Score: 46.8

Table 4.1 Hydrophobicity levels for each of the 20 amino acids (positive values are hydrophobic and negative values are hydrophilic)

Amino acid	Value	Amino acid	Value
Ala	1.8	Leu	3.8
Arg	−4.5	Lys	−3.9
Asn	−3.5	Met	1.9
Asp	−3.5	Phe	2.8
Cys	2.5	Pro	−1.6
Gln	−3.5	Ser	−0.8
Glu	−3.5	Thr	−0.7
Gly	−0.4	Trp	−0.9
His	−3.2	Tyr	−1.3
Ile	1.5	Val	4.2

```
O10J1_HUMAN    GNIIIVTIIRIDLHLH...TPMYFFLSMLSTSETVYTLVILPRMLSSLV
OLF15_MOUSE    GNLTIILLSRLDARLH...TPMYFFLSNLSSLDLAFTTSSVPQMLKNLW
OLF6_RAT       GNLAIISLVGAHRCLQ...TPMYFFLCNLSFLEIWFTTACVPKTLATFA
OLF1_CHICK     TNLGLIALISVDLHLQ...TPMYIFLQNLSFTDAAYSTVITPKMLATFL
FSHR_BOVIN     GNILVLVILITSQYKL...TVPRFLMCNLAFADLCIGIYLLLIASVDVH
OR             GNSLIVITVIVDPHLHSPMYFLLTNLSIIDMSLASFATPKMITDYLTG-H
RND_OR         PNLLLC- - - - - - - - - - - - - - - - - - - - - - - -
```

The alignment score between pHMM and the actual OR is 154.6, while the score for the randomized sequence is −5.6. In this case, the signal is much stronger, and it is clear that the OR sequence has a significant alignment with the 7-TM receptor family. Alignment with a pHMM has much more power than pairwise alignment since it includes the characteristics of all the sequences used to create the model; in this case, thousands of sequences.

4.5.2 Segmenting odorant receptors

Odorant receptors are 7-transmembrane proteins, meaning that each needs to cross the cell membrane seven times. As a consequence, the protein has to have seven hydrophobic segments (that do not react with the fatty cell membrane) alternating with seven hydrophilic segments (that do not react with the watery cytoplasm and extra-cellular environments). Every amino acid has its own characteristic level of hydrophobicity, from highly hydrophobic to highly hydrophilic. But because not every amino acid in a hydrophobic region of the protein will be highly hydrophobic (and vice versa for hydrophilic regions), we need to use HMMs to segment odorant receptors into their hydrophobic and hydrophilic segments.

Table 4.1 shows the hydrophobicity levels for each of the common amino acids (positive values are hydrophobic and negative values are hydrophilic).

We can convert the above OR amino acid sequence into a numeric sequence of 312 values of hydrophobicity (one for each of the amino acids). If we plot this numeric sequence, we obtain the plot in Figure 4.5. Although it does not

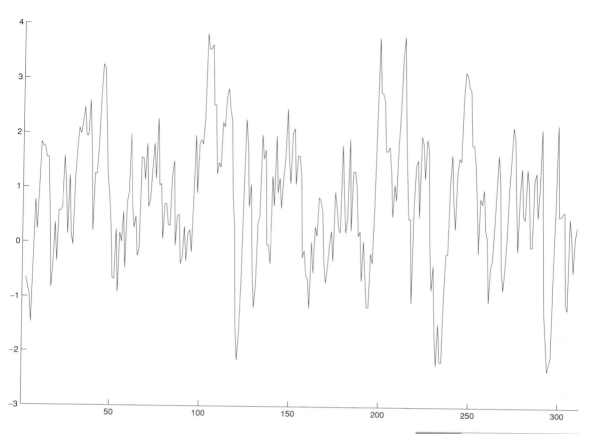

Fig. 4.5 The hydrophobicity profile of an OR receptor protein, obtained by replacing each of the 312 AAs with the corresponding values in Table 4.2

appear easy to distinguish the hydrophobic regions in this graph, we can smooth this plot by using a sliding window of 20 amino acids and reporting the average hydrophobicity level of each region. Because we do not necessarily need to know the hydrophobicity of each position, but rather that of stretches of the protein, this smoothing should make it easier to visualize hydrophobic segments. Figure 4.6 shows the effect of smoothing.

Although we can pick out a number of hydrophobic and hydrophilic peaks in these graphs simply by eye, an HMM can help us to exactly delineate these regions. We model the protein sequence as having been generated by a stochastic process that alternates between two hidden states: "out of membrane" and "in the membrane." Again, these states do not exclusively use hydrophobic or hydrophilic amino acids in the corresponding regions, but rather they have a bias for one type or the other. In each state, a different multinomial model picks amino acids with a different bias. If we are given these values, the Viterbi algorithm can be used to automatically segment the protein into its component regions; otherwise we will first have to estimate the emission matrices from the data, by using the EM algorithm.

Figure 4.7 shows the hidden Markov model used to produce the segmentation shown in Figure 4.6; emission counts (out of 312) are shown for each amino acid in the two states, but the transition probabilities are left off for readability.

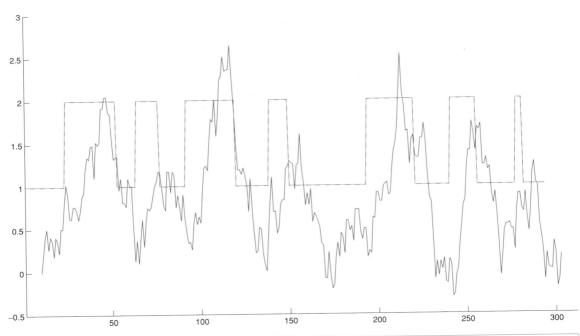

Fig. 4.6 The same hydrophobicity profile, after smoothing and segmentation by an HMM. Note that smoothing has the effect of emphasizing the periodic structure of the sequence

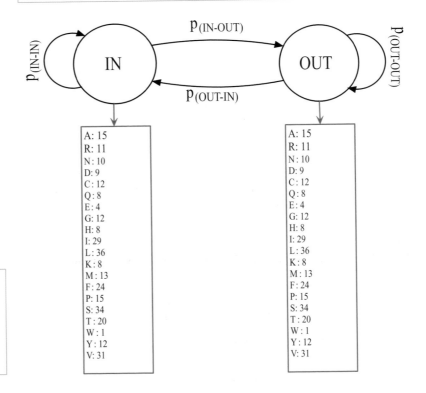

Fig. 4.7 HMM resulting from running the EM algorithm on the smoothed numeric sequence of hydrophobicity levels. The emission matrices show the number of times each amino acid is emitted (out of 312 AAs)

4.6* Algorithms for HMM computations

It is often the case that we are given the sequence **s** and the model parameters (E, T), and we need to compute the probability of the sequence under the model (the likelihood function). Alternatively, we may need to compute the most likely hidden sequence, **h**, to understand the statistical and biological properties of the data.

The probability of the sequence under the given model is

$$P(\mathbf{s}) = \sum_{\forall \mathbf{h}_j \in \mathcal{H}^n} P(\mathbf{s}, \mathbf{h}_j) = \sum_{\forall \mathbf{h}_j \in \mathcal{H}^n} P(\mathbf{s}|\mathbf{h}_j) P(\mathbf{h}_j),$$

where $\mathbf{h}_j \in \mathcal{H}^n$ indicates the jth element of $\mathcal{H}^n$. We will be interested in the most probable hidden sequence, $\mathbf{h}^*$:

$$\mathbf{h}^* = \arg \max_{\forall \mathbf{h} \in \mathcal{H}^n} P(\mathbf{s}, \mathbf{h}),$$

as discussed above. These summations both involve operating over an exponentially large space (in the length of the sequence), and can be solved with dynamic programming methods.

Maximum likelihood of the hidden sequence: Viterbi algorithm. The maximum likelihood hidden sequence can be found efficiently by exploiting a simple recursive relation, and the tabular computations typical of dynamic programming. The main idea is to introduce a slightly different function, V, from which it is easy to calculate the solution, and that can be computed recursively for increasingly long prefixes of the sequence. Such a function is denoted $V(k, i)$, and represents the probability of the most probable hidden sequence associated with the prefix $s(1 : i)$ and ending with state $h_i = k$.

We maintain a table V of size $|\mathcal{H}| \times (n + 1)$ where n is the length of the sequence. Each entry $V(k, i)$ is indexed by a position i in the sequence and a symbol k of the hidden alphabet. If we have this information for all possible symbols, we can compute the same quantities for the prefix of length $i + 1$, as follows:

$$V(l, i) = E(l, \mathbf{s}(i)) \max_k (V(k, i - 1) T(k, l)).$$

In other words, the information in each column is sufficient to compute the next column (a direct consequence of the Markov assumption).

Algorithm 4.1

Viterbi. Given a sequence **s** of length n, and an HMM with parameters (T, E):

- Create table V of size $|\mathcal{H}| \times (n + 1)$;
- Initialize: $i = 0$; $V(0, 0) = 1$; $V(k, 0) = 0$ for $k > 0$.
- For $i = 1 : n$, compute each entry using the recursive relation:

$$V(l, i) = E(l, \mathbf{s}(i)) \max_k (V(k, i - 1) T(k, l))$$
$$\text{pointer}(i, l) = \arg \max_k (V(k, i - 1) T(k, l)).$$

- Output: $P(\mathbf{s}, \mathbf{h}^*) = \max_k (V(k, n))$.

- Trace-back, $i = n : 1$, using: $\mathbf{h}^*_{i-1} = \text{pointer}(i, \mathbf{h}^*(i))$.
- Output: $\mathbf{h}^*(n) = \arg\max_k(V(k, n))$.

In practice, because the quantities involved can become very small, it is common to work with the logarithm of these probabilities, and a similar algorithm can be readily designed that makes use of this (numerically more stable) representation.

Probability of the sequence: forward algorithm. The probability of the sequence under a model, (E, T), can be found with the highly similar *forward* algorithm. In this case we use a function

$$F(k, i) = P\left(s(1 : i); h(i) = k\right), \tag{4.1}$$

representing the probability of the prefix of length i of the sequence, given that $h(i) = k$. As with the Viterbi algorithm, we compute the solution by filling a table, F, from left to right.

Algorithm 4.2
Forward. Given a sequence, $\mathbf{s}$, of length n, and an HMM with parameters (T, E):

- Create table F of size $|\mathcal{H}| \times (n + 1)$.
- Initialize: $i = 0$; $F(0, 0) = 1$; $F(k, 0) = 0$ for $k > 0$.
- For $i = 1 : n$, compute each entry using recursive relation:

$$F(l, i) = E(l, \mathbf{s}(i)) \sum_k (F(k, i - 1)T(k, l)).$$

- Output: $P(\mathbf{s}) = \sum_k F(k, n)$.

The time complexity of this algorithm, as with Viterbi, is linear in the length of the sequence. It is interesting to observe that the two recursive relations are essentially identical, with the exception that the maximization in the first algorithm is replaced by a summation in the second. This is not accidental, and reflects a deep algebraic connection between the two algorithms, one that we will not discuss in this book.

Tuning the parameters: expectation maximization. The maximum likelihood estimate of the parameters E and T, given only the observable sequence $\mathbf{s}$, cannot be computed exactly, because the likelihood function is not convex. However, heuristic methods can deliver solutions that are often good enough to be used in practice, corresponding to local maxima of the function. One of these methods is called the expectation maximization (EM) algorithm. Although we will not go in to the details of the approach, we will give a general intuition about how such an algorithm can work.

One important observation is that we can easily obtain exact estimates of E and T if we are given both $\mathbf{s}$ and $\mathbf{h}$; also we can obtain exact inference of $\mathbf{h}$ if we are given $\mathbf{s}$ and (E, T). Although we do not know how to optimally infer $\mathbf{h}$ and (E, T) simultaneously given $\mathbf{s}$ (that would be the result of optimizing a non-convex function), we can resort to an iterative procedure, by which we start with an initial guess of parameters (E, T), compute the best **h** for those parameters, then use it to get a better estimate of (E, T), and so on, until some stopping criterion is met. If things are done with some care, this process stops at a local maximum, and is often sufficient for our purposes. More details can be found following the links in Section 4.8.

4.7 | Exercises

(1) Using the lambda phage genome, segment it with a 4-state HMM, one biased towards each nucleotide. Do you find differences between these results and simply using a 2-state HMM?

(2) Draw the topology of a 2-state HMM emitting symbols from the alphabet $\{0, 1, 2, 3, \ldots, 9\}$, the two states being {even, odd}.

(3) Sketch the general architecture of an ORF finding HMM.

4.8 | Reading list

Many technical aspects of this chapter are based on the excellent presentation of HMMs in Durbin *et al.* (1998). This book is a modern classic, and is highly recommended to all statistics and computer science students interested in using HMMs as part of their research. The first uses of HMMs for segmentations of biosequences date back to Churchill (1989, 1992), The use of HMMs for gene finding and for gene family prediction were pioneered by David Haussler and his collaborators in a series of papers starting in the mid 1990s. Some of those ground-breaking papers are Haussler *et al.* (1993, 1994), and Krogh *et al.* (1994). An early discussion of pHMMs for multiple alignment can be found in Eddy *et al.* (1995). Baldi *et al.* (1994) is an early discussion of HMMs as models of biosequences. A discussion of HMMs for human gene finding can be found in Kulp *et al.* (1996). A classic tutorial on HMMs in the context of signal processing is Rabiner (1989). Eukaryotic gene finding with HMMs is discussed in Burge and Karlin (1997, 1998). A good and accessible survey of the biology of ORs can be found in Axel (1995). Our case study, and the data file available on the book's website, have been based for the data discussed in Zozulya *et al.* (2001). The database Pfam can be found at www.sanger.ac.uk/Software/Pfam/.

Links to these and many more papers, as well as to data, software, and websites, as well as to more background on HMMs, can be found on the book's website:

www.computational-genomics.net

Chapter 5

Are Neanderthals among us?
Variation within and between species

- Mutations and substitutions
- Genetic distance
- Statistical estimations: Kimura, Jukes-Cantor

In 1856, workers involved in limestone blasting operations near Düsseldorf, Germany, in the Neander Thal (Neander Valley) discovered a strange human skeleton. The skeleton had very unusual features, including a heavy brow-ridge, a large nose, receding chin, and stocky build. Initially neglected, the importance of the finding was recognized only many years later by the Irish anatomist William King. The skeleton belonged to an ancient species of hominid biologically different from modern humans. King called the specimen Neanderthal Man: man of the Neander Valley. The skeleton was dated to about 44 thousand years ago.

Since then, many other skeletons of the same species, *H. neanderthalensis*, have been discovered in Europe. Popular imagination has been captured by the image of these cavemen; the name itself has become a symbol of prehistoric humans. It has been possible to reconstruct the lifestyle of Neanderthals in prehistoric Europe based on the tools that they used, but one fundamental question remained: are Neanderthals our ancestors? Are modern Europeans the offspring of these primitive hominids? This question has divided scientists for decades, and has only been settled recently by genetic analysis.

Many other fundamental questions about human origins have been answered by modern genetics, as well as by recent fossil discoveries. The search for the oldest hominid fossils has continually revealed evidence that humans originated in sub-Saharan Africa. Beginning with the 1964 discovery of *H. habilis* by the archaeologist Louis Leakey (in Olduvai Gorge, Tanzania), ancient fossils of distinctly hominid form have been found all over the African continent. Radiocarbon dating of fossils from both *H. habilis* and *H. erectus* (another pre-historic hominid species) find that specimens of both species – as well as their stone tools – were present in Africa as long as 2 million years ago (MYA). Fossils of *H. erectus* dating from 1.6–1.8 MYA are found throughout the Old World; the famous Java Man and Peking Man specimens are the earliest known members of the genus *Homo* outside of Africa. Our next closest living relatives are the chimpanzee and bonobo, African apes that diverged from our lineage approximately 5 million years ago.

But when and where did our species, *H. sapiens*, first appear? The earliest skeletons from anatomically modern humans were found in southern Ethiopia and date to about 130 thousand years ago (KYA). Following this, fossil and archaeological evidence show that *H. sapiens* made it to Asia and Australia by about 60 KYA, Europe by 40 KYA, and the Americas – via Siberia – less than 30 KYA. We were not the only members of our genus inhabiting the earth during the last 130 thousand years. In Indonesia, *H. erectus* may have been present up until 27 KYA, and, as we said before, evidence has been found that *H. neanderthalensis* were living in Europe and Western Asia from 250 to 28 KYA.

In this chapter we will begin to learn how to address the questions of human origins using DNA sequence data. Rather than the very static view of the genome that we have presented in the preceding chapters, we now consider the dynamic nature of DNA: how sequences change over time and how we can use this information to infer the history and function of different parts of the genome. Variation data can also be used in medical research, forensics, and genome annotation. By the end of this chapter you will be able to provide a relatively conclusive answer to the question of our relations with Neanderthals, as well as confirm our African origins.

5.1 | Variation in DNA sequences

We can answer questions about human origins by exploiting the fact that every individual – whether comparing within or between species – has a slightly different genome sequence. Even siblings with the same parents will have differences between them. Variation in DNA accumulates via mutations, mistakes made by the cellular machinery that are then encoded in the genome. Variation in the exact configuration of DNA sequences can also be introduced by recombination (when the organism is diploid, i.e. has two copies of each chromosome); this phenomenon is a consequence of sexual reproduction. The analysis of variation, through comparison of two or more sequences, can provide us with a wealth of information about various aspects of genome structure, function, and history.

Mutations arise for many reasons. Generally, mutations occur because a mistake is made during the replication of the genome. Imagine how many mistakes you could make re-typing the approximately 2500 letters on this page. A human cell does this over and over for 3.5 billion letters. But the cell's proofreading machinery is very good. The best estimates of the human mutation rate calculate that there is only one mistake for every 200 million to 1 billion bases replicated. External factors, like chemicals or UV rays, can act to increase the rate of mutations by damaging DNA. Mutation rates differ between organisms and between the various genomes in single cells – in most animals the rate of mutation in the mitochondrial genome is an order of magnitude higher than in the nuclear genome, and in plants this is reversed.

Regardless of variation in mutation rates, new mutations at any one nucleotide position are relatively rare. As a consequence, most genetic differences between individuals are inherited mutations and not newly arisen variants. We will exploit this fact to study the history of individuals and species: shared mutations are indicative of shared ancestry.

Remark 5.1
Germline mutations. Mutations occur at every cell duplication because the genome must be replicated each time. Creating a fully grown human with trillions of cells, each of which dies off and is replaced multiple times during a lifetime, therefore introduces a number of mutations. This is one reason that cancer is largely an illness of the elderly. But mutations in our skin cells or heart-muscle cells are not passed on to our offspring: only mutations that occur in the germline cells (in the testes and ovaries) have any chance of spreading through the population. Of course for organisms that do not have a separate germline – such as plants – many additional mutations have the possibility of being passed on.

Every mutation first appears in a single individual – the mutation may be neutral (it has no effect), deleterious (it disrupts some biological function), or advantageous (it improves some biological function). Regardless of its effect, if the mutation is not passed on to a child, it is lost. Any difference among individuals at a specific position in the genome, whether it is at a frequency of 1% or 50% in a population, is called a *polymorphism*.

The most common types of mutations involve "point" mutations: the change of one base into another (e.g. A→T). When we find these mutations polymorphic within a species we call them SNPs (pronounced "snips"; single nucleotide polymorphisms). The various versions of the DNA sequence are called *alleles*, so that we might find a SNP with an A allele and a T allele at a certain position. A SNP usually refers to the location in a genome that is polymorphic; a SNP map for an organism lists all locations for which polymorphisms have been documented with sufficient frequency and is a very important research tool.

Example 5.1
Sequence polymorphism. In this artificial example, we have three sequences with six polymorphic positions. The last line represents a simple SNP map, highlighting the positions that are polymorphic in the sample. The different symbols used to mark polymorphic sites represent two different types of substitutions, as explained below.

G	T	C	C	T	T	C	A	T	A	A	T	C	A	T	C	A	C	G	G	G	A	C	T
G	A	C	C	T	T	C	A	T	A	A	C	C	A	T	C	A	C	G	G	G	A	C	T
A	A	C	C	T	T	C	A	T	A	A	C	C	A	T	C	T	C	C	G	G	A	C	C
×	○	–	–	–	–	–	–	–	–	–	×	–	–	–	–	○	–	○	–	–	–	–	○

SNPs account for a large part of genetic variation. In humans, for instance, there is on average one SNP every 1500 bases in the nuclear genome. In other words, any two sequences will differ at 0.067% of positions compared. It turns out that humans as a whole actually have very little polymorphism relative to the other great apes (and to many other species); the main reason for this is the relatively small number of humans that have inhabited the earth for the past 130 000 years.

A second major source of variation among human genomes involves short tandem repeats (STRs, or *microsatellites*). These are back-to-back (tandem) repeats of short DNA words such as CACACACA. Because of slippage during replication, the number of repeats of the word can vary. At some microsatellites, for instance, individuals may have as few as one or as many as 30 or 40 tandem repeats. The mutation rate at microsatellites is much higher than that for SNPs, making them very useful in identification, either for forensic or anthropological investigations (so-called "DNA fingerprints" often use microsatellites).

There are a number of other sources of genetic variation, but most occur more rarely. Most frequent of these are insertions or deletions (*indels*), where DNA sequences are either inserted or removed from the genome. These can be from one to one million bases long. Variation also comes from rearrangements such as inversions, duplications, and transpositions, where certain segments of the genome are "copied and pasted" or "cut-and-pasted" elsewhere during replication. Even whole genome duplications have been found to be polymorphic within certain plant species, but these are extremely rare events.

Remark 5.2
SNPs as point mutations. The definition of a "SNP" varies, but it is more common to reserve this word for only point mutations; some people also include single-nucleotide indels as SNPs. We stick to the first, more common definition.

Transitions and transversions. It is important to note that not all point mutations are equally likely, even among mutations with no effect. This is because nucleotides can actually be divided chemically into purines (A, G) and pyrimidines (C, T), as shown in Figure 5.1. (We will not worry about the specific chemical differences that distinguish these bases.) Mutations within the groups are called *transitions* (i.e. A → G, or C → T), and between groups are called *transversions* (e.g. G → C, or C → A). Although there are four possible transitions and eight possible transversions (or two and four, if we do not consider the direction of mutations), we often observe many more transitions than transversions. In humans, for instance, transition mutations are at least twice as likely as transversion mutations, resulting in many more SNPs that are A/G or C/T.

These differences in mutation rates are simply due to similarities in chemical structure within purines and pyrimidines, making it easier for transitions to occur; natural selection does not normally care whether a mutation is a transition or a transversion. Notice, however, that the genetic code is set up to be more robust to transitions: when only two synonymous codons code for the same amino acid they always differ by only one transition mutation. This necessarily means that transitions within coding sequences will be on average less harmful than transversions. Even in non-coding sequences, though, transitions outnumber transversions.

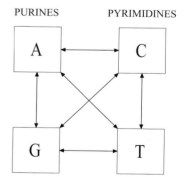

Fig. 5.1 Nucleotides can be divided into purines and pyrimidines. Substitutions within the same group are called "transitions," the ones across groups are called "transversions"

Example 5.2
Transitions and transversions in human mtDNA. If we perform a global alignment of the complete mitochondrial genome for two humans (GenBank accession numbers NC_001807 and AC_000021) we find 38 polymorphic positions. The table below shows the specific mutations found (rows indicate the first, columns the second genome). In total we have 36 transitions (17 A–G and 19 C–T) and two transversions. Note that we cannot distinguish the direction of mutations without extra information not provided here. Mitochondrial DNA will be discussed further in the next section.

	A	C	G	T
A		0	4	1
C	1		0	14
G	13	0		0
T	0	5	0	

DNA and amino acid substitution matrices. As we have shown in the above example, not all nucleotide mutations occur with the same frequency. Sometimes this is due to the chemical nature of the bases, and sometimes this is due to the deleterious consequences of the change in DNA sequence. Similarly, not all changes between amino acids are seen with equal frequency, often because the codon for two amino acids are multiple nucleotide-mutation steps away from each other (e.g. GCA and TGT), but also because some amino acids are more interchangeable than others due to their shared biochemical characteristics, such as size, polarity, and hydrophobicity.

Differences in mutation between nucleotides are often well described by simply considering transitions and transversions separately – although the default parameters in BLAST do not differentiate among these changes – but the situation for amino acids is much more complex. Due to the complexity of the genetic code and the various different chemical roles played by each individual amino acid, summarizing the mutation frequencies among amino acids necessitates a complete description of all of the pairwise mutation probabilities. This can be represented by a *substitution matrix*, identical to the ones described in Chapter 3 for alignment scoring. (Note that differences between individuals within a species are referred to simply as *mutations*, and differences between species as *substitutions*.) In the case of the alphabet of amino acids, $\mathcal{A}$, it is a 20 by 20 matrix, called an amino acid substitution matrix (because it is obtained from a comparison between species). Just as with the example given above for constructing a nucleotide substitution matrix from an alignment, so we can compare amino acid sequences to infer the amino acid substitution matrix. This idea originated with the pioneering work of Margaret Dayhoff, after whom the original substitution matrices were named.

Of course, the inference of substitution probabilities is somewhat self-referential: good alignments require substitution matrices, but substitution matrices need to be constructed based on good alignments. There are a few ways around this problem: one way is to start with very similar sequences where the alignment is obvious and unambiguous, and can be done with a simple scoring matrix. Consequently, we can use this alignment to obtain a first substitution matrix, use it to align slightly more divergent sequences, and so on. For any amount of divergence, we can then use a different matrix. There are two main families of such matrices for amino acid substitutions: PAM and BLOSUM.

PAM and BLOSUM. The most commonly used amino acid substitution matrices are called PAM (Percent or Point Accepted Mutation) and BLOSUM (BLOcks SUbstitution Matrix). While they differ slightly in how they are constructed and in how well they perform for any given alignment, these two types of matrices are largely similar. PAM matrices are constructed by comparing global alignments of very closely related sequences (less than 1% divergence) and tallying observed differences. The resulting matrix is known as PAM1 and is meant to be used for aligning sequences that have approximately 1% divergence. For more distant comparisons, extrapolations of PAM1 can be used (although it is not a linear extrapolation – PAM250 is not for proteins that are 250% divergent). BLOSUM matrices are built by direct observation of local alignments between sequences of differing similarity. For BLOSUM, the various different versions of the matrix are numbered by how similar the proteins should be. The default matrix used by BLAST, BLOSUM62, is built from a comparison of sequences that are a minimum of 62% identical. The choice of which matrix to use in any single case is therefore largely determined by the comparison being made.

5.2 Mitochondrial DNA: a model for the analysis of variation

In previous chapters we have discussed the advantages of mitochondrial genomes relating to their compactness. But mitochondrial DNA (mtDNA) is also ideal for studying human evolution, largely because of its high mutation rate. For this and a number of other technical advantages discussed below, we will focus on mtDNA in this chapter.

Mitochondria are organelles of eukaryotic cells involved in energy production. Largely because of their role in producing energy through oxidative phosphorylation, mitochondria contain a high number of mutagenic oxygen molecules that lead to a high rate of mutation. They have their own small circular chromosome (16 569 bases long in humans), containing 37 protein-coding and RNA genes (see map in Figure 5.2). Mitochondria also have a slightly different genetic code than the nuclear genome (see Exercise 1 of Chapter 2). Because we only inherit mtDNA from our mothers, we have only one version of it (as opposed to the nuclear genome, where we have one version from our mother and one from our father). Each cell contains multiple copies of mtDNA, which makes it easier to isolate and sequence.

A specific region of mtDNA is of particular interest for our analyses. This 1.1 Kb region is the only real stretch of non-coding sequence in the mitochondrial genome and is known as the *D-loop* or control region. Although the

Fig. 5.2 A simple map of mitochondrial genome. Human mtDNA has 16 569 bases with 37 genes (13 proteins, 22 tRNAs, and two rRNAs). At the top of the map the D-Loop is highlighted. It contains the replication start site, and on each side a hypervariable region (HVR) of a few hundred nucleotides. The replication start site is also conventionally used as the origin for numbering all sequence positions

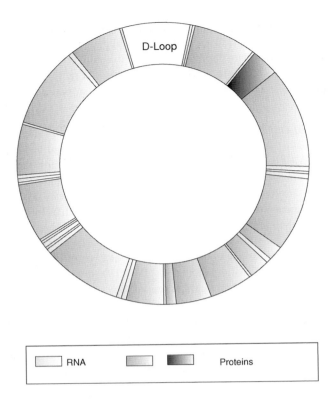

RNA   Proteins

D-loop does not contain any genes, it does contain necessary features including the origin of replication and the mitochondrial promoter. The origin of replication is where the replication of the circular genome begins; the promoter is where transcription of all of the mtDNA genes begins. In addition to these important sequences, the D-loop also contains two hypervariable regions with no known function: named hypervariable regions I and II (HVR-I and HVR-II). These regions are found on each side of the replication start site, and make up the majority of the D-loop (each having length between 400 bp and 500 bp). These regions show particularly high sequence variability among humans and are therefore ideal for studying the relationships among individuals.

Since by convention the circular mtDNA chromosome is presented in linear format starting from the origin of replication, the two HVRs have positions approximately 16 024–16 400 (for HVR-I) and positions 1–500 (for HVR II). The entire D-loop stretches from approximately position 16 024 to position 576. Of course numbering genomic positions is always somewhat arbitrary (since length might in principle change due to insertions and deletions). Because of this, numbering in human mitochondrial genomes is usually relative to the Cambridge Reference Sequence (CRS), the original mtDNA sequence obtained in 1981 by Fred Sanger's group in Cambridge, UK.

Technical advantages of mtDNA. There are two main technical advantages of using mtDNA over nuclear DNA. First, because mitochondria are only passed down through the mother, every individual will only have one version of mtDNA. Since we only have one version, we automatically know the haplotype of the mtDNA; that is, we know the configuration of polymorphisms on chromosomes. This turns out to be a huge technical advantage of mtDNA over nuclear DNA.

Consider a situation (completely realistic given today's sequencing technologies) where all you are told is that there are two polymorphisms present in a nuclear gene from a single individual. That is, there are two differences between the maternal and paternal copies of this gene that the person inherited. If there is an A/G polymorphism at one site and a C/T polymorphism at another site, there are two ways in which the sequences can be configured along the two parental chromosomes:

$$-A-C-$$
$$-G-T-$$

or

$$-A-T-$$
$$-G-C-$$

We can easily see that the number of possible configurations (called *haplotypes*) goes up exponentially with the number of polymorphisms considered. A major computational problem in genomics is to infer the haplotype of each of the sequences. For now, just be thankful that we do not have to worry about these issues because there is only one mitochondrial haplotype per person.

The second technical advantage inherent in studying mtDNA is the high copy number of these genomes in every cell. Because of this, it is relatively easy to extract DNA out of older tissues such as museum specimens or mummies. The skeletal remains of three Neanderthals are so well-preserved that careful extraction of tissue allows us to get DNA from the samples, even though these individuals each lived more than 30 KYA. The D-loops of these three Neanderthals have been sequenced and reported in the literature. Later in this chapter we will get these sequences from GenBank in order to determine whether *H. sapiens* and *H. neanderthalensis* were interbreeding in Europe thousands of years ago. Mitochondrial DNA sequences can also be used to determine our relationships to the other great ape species, and in the next section we begin to address the additional issues in comparing sequences among species.

5.3 Variation between species

In addition to studying variation within a species (such as humans), we are often interested in variation between species. The genetic differences between species are responsible for many of the behavioral, morphological, and physiological differences that we observe between species. Variation between species can also begin to tell us about the relationships among species – because more closely related species will have on average more similar DNA sequences, examining these sequences can tell us about how evolution has proceeded over millions of years. If we now want to know how distantly related the other great apes (chimpanzees, bonobos, gorillas, and orangutans) are to humans, we need to compare sequences between species. Key to understanding differences between species is knowing how many nucleotide substitutions separate any two DNA sequences.

The substitution rate. It is often useful to study the substitution rate between homologous sequences from different species. This can tell us about the time since divergence between the species, the biological function of genomic sequences (more on this in Chapter 6), and the relationships among species (Chapter 7). As mentioned earlier, every mutation originates in a single individual. This mutation may be lost immediately if the individual carrying it leaves no offspring, or it may rise to higher frequency, eventually becoming *fixed* throughout the species (that is, every individual in the species will have the new allele at the specific nucleotide position). The substitution rate is the rate at which species accumulate such fixed differences.

If mutations are neutral (i.e there is no effect of the mutation on the reproductive abilities of the organism), then a surprising relationship arises between the mutation rate and the substitution rate. Consider any new mutation: it is initially present at a frequency of $1/2N$ (where N is the number of individuals in the population, each of whom carries two copies of each nuclear gene). The chance that this new allele becomes fixed by random sampling alone is $1/2N$ – simply its initial frequency. Likewise, if a mutation is already present at 60% frequency it has a 60% chance of being fixed, and so on. So the substitution rate must take into account the number of new mutations created and the probability that any one of them is fixed. When there are N diploid individuals in a population and a rate, μ, of mutating to a new base, the substitution rate, ρ, is equal to

$$\rho = 2N\mu(1/2N) = \mu.$$

The above equation says that the substitution rate of new mutations is independent of the population size, and is simply equal to the (neutral) mutation rate. Larger populations create more mutations, but each has a lower chance of fixing; smaller populations have fewer polymorphisms, but each has a higher chance of fixing. We will see that when mutations are not strictly neutral the mutation rate and the substitution rate can be quite different, as new alleles can have an intrinsically better or worse chance of spreading.

A common confusion. Unfortunately, biologists have (at least) two uses for the phrase "substitution rate." Most of the time they take the time since divergence of two sequences from a common ancestor as a given and define the substitution rate, K, as simply the number of substitutions that have occurred between sequences (so it is not really a rate, *per se*, but a genetic distance). Generally K is expressed as the number of substitutions per site, so as to control for the length of the sequence compared.

If the divergence time, T, is known, however, then we can define the substitution rate as

$$\rho = K/(2T).$$

We divide by $2T$ because both lineages that come from a common ancestor can accumulate mutations independently. The parameter ρ is usually expressed as the number of substitutions per site per million years. For clarity, we will refer to ρ as the substitution rate and K as the genetic distance.

5.4 | Estimating genetic distance

The genetic distance between two homologous sequences is defined as the number of substitutions that have accumulated between them since they diverged from a common ancestor. Being able to estimate the true genetic distance between two sequences is crucial for the methods discussed here and in Chapters 6 and 7. Estimating this quantity exactly is not easy, though we can easily count the number of positions at which two sequences differ. The problem is that a simple count will be an underestimate of the true number of differences when multiple substitutions have occurred at the same site.

Consider the situation (illustrated in Example 5.3) in which multiple substitutions occur in the same position. Examination of the sequences at the beginning and the end of this time period will reveal either one substitution (if the second mutation is to a different base from the initial sequence) or zero substitutions (if the second mutation is to the same base as the initial sequence). This will occur with low frequency, but can be a real problem over long periods of time in under-counting the true number of substitutions and hence the time separating species. We can correct for multiple hits when estimating the genetic distance between two sequences by using a probabilistic model as we will see below.

Example 5.3

Multiple substitutions. Below we show how there can be six substitutions over time, yet only three would be visible by comparing the first sequence with the last one (time proceeds from the top sequence towards the bottom sequence). Multiple substitutions occurring at the same location end up being under-counted:

G	A	C	C	T	T	C	A	A	T	C	A	C	G	G	G	A	C	T	
T	T	C	C	T	T	C	A	A	T	C	A	C	G	G	G	A	C	T	
T	T	C	C	T	T	C	A	A	T	C	A	C	G	G	G	A	C	T	
T	T	C	C	T	T	C	A	A	T	C	A	C	G	G	G	A	C	T	
T	T	C	C	T	T	C	A	A	T	C	A	C	C	G	G	A	C	T	
T	T	C	C	T	T	C	A	A	T	C	T	C	C	G	G	A	C	T	
C	A	C	C	T	T	C	A	A	T	C	T	C	C	G	G	A	C	T	
1	0	0	0	0	0	0	0	0	0	0	1	0	1	0	0	0	0	0	Observed: 3
2	2	0	0	0	0	0	0	0	0	0	1	0	1	0	0	0	0	0	Actual : 6

At the extreme, two sequences are said to have reached "saturation" when there is on average at least one substitution per site across the sequence. We can see that in the limit the divergence between two homologous sequences will be such that only about a quarter of their sites match: a match this great can easily be obtained for two random sequences. Since the process of substitution is assumed to be random, both the true genetic distance, K, and the observed proportion of differences d are random variables. We are able to observe d, and can use it to estimate the hidden random variable K. There are various ways to infer K depending on what model of evolution we assume.

Possible evolutionary models go from the simple – where each substitution has the same probability – to the more complex – distinguishing between transitions and transversions, or even between substitutions that change the protein and ones that do not. We present here two simple models of sequence evolution. The next chapter will also include ideas about the effect of natural selection on genetic distances and substitution rates.

Sequence evolution can be regarded as a Markov process: a sequence at time (or generation) t depends only on the sequence at time (or generation) $t - 1$. It is not surprising, then, that both of the models we present are again based on the theory of Markov chains.

5.4.1   The Jukes–Cantor model

As mentioned above, a simple count of differences between two sequences does not tell the full story about their genetic distance. If even moderate amounts of time have passed, it is possible that many substitutions have occurred at the same position and can no longer be counted. On the other hand, if there are very few differences between sequences, it is likely that their count is an accurate estimate of the number of substitutions that have actually occurred.

How can we estimate the true number of substitutions given the observed differences between sequences? In 1969 Thomas Jukes and Charles Cantor proposed a probabilistic model to correct the observed number of differences to account for the possibility of multiple substitutions. Below we derive the famous Jukes–Cantor (JC) correction; for those who wish to skip the math, the equation is simply

$$K = -\frac{3}{4} \ln \left(1 - \frac{4}{3} d \right).$$

This says that the true number of substitutions per site between two sequences (K) can be estimated from the observed fraction of sites that differ (d).

Jukes–Cantor derivation

Let us assume that all positions in a sequence evolve independently, and focus on just one position. We are interested in the probability of a substitution occurring at this position in a given time, a probability we refer to as α. If we assume that all three possible substitutions from one base to any of the others are equally likely, we can describe the one-step Markov chain with the following transition matrix:

$$
M_{JC} =
\begin{array}{c c}
& \begin{array}{cccc} A & \quad C & \quad G & \quad T \end{array} \\
\begin{array}{c} A \\ C \\ G \\ T \end{array} &
\begin{array}{cccc}
1-\alpha & \alpha/3 & \alpha/3 & \alpha/3 \\
\alpha/3 & 1-\alpha & \alpha/3 & \alpha/3 \\
\alpha/3 & \alpha/3 & 1-\alpha & \alpha/3 \\
\alpha/3 & \alpha/3 & \alpha/3 & 1-\alpha.
\end{array}
\end{array}
$$

The theory of Markov processes says that the probability of a substitution after t time steps can be calculated as

$$M(t) = M^t.$$

This matrix can be written as

$$M^t_{JC} = \sum \lambda^t_i v_i v'_i. \tag{5.1}$$

where (λ_i, v_i) are the ith eigenvalue and eigenvector of the matrix M. It is also possible to prove that the eigenvalues are

$$\lambda_1 = 1$$
$$\lambda_{2,3,4} = 1 - \frac{4}{3}\alpha,$$

and the eigenvectors are independent of α:

$$v_1 = \frac{1}{4}(1, 1, 1, 1)$$
$$v_2 = \frac{1}{4}(-1, -1, 1, 1)$$
$$v_3 = \frac{1}{4}(1, -1, -1, 1)$$
$$v_4 = \frac{1}{4}(1, -1, 1, -1),$$

(Notice that there is triple degeneracy, and hence this is just one of the possible sets of eigenvectors for this matrix.)

By inserting these eigenvectors in Equation (5.1) we can see that $M_{JC}(t)$ can be written as

$$M_{JC}(t) = \begin{matrix} r(t) & s(t) & s(t) & s(t) \\ s(t) & r(t) & s(t) & s(t) \\ s(t) & s(t) & r(t) & s(t) \\ s(t) & s(t) & s(t) & r(t), \end{matrix}$$

where

$$s(t) = \frac{1}{4} - \frac{1}{4}\left(1 - \frac{4}{3}\alpha\right)^t.$$

This is the probability of a substitution being observed at a given position after a time interval of t time steps. It can be directly translated into a proportion of differences observed between two sequences, a quantity we call d. We now want to express t as a function of d. This is done by exploiting the approximation $\ln(1 + x) \approx x$ for small x, obtaining

$$t \approx -\frac{3}{4\alpha} \ln\left(1 - \frac{4}{3}d\right).$$

On the other hand, we estimate that if the probability of a substitution per time step is α, then over t time steps, we can expect the number of substitutions that occur (the genetic distance) to be

$$K = t\alpha,$$

this enables us to remove the number of time steps t, and conclude that

$$K \approx -\frac{3}{4} \ln \left(1 - \frac{4}{3}d\right).$$

This remarkable relation is known as the Jukes–Cantor formula. (We have assumed that $\frac{4}{3}\alpha$ is small, so this formula is more accurate for small α.)

This relation makes K tend to infinity when d tends to $\frac{3}{4}$, which is the distance we would expect to assign to unrelated sequences, and gives $K \approx d$ for very similar sequences, again what we would expect. Furthermore, this model predicts that after a very long time, any letter can be equally present at any location, implying that alignments would be trivial and the information about common ancestry would be lost.

Finally, we can also estimate the variance of K using the standard "delta method":

$$\mathrm{Var}(K) \approx \left(\frac{\partial K}{\partial d}\right)^2 \mathrm{Var}(d),$$

and since

$$\mathrm{Var}(d) = \frac{d(1 - d)}{n}$$

$$\frac{\partial K}{\partial d} = \frac{1}{1 - \frac{4}{3}d},$$

we obtain that

$$\mathrm{Var}(K) \approx \frac{d(1 - d)}{n(1 - (4/3)d)^2},$$

where n is the length of the sequence. These two quantities are plotted together in the example below, where multiple hits and the Jukes–Cantor correction are applied to artificial data.

Example 5.4
Simulating the Jukes–Cantor model of sequence evolution. We simulated the evolution of a sequence by using the JC model with an extremely high substitution rate to emphasize the effects of multiple hits. We started with a random sequence of length $n = 1000$ and performed one random substitution at each iteration, at random locations chosen uniformly. By keeping track of the differences between the current sequence and the original one at each iteration, we can plot (Figure 5.3) the true number of substitutions versus the observed number of differences. Averaging over ten experiments, we obtain the mean and variance of these values. Note that after 2000 substitutions, less than half are actually observable. Notice also that applying the JC correction, an almost linear relation between the two quantities is returned. This is not surprising, since the simulation was designed to follow the JC substitution model (equal probability of substitution among all symbols). Error bars were computed in the first plot by repeating the simulation ten times, in the second plot, by using the formula for the variance.

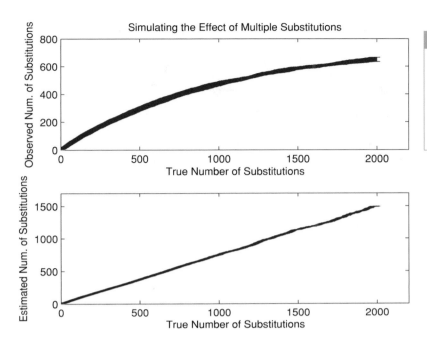

5.4.2 The Kimura two-parameter model

The Jukes–Cantor model assumes that all substitutions are equally likely, whereas we know that this is not the case. For example, we have seen in Example 5.2 that transitions are more likely to be observed than transversions. In order to account for this and other effects, the Japanese population geneticist Motoo Kimura proposed a model based on more than just the one parameter, α, indicating the general probability of substitution. In the widely used two-parameter model, we distinguish between transition and transversion probabilities.

If α is the probability of transitions $G \leftrightarrow A$ and $T \leftrightarrow C$, and β is the probability of transversions $G \leftrightarrow T, G \leftrightarrow C, A \leftrightarrow T$, and $A \leftrightarrow C$, we obtain the substitution matrix

$$
M_{K2P} = \begin{array}{c} \\ A \\ C \\ G \\ T \end{array}
\begin{array}{cccc}
A & C & G & T \\
1 - \alpha - \beta & \beta & \alpha & \beta \\
\beta & 1 - \alpha - \beta & \beta & \alpha \\
\alpha & \beta & 1 - \alpha - \beta & \beta \\
\beta & \alpha & \beta & 1 - \alpha - \beta.
\end{array}
$$

Now the probability of a substitution is $\beta + \beta + \alpha$ (two possible transversions and one possible transition). A similar analysis to the one above for Jukes–Cantor yields the following estimation for genetic distances:

$$
K = -\frac{1}{2} \ln\left(1 - 2P - Q\right) - \frac{1}{4} \ln\left(1 - 2Q\right),
$$

where P and Q are respectively the fraction of transitions and transversions. If we just count the overall number of substitutions and do not distinguish between these two types of mutation ($d = P + Q$), then we recover the Jukes–Cantor formula.

5.4.3 Further models of nucleotide evolution

More complicated models of nucleotide substitution can also be used, including models that distinguish among different types of transitions and transversions, and models that have a separate parameter for every pairwise substitution probability (this model is called the general time reversible or GTR model). Every model we have discussed (and those in general usage) have one important limitation: they assume that substitutions probabilities are symmetric, that $A \rightarrow T$ substitutions are just as likely as $T \rightarrow A$ substitutions. The same assumption applies to amino acid substitution matrices. Accumulating evidence suggests this may not always be true, but it remains to be seen how these asymmetries can be incorporated into estimates of genetic distance or even alignments.

5.5 | Case study: are Neanderthals still among us?

The discovery of Neanderthal skeletons in various parts of Europe raised many questions about human origins, among them the issue of our relation with this species. We can now answer many questions about human and primate origins by studying variation in the mitochondrial genome, either by using the whole genome or just the hypervariable regions.

In order to answer the question posed in this chapter's title, we used 206 modern human mtDNAs and parts of two Neanderthal mtDNAs, including that of the original individual from the German cave (all available on GenBank). Because only parts of the hypervariable regions are available for the Neanderthal, we extracted the corresponding regions from the available human sequences by using local alignment. This produced a homogeneous set of $206 + 2$ homologous (and hence comparable) sequences of about 800 bp each.

We computed the pairwise genetic distances between all 208 sequences, that is the proportion of sites at which the two sequences are different, corrected by the Jukes–Cantor formula. Even though we are comparing sequences within (at least one) species, the HVR is so quickly evolving that the use of the JC correction is recommended.

The average distance between any two *H. sapiens* sequences is 0.025, this being the number of substitutions per site (so out of 1000 bases, 25 will be different on average). The average distance between a Neanderthal and a modern human is 0.140, quite a bit higher. The resulting matrix of all of the pairwise differences can be visualized by means of multidimensional scaling, a statistical visualization method that enables us to embed the datapoints on a plane in a way that respects their pairwise distances, as seen in Figure 5.4. Distances in the figure reflect actual genetic distances between individuals. In Chapter 7 we will describe a more biologically meaningful ways of representing this type of data, namely phylogenetic trees. One such tree is already presented in Figure 5.5 to provide a more complete view of the data discussed in this chapter.

Examining the figure, it is easy to see that the Neanderthal sequences (the two star points on the top right) are very distant from the 206 *H. sapiens* sequences, all clustered on the left. We conclude that *H. neanderthalensis*

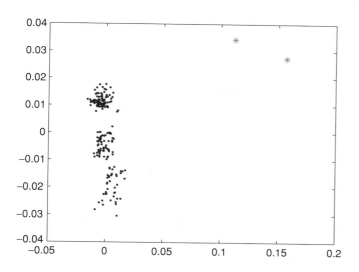

Fig. 5.4 Visualization of 208 mtDNA sequences. The cluster of 206 points on the left is entirely formed by *H. sapiens* data, whereas the two stars on the top-right represent the two Neanderthal sequences. Distances in this diagram directly reflect genetic distances between sequences

were indeed a different species, and that their DNA is different from that of modern humans (i.e. they are not a sub-population within modern humans). To better understand their role as possible European ancestors, we can examine the average distance between the two Neanderthals and humans on various continents. It turns out that they are related at approximately the same distance for all five continents, once more indicating that Neanderthals are not especially related to Europeans, or to any of the existing human populations. Their relation to us is simply one of a shared ancient common ancestor.

Out of Africa. If we compare the pairwise genetic distances among individuals living on specific continents, we find that Africans have the highest levels of variation on average (0.029, measured from 45 individuals). As a comparison, Native Americans have an average pairwise distance of 0.020 (measured from ten individuals). This suggests that Africa was likely to have been the continent where early humans evolved, in agreement with available fossil evidence: as humans left Africa they went through a population bottleneck that resulted in a loss of genetic diversity. If we combine this information with the results from Neanderthal mtDNA, we start to see a picture in which an ancient hominid species living in Africa (possibly *H. erectus*) gave rise to a wave of migration to Europe that produced Neanderthals, followed some time later by a second wave of migration out of Africa by modern humans, entirely replacing the Neanderthal in Europe.

Primate evolution. Finally, we can address questions about the evolution of the primates using mtDNA. Although we will study the details in Chapter 7, we show in Figure 5.5 a simple *phylogenetic tree* constructed using Jukes–Cantor estimates of distances between the Hyper Variable Region II of human, Neanderthal, chimpanzee, bonobo, gorilla, orangutan, and gibbon. The tree tells us that Neanderthals are indeed more closely related to modern humans than are any of the other extant Great Apes, including our closest living relatives,

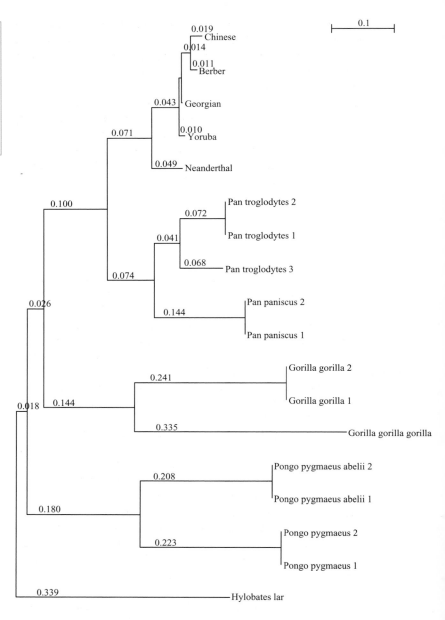

Fig. 5.5 Phylogenetic tree constructed using pairwise genetic distances between primate HVRs. The theory behind the construction and interpretation of such trees in presented in Chapter 7. Phylogenetic relations between species are represented by branches of the tree

the chimpanzees and bonobos. More details and examples of phylogenetic trees and how to interpret them are presented in Chapter 7.

5.6 | Exercises

(1) The complete mtDNA of a mammoth is available on Genbank (NC_007596), as is that of African and Indian elephants (NC_000934, NC_005129, NC_004921). A standard way to compare such sequences would involve the removal of the rapidly evolving HVRs, and the global alignment of the remaining sequence. This is done because we expect to have sufficient variation in the coding part of the genome, due to its length, and so we can afford removing the noisier parts. Which of the modern elephants seems to be more closely related to mammoths?

(2) Extinct saber-tooth tigers lived until 15,000 years ago, and many parts of their mtDNA are available. The 12S ribosomal RNA gene has accession number DQ097171 and can be compared to homologous sequences from various extant felines. What conclusions can you draw about their relations?

(3) The mtDNA sequences of blue whale, hippopotamus, and cow have accession numbers respectively NC_001601, NC_000889, NC_006853. Is the whale genetically closer to cows or to hippos?

5.7 | Reading list

The use of genetic techniques to address questions about the early history of modern humans was pioneered by Luigi Luca Cavalli-Sforza and his collaborators, and is presented in their book (Cavalli-Sforza *et al.*, 1996) (an account more suitable for a general audience is Cavalli-Sforza (2001)). The article Cavalli-Sforza (1998) discusses the impact of DNA techniques on population genetics. A book aimed at a general audience about mtDNA and early human migrations is the very readable Sykes (2002).

Large-scale whole-genome analysis of mtDNA for population genetics has become possible only in the past few years, for example see Ingman *et al.* (2000). The use of Neanderthal mtDNA fragments has been reported in various articles, see Krings *et al.* (1997, 2000), Ovchinnikov *et al.* (2000), Schmitz *et al.* (2002).

Saber-tooth tiger mtDNA sequences can be found in Barnett *et al.* (2005). The data used in this chapter are derived from various of the above papers and can be found on the website (Handt *et al.*, 1998; Ingman *et al.*, 2000).

The formulas for the calculation of genetic distances were introduced between 1969 and 1980. The celebrated Jukes–Cantor formula was introduced in 1969 (Jukes and Cantor, 1969) when Cantor was a student of Jukes at UC Berkeley. Motoo Kimura was an influential mathematical biologist, his contributions to the statistics of sequence evolution are countless, the results presented in this chapter can be found in Kimura and Ohta (1972), Kimura (1968, 1980). A general discussion of genetic distances and their calculation can be found in the very readable and complete book Felsenstein (2004).

The tree in Figure 5.5 was drawn with TreeView, a free software package created by Roderic Page. Links to this package, and to all of the above mentioned papers, datasets, and websites, can be found on the book's website:

`www.computational-genomics.net`

Chapter 6

Fighting HIV
Natural selection at the molecular level

- The neutral theory of evolution
- Substitution rates
- K_A/K_S: quantifying the amount of selection on a sequence

6.1 | A mysterious disease

In the spring of 1979 the Centers for Disease Control in the United States received reports of an unknown disease that affected young men and produced a wide range of symptoms, including rare forms of cancer. In 1981 the disease was named Acquired Immune Deficiency Syndrome (AIDS). It was recognized that transmission of this disease was largely sexual, but it was not until 1983 that the infectious agent – Human Immunodeficiency Virus (HIV) – was "simultaneously" identified by labs in France and the US (the sordid story of this inter-continental competition has been the subject of multiple books). Since the first cases were identified, 20 million people have died from AIDS worldwide.

At present there is no known cure for this disease and no effective vaccine against HIV infection. Large parts of the world are now facing an AIDS epidemic, with some African nations counting more than 60% of their population among the affected. Although methods exist to keep the virus in check, the high cost of these treatments means that most infected individuals in the developing world will die from AIDS. Indeed, this disease has now surpassed malaria as the number one killer in Africa.

Various aspects of the AIDS epidemic have caught scientists by surprise, including its sudden appearance, mysterious origin, and the difficulty in finding a cure or vaccine. In this chapter we will see one of the reasons why the fight against HIV and AIDS has been so difficult: the capability of the virus to constantly and rapidly evolve, evading our immune system as well as the action of drugs. We will address the appearance and origin of HIV and other viruses in the next chapter. In order to understand the insidious nature of this virus, we will need to address a number of issues, including how the human immune system works and how viruses mutate to escape it.

Yes, viruses do evolve: we can actually observe their genomes changing over very short periods of time. HIV, like other viruses, evolves during the course of infection of a single individual. In fact, the virus that eventually kills a patient is often quite different from the one that infected them. Viruses have very high mutation rates and very short generation times, characteristics that make it relatively easy for them to adapt in response to the human immune system. By evolving, HIV manages to remain one step ahead of our defenses.

HIV does not only evolve to evade our innate immune system, it also evolves in response to anti-viral drugs manufactured to fight infection. Shortly after many anti-viral drugs are introduced, drug-resistant versions of HIV appear. For instance, in 1987 a promising new drug called AZT was introduced in the fight against HIV. AZT interferes with a key enzyme involved in virus replication. After initial success with many infected patients, a new strain of HIV emerged that was resistant to the effects of AZT. HIV had managed to evolve around the anti-viral drug; this is what makes HIV so difficult to treat and prevent.

How exactly does HIV manage to evade our best attempts to destroy it? Which of its genes evolve in response to the immune system and which genes are so necessary to the viral function that they change very little? In the previous chapter we saw that DNA sequences evolve because mutations arise and can be passed to the next generation even if they have no effect on the function of the organism. However the process of natural selection can act to retard or accelerate the rate of evolution across a genome. This leaves a strong signature on both genes and non-coding regions.

Being able to understand how natural selection has shaped a genome can help us to understand the genome's functions, its interactions with the environment, and to some extent can help to reconstruct its past (or to better predict its future). Recognizing which parts of a viral genome are evolving the most slowly may point us to the most fundamental elements of organism function; recognizing which parts are evolving the fastest can lead us to the elements that are locked in an arms race with the immune system. Here we will discuss data analysis methods for analyzing and quantifying the effects of natural selection on a genome.

6.2 | Evolution and natural selection

The example of HIV illustrates the evolution of drug resistance in a virus, as well as the evolution of resistance to the host's immune responses. Many similar cases of drug resistance in viruses and bacteria have been documented, and all represent cases of adaptive natural selection on the part of the infectious agent.

By 1859, when Darwin's *On the Origin of Species by Means of Natural Selection* was published, many people already accepted the idea that species evolved over time. Darwin's contribution was to provide a framework for understanding how organisms adapt to their environment: evolution by natural selection. At the molecular level, natural selection acts (teleologically speaking) to both remove deleterious mutations – called negative or purifying selection – and to promote the spread of advantageous mutations – called positive selection. At the organismal level, natural selection is the process by which individuals who are best able to survive and reproduce leave more offspring for the next generation. This is how adaptations such as bird wings, whale flippers, and primate brains spread and flourish.

In order for evolution by natural selection to occur, two conditions must hold: individuals in a population must vary in the characteristics that are genetically controlled, and these characteristics must have differential effects on the survival or reproductive success (the fitness) among individuals. Under these conditions, the "fitter" individuals in a population will do better and leave more offspring, changing the genetic and genomic properties of a species. Evolution can also be driven by random effects, as mentioned in Chapter 5 and will be discussed later.

Generally speaking, these two axioms can be satisfied by systems other than living organisms. So-called genetic algorithms are computer programs that find optimal solutions to problems by keeping track of multiple, competing solutions undergoing repeated rounds of mutation and natural selection, much like living organisms. Viruses themselves are considered non-living entities by many researchers, yet they clearly can evolve over time in response to natural selection. Note that it is populations – not individuals – that evolve.

Much of the selection imposed on viruses comes from the attempts of the immune system to hunt and destroy them. The immune system must first recognize viruses as foreign invaders and then must find a way to either kill the virus or the cell it has infected. A number of features of viruses make them very hard to control in this manner. We next describe some of these features.

6.3 | HIV and the human immune system

HIV is a virus formed by a protein envelope containing two copies of its 9.5 Kb RNA genome (some viruses have DNA genomes; some have RNA). The genome contains only nine genes, some of which are encoded in overlapping sequences. HIV recognizes and infects the helper T cells of the human immune system. The human immune system's response to any infection is to find and kill infected cells, using helper T cells to identify the infected targets. One reason that HIV is such a difficult enemy to fight is because it infects the very cells that should be attacking it.

Infected cells become marked by small sub-sequences of viral proteins called *epitopes* that stick out of the cell membrane. If the immune system recognizes the specific epitope on an infected cell, it can kill it using special "killer" cells; if it cannot, then the virus is able to commandeer the cell's machinery to replicate itself. As a result, mutations that occur in the HIV epitope that make the virus invisible to detection by helper T cells that then communicate with killer cells are highly advantageous. It turns out that HIV is very good at producing new individuals with new versions of these protein epitopes.

A virus reproduces extremely quickly: one generation takes only 1.5 days and viral replication is quite error prone. It is estimated that the error rate for RNA viruses such as HIV is five mutations per 100 000 bases each generation (approximately 1000 times as high as the average mutation rate in humans).

Therefore, if we simply wait a few (viral) generations, the population of the virus found in an infected patient will contain a significant amount of genetic diversity. It is little wonder that any time the immune system figures out how to recognize viral envelope proteins, there is usually a version of the virus already in existence that is able to escape detection.

Like viruses, the human immune system is not static: it can change (within a single individual) to recognize new epitopes. This recognition may take a few days, but for many viruses (and for bacteria) leads to lifelong immunity. Unfortunately, HIV evolves so quickly that no immunity is permanent. The arms race between the host and virus continues throughout infection, but may slow down as the human immune system is finally defeated by HIV.

It is clear that having epitopes recognized by the immune system reduces the fitness of individual viruses; any new mutation that can evade detection will be selected for and the individual carrying it will give rise to huge numbers of offspring immune to the host's defenses, at least for a while. A study of the HIV genome should be able to detect the regions that are under such positive selection. As we will see, the HIV envelope proteins that contain the epitopes recognized by the immune system show clear signatures of adaptive natural selection.

6.4 Quantifying natural selection on DNA sequences

In the last chapter we saw that mutations originating in a single individual – as all mutations must – can eventually rise in frequency and become fixed throughout a species. Because this process happens within a single evolutionary lineage, we observe these fixed mutations as differences between species. And if mutations are neutral, that is they have no effect on the organism's probability of survival and reproduction, then we can exactly predict the rate at which mutations fix within a species, and hence the rate at which observable differences between species accrue. But all mutations are not neutral; most mutations that change amino acids will disrupt the function of proteins and will be selected against, as will non-coding mutations that affect gene regulation. Indeed, the best estimates are that between 80 and 90% of all new mutations that change the amino acid sequence of a protein are detrimental to organismal function.

How do we know which mutations are neutral and which are deleterious or advantageous? Many attempts have been made to actually measure the fitness of individuals with new mutations in the lab, but these experiments are only possible with very short-lived organisms that can be maintained in huge numbers. The simplest way, therefore, is to compare the rate of substitution of mutations that have the possibility of changing protein function with the rate in areas that have no effect on protein function. The most common way to do this is to compare the rate of *non-synonymous* to *synonymous* substitutions in a single gene.

Non-synonymous mutations to a DNA sequence are ones that change the amino acid sequence after translation. Synonymous mutations are those that change the sequence of the codon without changing the resulting amino acid. If we look at the genetic code in Chapter 2 (Table 2.2), we can see that most changes in the third position of codons do not change the amino acid coded for. Changes in the first codon position can sometimes (5% of the time) be synonymous, while changes in the second position are never synonymous. The assumption of our analyses will be that synonymous substitutions have no effect on protein function, and therefore on organismal fitness, while non-synonymous mutations will change the protein sequence, and *may* therefore have an effect on fitness. Because the rate of both non-synonymous and synonymous changes are proportional to the underlying mutation rate, the only difference in the observed substitution rates will be due to differing acceptance rates. This acceptance is a direct consequence of natural selection.

It is in fact not strictly true that all synonymous mutations are completely neutral (the synonymous codon bias observed in Chapter 2 can be caused by selection), but selection against them is so weak that we can ignore this effect for now. We may wonder why we cannot just compare the number of non-synonymous substitutions in any gene to the number of substitutions in a sequence that we know is completely free from selective constraint, such as the hyper-variable regions of the mitochondrial genome that we discussed in the last chapter. The reason is that the underlying mutation rate itself varies throughout the genome, and even along chromosomes. In order to make a fair comparison of the number of substitutions, therefore, we need to ensure that we are comparing regions with equivalent underlying mutation rates.

Because there are many more possible mutations in any coding region that are non-synonymous, we will actually compare the number of non-synonymous substitutions per non-synonymous site (denoted K_A) to the number of synonymous substitutions per synonymous site (denoted K_S). This allows us to correct for the fact that in most genes approximately 70% of all mutations will be non-synonymous.

The K_A/K_S ratio. The Japanese geneticist Motoo Kimura pointed out in 1977 that a comparison of the non-synonymous to synonymous substitutions in a gene can tell us about the strength and form of natural selection. Kimura started from the premise that advantageous mutations are extremely rare – proteins already function quite well, so the chance that any change to them is an improvement is very low (this premise is also borne out by laboratory experiments). He also surmised that deleterious mutations will have little if any chance of spreading through a population; these mutations will be selected against and will not rise in frequency. If both of these premises are true, then the great majority of differences between DNA sequences that we see will be completely neutral. The stronger the negative selection on a gene (i.e. the fewer changes allowed), the fewer non-synonymous substitutions will be observed.

Here is how Kimura described this set of relationships in terms of the ratio of non-synonymous to synonymous substitutions per site (K_A/K_S; sometimes also represented as d_N/d_S). (The "A" in K_A stands for "amino acid.") We saw in Chapter 5 that the rate of substitution equals the rate of mutation for neutral mutations. If the fraction of non-synonymous mutations in a gene that are neutral is f_0, then the number of non-synonymous substitutions observed in time t is

$$K_A = \nu f_0 t,$$

where ν is the total mutation rate. Likewise, the number of synonymous substitutions in the same period of time is

$$K_S = \nu t.$$

Because all synonymous mutations are neutral, $f_0 = 1$. This implies that the number of synonymous substitutions is limited solely by the mutation rate. The ratio K_A/K_S then tells us about the fraction of non-synonymous mutations that are neutral, and consequently the strength of selection:

$$K_A/K_S = f_0.$$

The stronger the negative selection on a gene, the fewer non-synonymous mutations will be neutral, resulting in a smaller f_0; as a consequence, K_A/K_S will be less than 1. Data from thousands of comparisons of genes show that in the vast majority of cases K_A/K_S is well below 1, usually between 0 and 0.3. (K_A/K_S is not always constant across an entire gene; later in this chapter we will see how it can vary according to the region of the protein we are examining.)

Under the framework we have defined so far, K_A/K_S can be no greater than 1; indeed, it will only be 1 when all non-synonymous mutations are neutral. But if we allow for advantageous non-synonymous mutations – which can substitute faster than synonymous mutations – K_A/K_S can be greater than 1. Representing the proportion of mutations that are advantageous as α, the number of non-synonymous mutations is then

$$K_A = \nu(f_0 + \alpha)t;$$

and K_A/K_S would be equal to $f_0 + \alpha$, a combination of neutral and advantageous substitutions.

If we thus consider all types of mutations, we can use K_A/K_S ratios to tell us only about which form of natural selection has the biggest effect on genes. If $K_A/K_S < 1$, then negative selection predominates; this does not mean that positive selection has not also contributed to sequence divergence, only that it has been a small part. Conversely, if $K_A/K_S > 1$, then positive selection predominates, although this does not mean that all mutations are allowed or are advantageous. We can see from these relationships that when $K_A/K_S = 1$ it does not necessarily mean that a gene is under no selective constraint, only that positive and negative selection may be canceling each other out.

Of course it is important to be able to estimate K_A/K_S with accuracy and confidence, and this is often far from simple in practice. As we saw in Chapter 5, we may even need to apply corrections to account for the possibility of multiple substitutions, especially multiple synonymous substitutions. Estimation of this ratio can be done either by fast approximate methods, or by more complex statistical approaches based on maximum likelihood. Next we describe one of the most widely used approximate algorithms.

6.5 | Estimating K_A/K_S

The simplest class of estimation methods separately counts the number of synonymous and non-synonymous *sites* in the two sequences (S_c and A_c) and the number of synonymous and non-synonymous *differences* between the two sequences (S_d and A_d). By adjusting for the number of possible sites that can produce non-synonymous and synonymous changes, we can calculate the non-synonymous and synonymous substitutions *per site*. These are necessary to obtain a normalized ratio (after correction for multiple hits) of K_A and K_S.

The simplest methods (such as the popular algorithm by Masatoshi Nei and Takashi Gojobori) assume that the rate of transversions and transitions are the same, and that there is no codon usage bias. More complex algorithms take into account transition and transversion biases, as well as codon and nucleotide usage biases. We describe the simple Nei and Gojobori algorithm below.

Algorithm: Nei and Gojobori. In order to compute the proportion of synonymous and non-synonymous substitutions we need to start with an alignment of homologous DNA sequences. Given the alignment, there should be a one-to-one correspondence between codons in the two sequences (if there are gaps in either of the two sequences, those codons are not compared and are not included in further calculations). It is now possible to separately count both the number of non-synonymous and synonymous sites and the number of non-synonymous and synonymous differences between sequences. We should say that the idea of either a non-synonymous or synonymous "site" is artificial, as really only mutations can be defined as amino acid changing or not. But, for both algorithmic and semantic convenience, researchers define sites by their propensity to produce non-synonymous or synonymous changes. This is the first step in our algorithm.

Step 1: Counting A and S sites. It is useful to start by focusing our attention on just one pair of corresponding codons, as all the quantities defined on individual codons will be readily generalized to the case of longer sequences. Here is an alignment:

        TTT
        TTA .

We assume each protein-coding DNA sequence is a sequence from the codon alphabet $\mathcal{C}$, with the kth codon denoted by c_k. We define the number of synonymous sites in the kth codon as $s_c(c_k)$ and that of non-synonymous sites as $a_c(c_k) = 1 - s_c(c_k)$. We denote by f_i the fraction of changes at the ith position of a given codon ($i = 1, 2, 3$) that result in a synonymous change (not to be confused with the fraction of neutral mutations, f_0, used above). The $s_c(c_k)$ and $a_c(c_k)$ for this codon are then given by $s_c(c_k) = \sum f_i$ and $a_c(c_k) = (3 - s_c(c_k)) = (3 - \sum f_i)$, respectively.

Example 6.1

Counting $s_c(c_k)$ and $a_c(c_k)$. In the case of codon TTA (Leucine), $f_1 = 1/3$, $f_2 = 0$, and $f_3 = 1/3$. In other words, one change at the first position, no changes at the second, and one change at the third do not change the amino acid and are hence synonymous (see the genetic code table in Chapter 2 to verify this for yourself). Thus, $s_c(\text{TTA}) = 2/3$ and $a_c(\text{TTA}) = 7/3$.

For a DNA sequence of r codons, the total number of synonymous and non-synonymous sites is therefore given by

$$S_c = \sum_{k=1}^{r} s_c(c_k)$$
$$A_c = (3r - S_c),$$

respectively. So S_c and A_c are properties of individual sequences, more precisely properties of the specific codon composition of a sequence.

Since these models are always used when comparing two sequences, we will define the averages of S_c and A_c for the two sequences:

$$\hat{S}_c = (S_{c1} + S_{c2})/2$$
$$\hat{A}_c = (A_{c1} + A_{c2})/2.$$

These are the quantities that we will use in calculating K_A and K_S.

Remark 6.1

Stop codon. Typically the stop codon is left out of all calculations, since it is impossible to define non-synonymous and synonymous changes at this position.

Step 2: Counting A and S differences. We denote by $s_d(c_k)$ and $a_d(c_k)$ the number of synonymous and non-synonymous differences for the kth codon pair in the alignment. When there is only one nucleotide difference, we can immediately decide whether the substitution is synonymous or non-synonymous.

Example 6.2

Synonymous and non-synonymous substitutions. If the codons compared are

    GTT   (Val)

    GTA   (Val),

there is only one difference, and it is synonymous; hence $s_d = 1$ and $a_d = 0$.

When two nucleotide differences exist between the two codons under comparison, there will be two possible ways to obtain the observed differences. That is, we can think of two possible pathways of evolution leading from the first to the second codon, depending which one of the two mutations came first (we are considering here only the shortest pathways between two codons). Notice that depending on the order of substitutions, a certain difference can be synonymous or not, as can be seen in the example below. For simplicity, we assign equal probability to both pathways, compute the values s_d and a_d for each pathway, and then average them.

Example 6.3
Synonymous and non-synonymous substitutions. For example, in the comparison of

    TTT

    GTA,

the two possible pathways are

>   pathway 1   TTT (Phe) ↔ GTT (Val) ↔ GTA (Val)
>   pathway 2   TTT (Phe) ↔ TTA (Leu) ↔ GTA (Val) .

Pathway I involves one non-synonymous and one synonymous substitution, whereas pathway II involves two non-synonymous substitutions. We assume that pathways I and II occur with equal probability. The s_d and a_d then become 0.5 and 1.5, respectively.

When there are three nucleotide differences between the codons compared, there are six different possible pathways between the codons, and in each pathway there are three mutational steps. Considering all these pathways and mutational steps, we can again evaluate s_d and a_d in the same way as in the case of two nucleotide differences, by averaging the s_d and a_d scores of each pathway with equal weight.

As before, once we can compute s_d and a_d for each codon pair in the alignment, we can easily obtain the same values for the entire sequence by summing up the contribution of each. The total number of synonymous and non-synonymous differences between the two sequences is then

$$S_d = \sum_{k=1}^{r} s_d(c_k)$$

$$A_d = \sum_{k=1}^{r} a_d(c_k),$$

where $s_d(c_k)$ and $a_d(c_k)$ are s_d and a_d for the kth codon pair, respectively, and r is the number of codons compared. Note that $S_d + A_d$ is equal to the total number of nucleotide differences between the two DNA sequences compared.

Step 3: Computing K_A and K_S. We can now estimate the proportion of synonymous (d_s) and non-synonymous (d_n) differences by the following equations:

$$d_s = S_d / \hat{S}_c$$

$$d_a = A_d / \hat{A}_c,$$

where $\hat{S}_c$ and $\hat{A}_c$ are the average number of synonymous and non-synonymous sites for the two sequences compared. To estimate the number of synonymous substitutions (K_S) and non-synonymous substitutions (K_A) per site, we use the Jukes and Cantor correction:

$$K = -\frac{3}{4} \ln \left(1 - \frac{4}{3} d \right)$$

for both d_s and d_a, hence obtaining K_S and K_A.

Algorithm 6.1

Nei–Gojobori, 1986. The table below shows the steps involved in the computation of K_S and K_A using the Nei–Gojobori method:

Input: two homologous ORF sequences
Output: K_A and K_S
Global alignment of sequences
For each codon-pair with no gaps
    Compute $s_c(c_k)$ and $a_c(c_k)$ for both sequences
    Compute $s_d(c_k)$ and $a_d(c_k)$
Compute: $S_c = \sum_{k=1}^{r} s_c(c_k)$
$A_c = (3r - S_c)$
$\hat{S}_c = (S_{c1} + S_{c2})/2$
$\hat{A}_c = (A_{c1} + A_{c2})/2$
$S_d = \sum_{k=1}^{r} s_d(c_k)$
$A_d = \sum_{k=1}^{r} a_d(c_k)$
$d_s = S_d/\hat{S}_c$
$d_a = A_d/\hat{A}_c$
$K_S = -\frac{3}{4} \ln\left(1 - \frac{4}{3}d_s\right)$
$K_A = -\frac{3}{4} \ln\left(1 - \frac{4}{3}d_a\right).$

The computation of the codon quantities $s_c(c_k)$, $a_c(c_k)$, $s_d(c_k)$, and $a_d(c_k)$ is performed as described above, and could be precomputed and stored in a table prior to seeing the input sequences. That part of the computation is general, and is simply a function of codon pairs. Given a global alignment of two ORFs, then, we can readily perform the summations shown in the second part of the table, and hence the cost is linear in the length of the sequences.

6.6 | Case study: natural selection and the HIV genome

The genome of HIV has been sequenced hundreds of times since 1985, so that it is possible to study the differences between many individual genomes, and to gain a general understanding of how this virus evolves. By applying many of the algorithms and statistics we have learned over the first six chapters of this book, we can find genes, align their sequences, count their differences between individuals, and quantify the effect of natural selection on the HIV genome.

HIV (like many other viruses) evades the immune system by constantly evolving. In other words, HIV is a moving target. In particular, there are specific regions of its proteins that are recognized and attacked by our immune system, and these are the regions that are expected to show a signature of adaptive evolution due to the advantage accrued by novel variants. This process is balanced by the need of the virus to maintain its biological functions. Other regions are therefore under predominantly negative selection and remain invariant, because they have important biological functions and are likely not involved in interactions with the immune system. An analysis of K_A/K_S in different genes and different parts of a single gene can reveal those regions of

Table 6.1 | Main ORFs found in HIV1 genome (accession number NC-001802), with their length in base pairs, start and stop positions, and the reading frame (RF) in which they are found. We also report the name of the protein encoded by the relative gene, and an estimate of the K_A/K_S ratio of each gene, obtained comparing two different sequences of HIV, see main text for details

Start	Stop	Length	RF	Protein name	K_A/K_S
5377	5593	216 bp	1	TAT (part of)	0.16/0.15
5608	5854	246 bp	1	VPU	–
1904	4640	2736 bp	2	GAG-POL-II	0.024/0.20
5105	5339	234 bp	2	VPR (part of)	0.05/0.50
5771	8339	2568 bp	2	ENV (precurs. of 2)	0.13/0.27
336	1836	1500 bp	3	GAG-POL-I	0.05/0.22
4587	5163	576 bp	3	VIF	0.06/0.21
8343	8712	369 bp	3	NEF (part of)	0.09/0.31

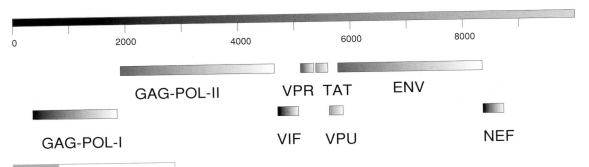

Fig. 6.1 Genome of HIV1. Note the ENV gene and the GAG-POL-I gene, used below in the sliding window analysis, in Figure 6.2. The details of these ORFs can be seen in Table 6.1

the HIV genome undergoing adaptive evolution. Here we go through the steps necessary to conduct a genome-wide analysis of natural selection in HIV.

ORF finding. The HIV genome has nine open reading frames but 15 proteins are made in all (some genes are translated into large polyproteins which are then cleaved by a virus-encoded protease into smaller proteins). Some ORFs overlap slightly, and there are also some introns. All these factors complicate the detection of genes (see Figure 6.1 for a diagram of the HIV genome).

If we apply the ORF-finding algorithm discussed in Chapter 2 on an HIV genome downloaded from GenBank (accession number NC_001802), we obtain the eight ORFs reported in Table 6.1. Note that there are more genes in the HIV genome, but we have missed some protein-coding regions because of limitations of our simple gene-finding strategy: for example there are two genes containing introns in HIV that cannot be detected by simple ORF finding (HMMs should be used for this). We also report the length of the ORF, the reading frame (RF) on which it is found, and the protein encoded by it. The last column reports the K_A/K_S ratio as computed by the Nei–Gojobori algorithm (see below for details).

K_A/K_S *ratio.* In order to measure natural selection on each of the eight ORFs that have been identified, we used a second HIV genome (GenBank accession numbers AF033819 and M27323).

After aligning the corresponding ORFs, we used the Nei–Gojobori algorithm outlined earlier in this chapter to calculate K_A/K_S for each ORF (see Table 6.1). We can see that K_A/K_S ranges from 0.1 to 1.0, indicating a wide range of evolutionary constraints. However, we should keep in mind that we are averaging over entire genes to calculate these values, so there may still be smaller sections of these genes evolving at a very high rate, possibly with a ratio significantly greater than 1. We can detect such regions using a sliding-window analysis as described below.

Natural selection on HIV epitopes: the ENV gene. The *ENV* gene codes for the envelope glycoprotein gp160, which is a precursor to two proteins: gp41 and gp120. The gp120 protein is embedded in and extends exterior to the viral outer envelope and is primarily responsible for binding to receptors on T-cells. (In fact, mutations in the human receptor protein recognized by gp120, *CCR5*, are known to confer increased immunity to HIV.) Additionally, due partly to its physical location in the viral envelope, gp120 is recognized by the immune system as an indicator of infection. So selection on gp120 acts both to maintain continuing recognition of host cells and simultaneously to avoid detection by the immune system. These roles are carried out by different parts of the gp120 protein, and we therefore expect that simply measuring K_A/K_S across the whole gene will obscure both processes by giving us an average value (we observed an average score of 0.5 for the entire gp120 ORF). To avoid this we can measure the effect of selection on smaller regions of the gene, by computing K_A/K_S in sliding windows.

Sliding window analysis. For the analysis of single genes – especially long ones – we can measure K_A/K_S by taking smaller windows of only a fraction the size of the gene, and computing the ratio for just the window. By sliding this window along the sequence (as we did for GC-content in Chapter 1), we gain a good heuristic feeling for the range of values of K_A/K_S, and therefore of selection, across the gene. The size of the windows used is quite important: windows that are too small give highly noisy results, while windows that are too large can hide the local effects of selection by averaging together variable and stable regions. The step size taken in sliding the window across the sequence can similarly have an effect on the patterns revealed. It is important to remember, however, that while sliding-window plots are very valuable for visualizing patterns in data, they are not necessarily statistically rigorous analyses. In this case, however, they enable us to see the varying levels of selective pressure on different parts of the envelope protein.

After a pair of *ENV* sequences are aligned, a window with length L moves along the length of the pair in steps of size m. We calculate the K_A/K_S ratio for each window (see Figure 6.2). As expected, the rate of non-synonymous substitutions is greater than the rate of synonymous substitutions in some regions of *ENV* – a clear indication of positive selection, although the average over the entire gene is below 1. These may be the regions that are known to be recognized by the human immune system. There are also many regions with

Fig. 6.2 Sliding window analysis of two HIV proteins, ENV and GAG (using genomes AF033819 and M27323). Window size is 60 codons. Although most of the protein sequence has K_A/K_S values below 1, a few parts have higher values. The red line indicates K_A, the blue line K_S, the green line the ratio K_A/K_S.

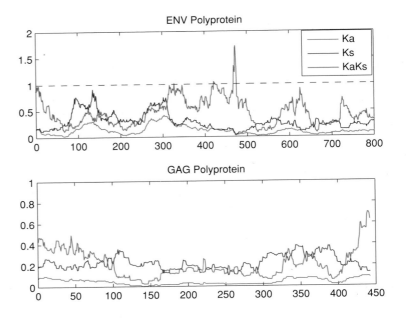

K_A/K_S less than 1, and these are the regions necessary for the virus to recognize the receptors of its host cells. As we observed earlier, the average ratio for the entire gene is less than 1; clearly, sometimes finer-scale analyses are necessary to uncover the true story of natural selection.

GAG polyprotein. GAG is one of the three main genes found in all retroviruses (along with ENV and polymerase). It contains around 1500 nucleotides, and encodes four separate proteins which form the building blocks for the viral core. This protein contains additional epitopes recognized by the human immune system, and hence it is under constant pressure to escape by evolving. We repeated the same analysis of K_A/K_S with this protein (see Figure 6.2). The results also show regions of higher divergence, mixed with more stable regions.

6.7 | Exercises

(1) Measure the K_A/K_S ratio for various mtDNA genes, comparing human with mouse, as well as with chimpanzee (make sure to use the correct genetic code). What can you conclude about natural selection?

(2) Repeat the same exercise, this time using viral genomes (HIV or SARS, which is discussed in detail in Chapter 7). Compare the results with those obtained for mtDNA.

(3) Practice with free online software tools for measuring K_A/K_S (information about these packages can be found in the book's website).

6.8 Reading list

The first genomic sequence of HIV was obtained in 1985 and was published in the journal *Cell* (Wain-Hobson *et al.*, 1985). A survey of HIV can be found in Greene, (September 1993). Two survey papers on the K_A/K_S ratio can be found in Hurst (2002) and Yang and Bielawski (2000). More discussions can be found in Muse (1996) and Tzeng *et al.* (2004), and additional readings can be found in Kumar (1996).

The original papers that introduced this kind of analysis and the algorithms we use here are Miyata and Yasunaga (1980) and the classic article by Nei and Gojobori (Nei and Gojobori, 1986). More advanced and recent discussions revolve around the issue of estimating the ratio at single codon, using multiple alignments, see for example Suzuki and Gojobori (1999), while estimates of variance are found in Ota and Nei (1994). Also of interest is Thorne *et al.* (1991).

A freely available software tool that also computes the K_A/K_S ratio is MEGA, referenced via the book's website. A phylogenetic analysis of the various strains of HIV (and a discussion of the origins of this virus) are the topic of Exercise 2 in Chapter 7 and can be found on the book's website. Links to software packages, and to all of the above-mentioned papers, datasets, and websites, can be found on the book's website:

www.computational-genomics.net

Chapter 7

SARS–A post-genomic epidemic
Phylogenetic analysis

- Phylogenetic trees
- The neighbor-joining algorithm
- The Newick format for representing trees

7.1 | Outbreak

On February 28, 2003 the Vietnam French Hospital of Hanoi, a private hospital with only 60 beds, called the World Health Organization (WHO) with a report of patients who had unusual influenza-like symptoms. Hospital officials had seen an avian influenza virus pass through the region a few years earlier and suspected a similar virus. The pathogen seemed highly contagious and highly virulent, so they asked that someone from the WHO be sent to investigate. Dr. Carlo Urbani, an Italian specialist in infectious diseases, responded.

Dr. Urbani quickly determined that the Vietnamese hospital was facing a new and unusual pathogen. The infections he observed were characterized by a fever, dry cough, shortness of breath, and progressively worsening respiratory problems. Death from respiratory failure occurred in a significant fraction of the infected patients. For the next several days, Dr. Urbani worked at the hospital documenting findings, collecting samples, and organizing patient quarantine. He was the first person to identify and describe the new disease, called Severe Acute Respiratory Syndrome, or SARS. In a matter of weeks, Dr. Urbani and five other healthcare professionals from the hospital would be dead.

By March 15 the WHO had already issued a global alert, calling SARS a "worldwide health threat." They warned that possible cases had been identified in Canada, Indonesia, Philippines, Singapore, Thailand, and Vietnam.

The origin of the epidemic. Although the origins and cause of SARS were still unknown in March of 2003, it would not be long before the analysis of multiple SARS genomes revealed the story of how this disease had originated and traveled to many countries.

We now know that the first cases of what was to become known as SARS appeared as early as November 2002 in the Chinese province of Guangdong. A few months later the first major outbreak of SARS hit Guangdong: more than 130 infected patients were treated, 106 of whom had acquired the disease while in a hospital in the city of Guangzhou (the rest of the world was unaware of this). A doctor who worked in this hospital visited Hong Kong and checked into the city's Hotel Metropole on February 21, 2003. He was eventually hospitalized with pneumonia during his visit to Hong Kong and died. A number of other travelers staying on the ninth floor of the Metropole became infected and left Hong Kong as disease carriers. One of these was an American businessman named Johnny Chen; he would be the first patient treated in the Vietnam French Hospital of Hanoi (before dying Mr. Chen infected at least 80 people, including half of the hospital workers who cared for him). Other infected travelers from the Metropole would bring SARS to Canada, Singapore, and the United States. By late April 2003, over 4300 SARS cases and 250 SARS-related deaths had been reported to the WHO from over 25 countries around the world. Most of these cases occurred after exposure to SARS patients in household or hospital settings. Many of these cases would later be traced, through multiple chains of transmission, to the doctor from Guangdong province who visited Hong Kong. (On April 5, 2003 China apologized for its slow response to the outbreak.)

In response to the outbreak – and while struggling to control the spread of the pathogen – the WHO coordinated an international collaboration that included clinical, epidemiological, and laboratory investigations to identify the exact cause of the disease, as well as its origin. In the third week of March 2003 laboratories in the United States, Canada, Germany, and Hong Kong independently isolated a novel coronavirus (SARS-CoV) from SARS patients. Evidence of SARS-CoV infection has since been documented in SARS patients throughout the world, indicating that the new virus is in fact responsible for the syndrome.

Coronaviruses are RNA viruses common in humans and animals; they are called coronaviruses because their distinctive halo of spiky envelope proteins resembles a crown. Some of these viruses cause common colds and are responsible for 15–25% of all upper respiratory tract infections, as well as being the cause of important diseases of livestock. In April 2003 scientists from Canada announced the completion of the genome sequence of the SARS virus. *Phylogenetic* analyses revealed the most closely related coronavirus to be one that infected a small mammal (not a bird as initially suspected), the palm civet. Not coincidentally, the palm civet is a part of the diet in the Guangdong province of China.

Phylogenetic analysis of the SARS epidemic. While SARS was still spreading, and television was filled with images of people wearing surgical masks in the streets, scientists were already discussing the significance of the SARS genome. Multiple laboratories around the world were racing to find the origin and ultimately a cure for SARS.

In May of 2003, two papers were published in the journal *Science* that reported the first full genome sequences of SARS-CoV. The agent of the epidemic turned out to be a 29 751 base pair coronavirus that was substantially different from any known human virus; the conclusion, therefore, was that SARS was derived from some non-human virus. Jumping the species barrier is not uncommon for viruses, as quite a number of examples of such zoonotic infections are known (HIV is one other such example). By 2003 the virus had spread to

Africa, India, and Europe, so genome sequences of additional SARS viruses were available from individuals around the world. All of these data were available online, and became a leading example of how virology and medicine can benefit from genomic tools.

Many important questions can be answered by analyzing large sets of complete viral genomes. In this chapter we will present the tools to answer some of them. What kind of virus caused this epidemic? What organism was the original viral host? What was the time and place of the crossing of the species barrier? What are the key mutations that made this switch possible? What was the route of transmission of SARS from the time it crossed the species barrier to its spread around the world?

In order to answer these questions, we will first examine some key algorithms of *phylogenetics*, and then will apply these algorithms to the very SARS data that were obtained in the spring of 2003. (All of these sequences are available from GenBank, and on this book's website.) Phylogenetics – the study of relationships among individuals and species – forms a crucial set of tools in computational genomics, needed for everything from building the tree of life, to discovering the origins of epidemics, to uncovering the very processes that shape genomes. We now take a general look at the algorithms and statistical models that are used to analyze phylogenetic relationships.

7.2 | On trees and evolution

The trajectory followed by the SARS virus during the winter and spring of 2003 can be likened to a tree. All of the SARS viruses in the world are related to one another: starting from the single virus that appeared in China, the network of relationships branched over and over again as SARS was passed from person to person. The result of this branching process can be envisioned as a graph with a tree-like structure, and we can infer this tree from the DNA differences between the different SARS genomes (see for example Figure 7.2).

Traditionally, the evolutionary history connecting any group of species or individuals (not just viruses) has been represented by means of a tree, which mathematically is a special type of graph. (We can also represent the relationships among related genes, or other groups using trees; we will call any such units under comparison *taxa*.) We are able to draw such trees because all of the species on earth share a common ancestor, as do all of the individuals within a species. The use of trees to represent relationships among species dates at least to the time of Charles Darwin. Note however that the relation among some genes or species can be more complex than a tree, and we may need to resort to phylogenetic *networks* on these occasions, due to the role of recombination or inter-specific hybridization. In this book we will not explore this important issue further, but will only use phylogenetic trees.

The structure of phylogenetic trees. Whatever taxa we wish to represent the relationships among, a phylogenetic tree attempts to represent both the ordering of relationships (A is closer to B than it is to C), and the distance separating any two groups (i.e. the time since they diverged). The simplest tree contains only two taxa (whether the taxa represent species, individuals, genes, etc.), and is represented in Figure 7.1. The two taxa are called the *external nodes* (or *leaves*), and they are connected by *branches*. Their common ancestor is an *internal node*. In the case of two taxa there is only one possible topology, or ordering of relationships. However, the length of time since the common ancestor can cover a huge range, from one day to one billion years. If both of these taxa are extant (that is, present now), then the time back to the ancestor must be the same for both lineages.

When we have more than two taxa, we must define a number of additional characteristics of trees. Bifurcating trees are those in which every internal node has exactly degree 3 (except for the root node – defined below), and every external node has exactly degree 1. (The degree of a node is the number of branches connecting to it.) Multifurcating trees can have interior nodes with a degree higher than 3. In evolutionary trees, the external nodes represent existing taxa, while the internal nodes represent their ancestors (typically, but not necessarily, extinct). Bifurcating trees can thus be thought of as requiring that every ancestor leads to only two descendants. Note that we normally assume that the true tree is bifurcating, that one ancestor leads to only two descendants at splitting; however, we can sometimes use multifurcating trees to represent uncertainty in the order of splitting events.

Rooted vs unrooted trees. We can also define a phylogenetic tree as either *rooted* or *unrooted*. In a rooted tree we define a special internal node called the root. The root node is the common ancestor to all the other nodes in the tree and all evolutionary paths lead back to the root (the root node has a degree of 2, as can be seen in Figure 7.2). When we have a rooted tree, we can consider its branches to have an orientation going from the root to each external node. Unrooted trees, on the other hand, are un-oriented; they show the topological relationships among taxa, but are agnostic with respect to the identity of the common ancestor of all taxa (see Figure 7.3).

The task of finding the root (choosing an edge of an unrooted tree where to place the root node) requires external biological information, or at least some assumptions about where the root should be placed. The root is typically defined by including in the dataset one or more taxa that are known to be the result of an earlier split, and hence to be more distantly related to each of the other taxa. This external taxon (or taxa) is called an *outgroup*. The branch of the tree

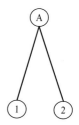

Fig. 7.1 A simple tree with only two leaves: nodes 1 and 2. Node A is the root of the tree

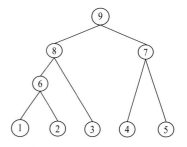

Fig. 7.2 A bifurcating rooted tree with five leaves, three internal nodes, and one root

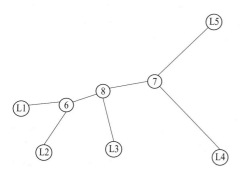

Fig. 7.3 An unrooted tree with five leaves and three internal nodes

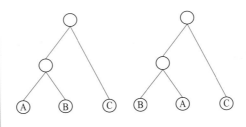

Fig. 7.4 These two trees are mathematically different, but they are biologically equivalent: the order in which the children of a node are represented is irrelevant, and hence phylogenetic trees are to be considered invariant with respect to changes of this order

where the outgroup joins the rest of the taxa then is considered to contain the root node. Additional methods for defining the root based on the structure of the tree are also used, and we discuss some of them below.

Finally, we must underscore an important component of these graphs: any rotation of branches about an internal node does not change the relationships among taxa. No matter the exact order in which we list the taxa from left to right, the tree represents the same set of phylogenetic relationships (see for example Figure 7.4).

The number of possible trees. The algorithmic and statistical problem of reconstructing a phylogenetic tree from a set of related DNA sequences is greatly complicated by the huge number of possible trees. The number of possible tree topologies is a function of n, the number of taxa in the tree, and depends on whether a tree is rooted or unrooted. The number of unrooted trees for $n \geq 3$ is

$$\frac{(2n-5)!}{2n-3(n-3)!}.$$

The number of rooted trees for $n \geq 2$ is

$$\frac{(2n-3)!}{2n-2(n-2)!}.$$

We can see that there is only one possible unrooted tree for the case of three taxa; the same holds for the case of two taxa in a rooted tree. For either kind of tree, the number of possibilities increases very quickly as n rises. For five taxa there are already 105 rooted trees, and for ten taxa there are 34 459 425 rooted trees. Only one of these is the true tree of evolutionary relationships, and inferring it from data is one of the main tasks of phylogenetic analysis.

Representing trees. There are various ways to non-graphically represent a tree, $\mathcal{T}$. A simple representation is – as with other graphs – by listing its nodes and the neighbors of each node. For oriented trees (those with a root) it is even easier: we only need to list the descendants of each node. So if we number the external nodes from 1 to n, for a bifurcating tree, there will always be $n-1$ internal nodes, and hence a matrix of all internal nodes and their children will be $(n-1) \times 3$ and will suffice to fully specify the tree topology (see the next example). Note that in this chapter we will denote by $\mathcal{T}$ both the graph itself and its representation in one of the various equivalent non-graphical formats.

Example 7.1

Tree representation as an array. The topology of the 5-taxa rooted tree in Figure 7.2 can be represented by the array:

9	8	7
8	3	6
7	4	5
6	1	2
5	–	–
4	–	–
3	–	–
2	–	–
1	–	–,

where each entry in the left-most column represents a node (internal and external), and the two corresponding entries on the same row represent its children. External nodes (here 1–5) have no descendant nodes, and hence the last five rows could be omitted. Note that this representation only works for rooted trees and is not the most intuitive one for biological interpretation; however, it is often used in implementation. If we also want to specify the distance between nodes (the branch lengths), we can either add this information to the above matrix, in the two right-most columns, or create a separate array that contains the distance from each node to its direct ancestor.

The example above shows one of the many possible representations of a tree. Another, more intuitive, representation of directed trees exploits the relationship between parental nodes and their descendants, using parentheses. In this representation, the tree T would be represented as

$$(((1, 2), 3), (4, 5)).$$

This is the same tree that appears in Figure 7.2. A popular standard tree file format called *Newick Format* is based on this idea, and is described in Section 7.5.

7.3 Inferring trees

7.3.1 Introduction to phylogenetic inference

As we have seen, the relationships among organisms can be viewed as a tree, and this representation is likely to be a very close, if not exact, model for the true relationships among species, individuals, and even genes. But the underlying, true tree is unknown. Yes, in the case of SARS we might have been able to re-create the true tree if we had known of the original infection and tracked its passing from one person to the next; but more often than not we are simply presented with organisms in the present day and asked to infer the most likely set of relationships connecting them. Just a few years ago this task would have been done largely by tracking changes in morphological characters: visible differences in the organisms that might tell us about their underlying genetic relatedness. Starting in the 1980s, and concomitant with technological advances in DNA sequencing technologies, inferring phylogenetic trees became a task inextricably linked to the analysis of DNA. More recently, it has been based on whole-genome comparisons.

There is always a true tree (or tree-like diagram) that describes the relationships among organisms. This unknown tree can be inferred from a comparison of the DNA sequences of these organisms because the sequences are always changing, leaving behind a trail of mutations that will be present in the descendants of mutant genes and absent from all other individuals. (Note that this line of reasoning relies heavily on the fact that mutation is rare, and will therefore lead unrelated individuals to the same sequence extremely infrequently.) If a gene or any segment of DNA did not change over time, we would have no record of its past. But mutation ensures that there is a traceable history of relationships.

Within a set of organisms we expect that every gene that they share will lead us to the same or very similar trees. Each of the genes might mutate and evolve at a different rate, but all of the genes will be inherited as a group and will be passed to descendants together, resulting in the same tree. Recombination between sequences within a species can cause two genes (or different parts of the same gene) to have different histories, but as we said earlier we will ignore this complication for now. So regardless of the exact DNA sequence we choose to examine, we expect to obtain the same tree from our analyses. And the more sequence we examine – and hence the more mutations – the more power we gain to resolve relationships between closely related organisms. However, although the true tree reflects the fact that the organisms at the external nodes are all equally distant from their common ancestor (in terms of time), different genes evolve at different rates, and different species may even have different mutation rates. As a result, though all of the external taxa in the true tree are the same distance from the root node, the vagaries of mutation mean that inferred trees may include some very long branches and some very short branches. All of the external taxa may therefore not necessarily be the same measured genetic distance from the root (a fact that can be very interesting for the study of changes in mutation or substitution rates).

Given a set of taxa and homologous sequences from each of them, there are a number of common ways to reconstruct their phylogenetic relationships. The methods can be broadly divided into two groups: those that rank all possible trees using some criterion in order to find the optimal one; and those that directly build the tree from the data (without explicitly stating a scoring function). Within the first group, criteria used often center around finding the tree with the smallest number of necessary mutations to explain the data (via likelihood and other methods). Given the huge number of possible trees, these methods can take a very long time to find the best tree, and even then may not necessarily find this tree because of the approximations that must be used to speed up the search. However, likelihood-based methods are favored for in-depth phylogenetic analyses. The second group includes phylogenetic methods that are themselves both criteria and algorithms for building trees, and are often based on computing the pairwise distance between taxa as a first step. They are typically very fast and have hence become extremely popular in genomic analyses. Although not necessarily as well behaved statistically as other methods, the most popular of these so-called "distance" methods (the *neighbor-joining* algorithm) is surprisingly robust and accurate. It is guaranteed to infer the true tree if distances used reflect the true distances between sequences, a result that is often not guaranteed by more statistically sophisticated methods.

7.3.2 Inferring trees from distance data

For a set of n taxa $\{\tau_1, \ldots, \tau_n\}$, we represent the genetic distance between them as a matrix of pairwise distances, D, usually taken from pairwise alignments and corrected for multiple substitutions by schemes such as Jukes–Cantor (with each distance measure between taxa given by $d(i, j)$). Given a distance matrix, simple and efficient algorithms can be used to infer the tree as long as these distances are *additive* (a notion defined shortly below) and often even when they are not.

Additivity and distance matrices. If the branches within a tree each have a specified length, then the distance between any two nodes can easily be computed as the total length of the (unique) path connecting them (see Figure 7.5 for an example).

In this way a tree can specify a distance matrix between its leaf nodes. However, not all distance matrices have this "additivity" property. Intuitively, the notion of additivity means that a certain distance can be represented by a tree. Formally, this translates into a technical condition that is stated below, and that motivates the algorithmics used in this chapter. Biologically, additivity is an important property for a distance matrix: the actual number of substitution events separating two taxa from their last common ancestor (their genetic distance) forms an additive distance. One of the attractions of using substitution models such as Jukes–Cantor is that they attempt to make the distance matrix more additive, and hence they make inference of the tree easier.

We can represent the distances within the tree of Figure 7.5 with the following distance matrix:

	L1	L2	L3	L4	L5
L1	0	2	4	6	6
L2	2	0	4	6	6
L3	4	4	0	6	6
L4	6	6	6	0	4
L5	6	6	6	4	0

Definition 7.1

Additive tree of a distance matrix. Let D be a symmetric $m \times m$ matrix where the numbers on the diagonal are all zero and the off-diagonal numbers are all strictly positive. Let T be an edge weighted tree with at least m nodes, where m distinct nodes of T are labeled with the rows of D. Tree T is called an *additive tree* for matrix D if, for every pair of labeled nodes (i, j), the path from node i to node j has total weight (or distance) exactly $d(i, j)$.

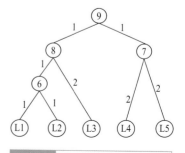

Fig. 7.5 A rooted tree with length-annotated branches.

Definition 7.2
Length of a tree. We also define the *total length* of a tree as the sum of all the branch lengths.

7.3.3 The neighbor-joining algorithm

The most popular distance-based method for inferring phylogenetic trees is known as *neighbor-joining*. The neighbor-joining (NJ) algorithm was first described by Naruya Saitou and Masatoshi Nei in 1987 (this is the same Nei as in the Nei–Gojobori method discussed in Chapter 6). NJ is a greedy algorithm that starts with an initial star phylogeny (one in which all taxa are connected directly to a single root node) and proceeds by iteratively merging pairs of nodes. The criterion with which each pair of nodes is selected is the key to its success: it identifies nodes that are topological neighbors in the underlying tree by using a mathematical characterization that is valid for all additive distance matrices.

After selecting the two taxa, they are merged into a single taxon, which will be further treated as a new single taxon. A new modified distance matrix is then created, where the distances of other taxa to the composite taxon are calculated. This process is repeated until all of the taxa have been joined together. Because NJ produces unrooted trees, an outgroup or other method is needed to specify the root node. As noted earlier, if the distance matrix used to build the tree is additive, then NJ will give the true tree; if, however, it is non-additive (i.e. there is noise in the data), there can be ambiguities in the inferred tree. Below we provide details for the calculation and construction of trees with NJ (using the corrected method published by James Studier and Karl Keppler), including some of the necessary background that makes it clear how NJ works. The reader can safely skip this technical part if they prefer.

Finding branch lengths. The lengths of individual branches in an unrooted tree with three external taxa can be computed from pairwise distances for additive matrices. To see this, imagine first that we have three taxa in an unrooted tree with known distances on all branches. Consider this unrooted tree joining taxa A, B, and C, with the length of each branch L_x, L_y, and L_z respectively (see Figure 7.6); then:

$$L_x + L_y = d_{AB}$$
$$L_x + L_z = d_{AC}$$
$$L_y + L_z = d_{BC}.$$

The solution for this system is

$$L_x = \frac{(d_{AB} + d_{AC} - d_{BC})}{2}$$
$$L_y = \frac{(d_{AB} + d_{BC} - d_{AC})}{2}$$
$$L_z = \frac{(d_{AC} + d_{BC} - d_{AB})}{2}.$$

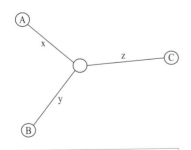

Fig. 7.6 Illustration of the 3-point formula

This formula is called the *3-point formula*, and shows how we can infer the individual branch lengths on a tree from a set of pairwise distances.

A test of neighborliness for two taxa. Neighbor-joining proceeds by finding neighbors in the tree, and iteratively joining them until the whole tree is complete. In order to do this, NJ must be able to identify these neighboring taxa. It is a remarkable property of additive distances that it is possible to devise a test to find nodes that are neighbors in the underlying tree.

Consider two taxa, τ_1 and τ_2, that are joined to the vertex V and two other generic neighbor nodes τ_i and τ_j (as in Figure 7.7). Then the following inequality holds when τ_1 and τ_2 are neighbors:

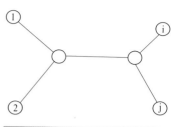

Fig. 7.7 The 4-point condition, used in the development of the neighbor-joining algorithm

$$d(\tau_1, \tau_2) + d(\tau_i, \tau_j) < d(\tau_1, \tau_i) + d(\tau_2, \tau_j).$$

This can be seen from Figure 7.7. In words, the sum of the distances between τ_1, τ_2, τ_i, and τ_j should be minimized when neighbors are paired in the summation. This leads to a criterion for detecting neighbors when there are an arbitrary number of external nodes in a tree. First, define the total distance from taxon τ_i to all other taxa as

$$R_i = \sum_{j=1}^{n} d(\tau_i, \tau_j),$$

where the distance $d(\tau_i, \tau_i)$ is naturally interpreted as 0. We also define the "neighborliness" between two taxa to be

$$M(\tau_i, \tau_j) = (n-2)d(\tau_i, \tau_j) - R_i - R_j, \qquad (7.1)$$

where we are minimizing both the distance between external nodes and the total distance in the tree. For any two nodes τ_i and τ_j that are neighbors, we require that

$$M(\tau_i, \tau_j) < M(\tau_i, \tau_k) \ \forall k \neq j.$$

This gives us the crucial piece of the NJ algorithm: from the distance matrix D that contains all of the pairwise distances $d(\tau_i, \tau_j)$, compute a new table of values for $M(\tau_i, \tau_j)$. Then choose to join the pair of taxa with the smallest value of $M(\tau_i, \tau_j)$. We call this the *4-point condition*.

Joining neighbors in the tree. The NJ algorithm chooses to merge two nodes that satisfy the criterion above into a new node, V, and then computes the distance between V and all of the other nodes, as well as the length of the newly created branches to τ_i and τ_j using the 3-point formula. It then recomputes M (now using V as an external taxon) and iterates.

We calculate the distance from the new node V to each of the remaining external nodes as

$$d(V, \tau_k) = \frac{1}{2}[d(\tau_i, \tau_k) + d(\tau_j, \tau_k) - d(\tau_i, \tau_j)] \ for \ k \neq i, j. \qquad (7.2)$$

The 3-point formula described above gives us the branch lengths from V to the joined neighbors τ_i and τ_j. The branch lengths from τ_i to V and τ_j to V are given by

$$L(\tau_i, V) = \frac{d(\tau_i, \tau_j)}{2} + \frac{R_i - R_j}{2n - 2} \qquad (7.3)$$

$$L(\tau_j, V) = \frac{d(\tau_i, \tau_j)}{2} + \frac{R_j - R_i}{2n - 2}. \qquad (7.4)$$

Below we summarize the various steps of the algorithm.

Rooting the tree. The procedure described above constructs an unrooted tree. In order to define a root node, we need to specify an outgroup, so that the root is assumed to be on the branch connecting the outgroup to the rest of the tree. The midpoint of this branch is a possible choice for the root, but other criteria may be used, for example some aimed at producing a more balanced tree. Here we simply apply so-called midpoint rooting to all of the trees we construct.

NJ algorithm. Input: an $n \times n$ distance matrix, D, and the specification of an outgroup.
Output: a rooted phylogenetic tree, $\mathcal{T}$, represented by a table of relationships, T, and a separate array with all branch lengths, TD:

Step 1: Given a pairwise distance matrix for n taxa, D, compute a new table of values of $M(\tau_i, \tau_j)$ as defined in equation (7.1). Choose the smallest value in this matrix to determine which two taxa to join.

Step 2: If τ_i and τ_j are to be joined at a new vertex V, first calculate the distance from V to the remaining external nodes using equation (7.2). Use these values to update the distance matrix, D, replacing τ_i and τ_j by V.

Step 3: Compute the branch length from τ_i to V and τ_j to V using equations (7.3) and (7.4). Set the values of $T(V, 1) = \tau_i, T(V, 2) = \tau_j, TD(\tau_i) = L(\tau_i, V)$ and $TD(\tau_j) = L(\tau_j, V)$. These describe the tree topology and branch lengths.

Step 4: The distance matrix now includes $n - 1$ taxa. If there more than two taxa remaining, go back to step 1. If only two taxa remain, join them by a branch of length $d(\tau_i, \tau_j)$.

Step 5: Define a root node on the branch connecting the outgroup to the rest of the tree.

UPGMA. The NJ algorithm reduces to a simpler method, called UPGMA (Unweighted Pair Group Method with Arithmetic Averages), in the case when the matrix M is defined to be equal to the distance matrix D. This means that the distance from the leaf taxa to the root is the same for all taxa, a condition called *ultrametricity*. While this condition must hold for the true tree, in practice it is almost never true of DNA sequence data and therefore leads to erroneous inference of phylogenetic trees. However, UPGMA was an early distance-based phylogenetic method, and is related to the hierarchical clustering algorithm discussed in Chapter 9.

7.4 Case study: phylogenetic analysis of the SARS epidemic

7.4.1 The SARS genome

The genome sequence of SARS-CoV obtained by the Canadian group in April 2003 is a 29 751 bp, single stranded RNA sequence. It can be accessed via GenBank (accession number AY274119.3), and a map of its genes is provided in

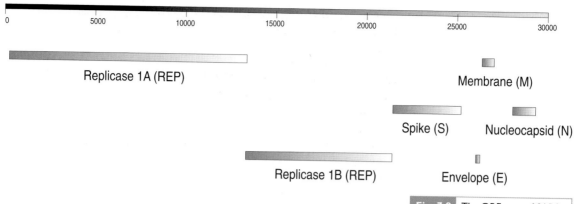

Replicase 1A (REP)

Membrane (M)

Spike (S) Nucleocapsid (N)

Replicase 1B (REP) Envelope (E)

Figure 7.8. Its GC content is approximately 41%, within the range for published complete coronavirus genome sequences (37–42%). It has a structure typical of coronaviruses, with five or six genes in a characteristic order. Using the methods described in Chapter 3 we can easily find most of these genes. Notice however that – as with HIV – things can be a little more complicated in viruses, with overlapping ORFs and other problems that can prevent simple ORF-finding methods from identifying all coding regions.

Fig. 7.8 The ORF map of SARS genome. Two-thirds of the genome contains the gene for the replicase protein, the remaining third various key genes, including spike and envelope. The order of these genes is typical of other coronaviruses

7.4.2 Reconstructing the epidemic

During the SARS epidemic, many of the key questions about its origin and nature could be answered by genomic sequence analysis. The sequence of SARS was obtained and published by various groups in early 2003, and was used as the basis for investigation into the origin and spread of the epidemic. The entire epidemic can now be re-created with the many viral sequences available in GenBank. By building a phylogenetic tree of the isolates from known dates and places, we can observe the crucial role played by the Hotel Metropole. We have chosen 13 sequences for which we could find date and location of the sample (see Table 7.1), and use them to demonstrate how sequence information can illuminate the unfolding of an epidemic.

Identifying the host. The SARS virus was recognized early on as a corona-virus, having the same genes in the same order as other known coronaviruses. It was, however, very different from any other known human coronavirus, and hence its origin was likely to be from another animal. A NJ tree of the spike proteins for various animal coronaviruses, including the coronavirus found in the palm civet, leaves little doubt about the closest relative of SARS coronavirus. SARS appears most closely related to the Himalayan palm civet coronavirus (Figure 7.9), and is quite distantly related to other human coronaviruses.

The disease was not carried by birds but it originated in the palm civet, and later adapted to be spread from human to human.

The epidemic tree. Using the 13 genomes in Table 7.1, a neighbor-joining tree of the spike protein was constructed (see Figure 7.10). The distance matrix was obtained by Jukes–Cantor corrections on genetic distance calculated from global alignments of the spike nucleotide sequence.

Table 7.1 Name, location, and sampling date of SARS virus isolates used in our case study

Name of isolate	Acc. number	Date	Location
GZ01	AY278489	DEC-16-2002	Guangzhou (Guangdong)
ZS-A	AY394997	DEC-26-2002	Zhongshan (Guangdong)
ZS-C	AY395004	JAN-04-2003	Zhongshan (Guangdong)
GZ-B	AY394978	JAN-24-2003	Guangzhou (Guangdong)
HZS-2A	AY394983	JAN-31-2003	Guangzhou Hospital
GZ-50	AY304495	FEB-18-2002	Guangzhou (Guangdong)
CUHK-W1	AY278554	FEB-21-2003	Hong Kong
Urbani	AY278741	FEB-26-2003	Hanoi
Tor 2	AY274119	FEB-27-2003	Toronto
Sin2500	AY283794	MAR-01-2003	Singapore
TW1	AY291451	MAR-08-2003	Taiwan
CUHK-AG01	AY345986	MAR-19-2003	Hong Kong
CUHK-L	AY394999	MAY-15-2003	Hong Kong

We can read the entire story of the epidemic on this tree. Using the palm civet as an outgroup, we see that all the early cases occurred in the Guangdong province, and that the Hotel Metropole coronavirus is almost identical to one of these sequences (i.e. there is no discernible genetic distance between them; Figure 7.10). The rest of the world-wide epidemic is seen to be nested within these initial infections: the events in Singapore, Hanoi, Taiwan, and Toronto can all be traced to the Hong Kong hotel and/or Guangdong. (The sequence of the Hanoi coronavirus is now called the Urbani strain.) The main question that remains is: When did the epidemic start? The answer can be found in the data from Table 7.1.

Date of origin. Because we know the date of collection of each of the SARS viruses for which we have sequence, we are able to observe the progression of mutations over time. For convenience, we again use the ORF corresponding to the spike protein. Relative to the sequence from the palm civet, we see that genetic distance (the y-axis of Figure 7.11) increases with time, in a roughly linear manner (time is along the x-axis, with the 0 point representing January 1, 2003). If we interpolate a least-squares line through these data, we can estimate the approximate date for the origin of the epidemic. Any date compatible with zero distance from the palm civet is a plausible start date for the epidemic, and we estimate it to be an interval centered around September 16, 2002 (106 days before January 1, 2003). The 95% confidence intervals are also shown in Figure 7.11. The method we have used is rather crude, and relies on many assumptions that we cannot verify, yet it delivers a very plausible estimate since the earliest reported cases can be traced back to the second half of 2002.

Area of origin. Even though we now know that the Guangdong province was the area of origin of the epidemic, we can use the same method as presented in Chapter 5 for the origin of humans to look for the likely area of origin of

Fig. 7.9 Phylogenetic tree connecting various coronaviruses. Clearly the closest relative to SARS is not a bird virus, but that of palm civet

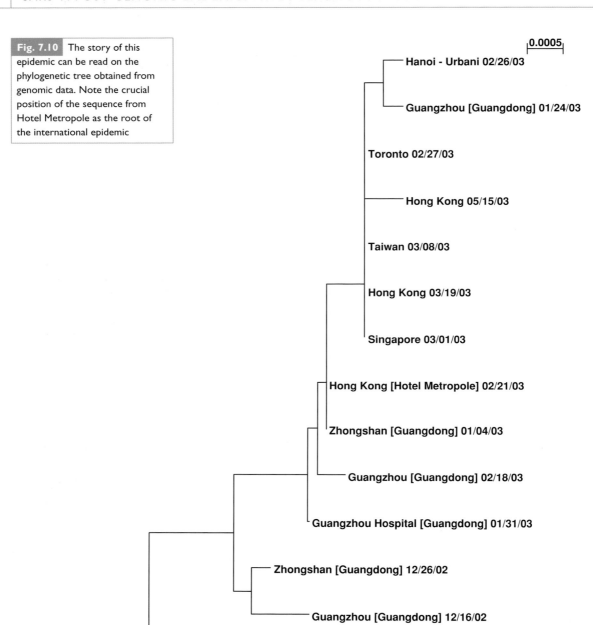

Fig. 7.10 The story of this epidemic can be read on the phylogenetic tree obtained from genomic data. Note the crucial position of the sequence from Hotel Metropole as the root of the international epidemic

0.0005

Hanoi - Urbani 02/26/03

Guangzhou [Guangdong] 01/24/03

Toronto 02/27/03

Hong Kong 05/15/03

Taiwan 03/08/03

Hong Kong 03/19/03

Singapore 03/01/03

Hong Kong [Hotel Metropole] 02/21/03

Zhongshan [Guangdong] 01/04/03

Guangzhou [Guangdong] 02/18/03

Guangzhou Hospital [Guangdong] 01/31/03

Zhongshan [Guangdong] 12/26/02

Guangzhou [Guangdong] 12/16/02

Palm Civet

SARS. We again take the high nucleotide diversity between sequences in Guangdong as an indication that the virus originated there, with the lower diversity outside this area a result of the subsequent international spread of the single Hotel Metropole strain. Using the genetic distance matrix, we plot (by multidimensional scaling) each sequence as a point. Figure 7.12 shows clearly that there is more diversity among the Guangdong sequences than among all the sequences collected abroad. Of course the tree of Figure 7.10 is another way

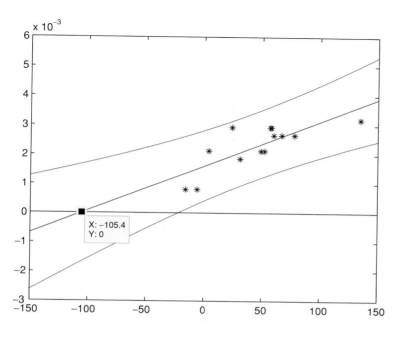

Fig. 7.11 The genetic distance of samples from the palm civet increases roughly linearly with time

Fig. 7.12 Multidimensional scaling visualization of the genetic distance between spike genes shows that the international epidemic sequences are not as diverse as those found in the Guangdong province of China

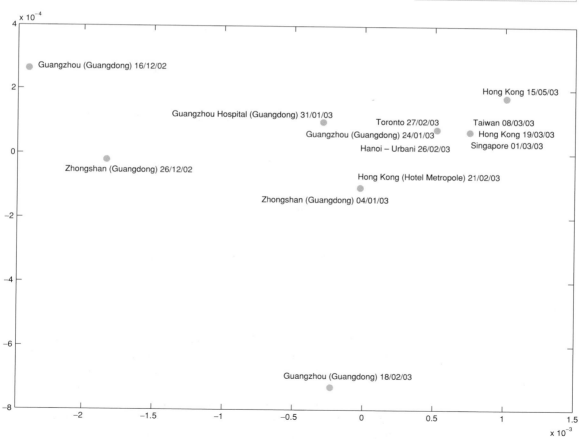

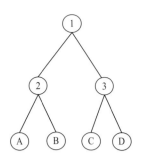

Fig. 7.13 The Newick representation of this tree is ((A, B), (C, D));

of expressing the same information by looking at the lengths of branches separating the various viruses. Both the phylogenetic tree and the multidimensional scaling therefore strongly suggest that Guangdong Province was the area of origin for SARS.

7.5 | The Newick format

As an alternative to the rather awkward matrix tree representation introduced in the beginning of this chapter, the Newick format makes use of the correspondence between trees and nested parentheses. This becomes very useful for representing trees in computer-readable form. For example, the tree in Figure 7.13 can be represented in the previously introduced format by the array in (7.5):

$$
\begin{array}{ccc}
1 & 2 & 3 \\
2 & A & B \\
3 & C & D \,.
\end{array}
\qquad (7.5)
$$

In the Newick format this tree is represented by the following sequence of printable characters:

((A, B), (C, D));

the convention is that the tree file must end with a semicolon. Interior nodes are represented by a pair of matched parentheses. Between them are representations of the nodes that are immediately descended from that node, separated by commas. In the above tree, the immediate descendants of the root are two interior nodes. Each of them has two descendants. In our example these happen to be leaves, but in general they could also be interior nodes and the result would be further nesting of parentheses. Leaves are represented by their names. A name can be any string of printable characters, except blanks, colons, semicolons, parentheses, and square brackets. Any name may also be empty; a tree like:

((,), (,));

is allowed in the file format. Note also that trees can be multifurcating; that is, nodes can have more than two children.

Branch lengths can be incorporated into a tree by putting a real number, with or without decimal point, after a node and preceded by a colon. This represents the length of the branch immediately above that node. Thus the above tree might have lengths represented as

$((A : 1.0, B : 1.0) : 2, (C : 1, D : 1) : 2);$

The tree starts on the first line of the file, and can continue to subsequent lines. It is best to proceed to a new line, if at all, immediately after a comma. Blanks can be inserted at any point except in the middle of a species name or a branch length. Names can also be assigned to interior nodes: these names follow the right parenthesis for that interior node, as in

((A, B)2, (C, D)3);

7.6 | Exercises

(1) Using the mtDNA data discussed in Chapter 5, create a tree comparing human and apes. Discuss the position of Neanderthal. Compare the trees obtained with and without the Jukes–Cantor correction.

(2) The mysterious origins of HIV, described in Chapter 5, have been the subject of many investigations. In particular, the relation between HIV and a similar virus found in monkeys, SIV, has been debated and studied in depth. Genomic analysis of various strains of HIV and SIV can be used to settle the question. The data are available on the book's website, both for complete genomes and just for the ENV protein. Using the free package Phylip, construct the phylogenetic tree of various strains of HIV and SIV. This tree should show that the virus crossed the species barrier twice, once leading to the HIV1 epidemic and the second time leading to the HIV2 epidemic. The book's website contains a reconstruction of the tree as a reference.

(3) Construct the tree of the odorant receptors and related proteins, as discussed in Chapter 4 (dataset available on the book's website).

7.7 | Reading list

The genome sequence of the SARS-associated coronavirus was first reported in Marra *et al.* (2003) and Rota *et al.* (2003) and its evolution discussed in Guan *et al.* (2003) and Consortium (2003). The timing of the last common ancestor of SARS viruses can be found in Zeng *et al.* (2003) and Lu *et al.* (2004) and the estimation of the area of origin is discussed in Zhang and Zheng (2003). Its phylogeny with other coronaviruses is presented in Eickmann *et al.* (2003) and in Lei *et al.* (2003), and a more general discussion of viral evolution can be found in Holmes and Rambaut (2004). The story of Carlo Urbani's death can be found in Reilley *et al.* (2003).

A complete textbook on phylogenetic tree inference is the excellent Felsenstein (2004), which should be considered the starting point of any investigation into the algorithmic and statistical issues concerning computational phylogenetic analysis. A classical reference on the construction of phylogenetic trees is Fitch and Margoliash (1967). The neighbor-joining algorithm was introduced in Saitou and Nei (1987).

Interesting introductory readings on phylogenetic topics are Doolittle (2000) (on the tree of life) and Cann and Wilson (2003) (on human origins). A discussion of the phylogenetic tree of HIV can be found on the book's website.

Freely available packages for phylogenetic analysis include CLUSTALW Thompson *et al.* (1994) and Phylip, the phylogeny inference package created by J. Felsenstein (Felsenstein, 2004). Very popular tree visualization tools include NJPLOT, UNROOTED, and TreeView, whose complete references and web coordinates are available via the book's website.

Links to software packages, and to all of the above-mentioned papers, datasets, and websites, can be found on the book's website:

www.computational-genomics.net

Chapter 8

Welcome to the Hotel *Chlamydia*
Whole genome comparisons

- Genome rearrangements
- Orthology and paralogy
- Synteny blocks, inversions, and transpositions

8.1 | Uninvited guests

Every human being has multiple species of bacteria living within them. Most of these bacteria, such as *E. coli*, are not harmful to us and are considered beneficial *symbionts*. The bacteria help us to digest certain foods or supply us with vitamins that we cannot make on our own, and we provide them with the nutrients and environment they need to survive. The benefits of having bacterial symbionts extend beyond the production of necessary chemicals. These bacteria actually prevent infection by other pathogenic bacteria simply by virtue of having already established their presence in our gut. In fact, after taking a course of antibiotics it is often recommended that people eat foods like yogurt to re-populate their stomach and intestines with symbiotic bacteria.

Although there are many well-known examples of beneficial symbiotic relationships in nature, they tend to be interactions between free-living organisms such as bees and flowers or birds and rhinoceros (the appropriately named tick-bird eats ticks off the back of the rhino). As with our relationship with *E. coli*, however, there are many symbionts that are hidden from view because they live within their hosts. These symbionts often aid their hosts in digestion and benefit themselves by living in the stomach of a mobile organism. For instance, termites have specific protozoa (a type of single-celled eukaryote) living in their digestive tract to help with the digestion of wood. Without the protozoa, the termite would lose the ability to process its main source of nutrients.

Some symbionts have even moved permanently into the cells of their hosts; they have become completely dependent on the host to provide them with nutrients. In the process, the genomes of these intracellular symbionts have undergone dramatic changes. Because many of the chemicals that they previously had to synthesize themselves are now provided by their hosts, symbionts often lose the genes underlying whole biochemical pathways. There is no longer any natural selection to maintain the function of these genes, and so mutations that destroy them are simply ignored. As a result, intracellular symbiont genomes are some of the smallest known, both in total size and in the number of genes.

Chlamydia trachomatis is an intracellular symbiont of humans that does not provide any benefit to the host – it is a *parasite* (*Mycoplasma genitalium*, which we introduced in Chapter 1 as having the smallest genome known, is also a parasite of humans). *Chlamydia* (a bacterium) is the most common sexually transmitted disease in the United States, with an estimated 3 million new infections each year. It has lost the ability to make many biochemical products, so that it can live only in specific cells of humans. It cannot even be kept alive in the lab. Because of this simplified lifestyle scientists believed for some time that it was a virus.

Chlamydia pneumoniae is a related bacterial parasite of humans, infecting cells in the respiratory tract; it causes both pneumonia and bronchitis. As with *C. trachomatis*, it shows very reduced metabolic and biosynthetic functions and has a very small genome (both genomes are approximately 1 Mb in length). Six different *Chlamydia* species have now been fully sequenced. They are all obligate intracellular symbionts, though not all are harmful to their hosts. All of the species show slight differences in the number and identity of genes that have been lost since their most common ancestor, but their overall genome organization is quite similar. The intracellular lifestyle of *Chlamydia* appears to date back 700 million years, with the emergence of the first eukaryotes. Both mitochondria and chloroplasts are thought to be derived from intracellular bacterial symbionts that lost so many of their genes that they became an essential part of the eukaryotic cell. As with both mitochondria and chloroplasts, *Chlamydia* are locked into a symbiotic relationship with their eukaryotic hosts, and it appears that *Chlamydia* are quite closely related to the cyanobacterial ancestors of plant chloroplasts.

In this chapter we address the challenges inherent in making whole genome comparisons. The *Chlamydia* genomes make a perfect case study because of their small size and relatively slow rate of genome evolution – although nucleotide substitutions occur at an average rate, *Chlamydia* show very few genome rearrangements and very few instances of horizontal gene transfer. There are now many other species in which whole-genome comparisons can be made, and *Chlamydia* provides us with a simple example of the questions that can only be answered by this kind of analysis.

8.2 | By leaps and bounds: patterns of genome evolution

In this chapter we want to make comparisons between DNA sequences at a different resolution than we have previously discussed. Instead of focusing on small differences between homologous genes, we will look at large-scale features of genome evolution. These comparisons can tell us about changes in the gene content of genomes as well as changes in the relative position of genes in a genome. Whole genome comparisons provide useful information for understanding evolution and for understanding sequence and gene function. The statistical and algorithmic tools required for many aspects of whole genome comparisons build upon and expand those tools needed to compare much shorter sequences; we provide an overview to a handful of these methods.

The evolutionary trajectory of a genome in sequence space is not determined solely by the steady accumulation of independent nucleotide substitutions, insertions, and deletions. To be sure, single nucleotide polymorphisms do form the bulk of genetic variability between individuals of the same species, but often other, less local transformations of the genome can be observed both within and (more frequently) between species. For example, the transfer of long sequences between species (horizontal gene transfer) is much more common than previously thought, accounting for up to 20% of the *E. coli* genome. Sequence rearrangements due to reshuffling within a genome are also common: inversions occur when an entire segment of DNA is "flipped" around (Figure 8.3), and transpositions occur when DNA is cut-and-pasted from one location of the genome to another. Whole chromosomes can break apart and re-form by sticking novel combinations of chromosomal pieces together, and even whole genomes can be duplicated, resulting in *polyploid* individuals.

Furthermore, the gene content of genomes can change without the drastic effects of large duplications, deletions, or horizontal gene transfers. Single genes are often gained or lost via small-scale duplications or deletions. Typically, gene duplication results in the presence of two copies of the original gene, one of which may then diverge in function. Small deletions or single frameshift mutations are also sufficient to turn functioning genes into pseudogenes; it appears that such gene loss is quite common, either because genes are redundant in function or because the environment has changed in such a way that the genes are no longer needed. Gene gain and loss results in many differences between genomes, both in total gene number and in the identity of genes carried in individual genomes.

Comparative genomics, or the study of large differences between whole genomes, can tell us much about the organization, function, and evolution of genomes. In this chapter we learn multiple methods in comparative genomics by examining the key steps in an analysis of multiple *Chlamydia* genomes. We begin by comparing the genes contained within various *Chlamydia* genomes.

8.3 | Beanbag genomics

To some extent, the comparison of whole genomes often boils down to many comparisons of the individual genes within each genome. While this approach is akin to treating a genome as simply a beanbag full of genes, it is frequently the most manageable and informative thing to do. Because of the multiple inversions, transpositions, duplications, deletions, and other chromosomal rearrangements that can occur in evolution, an alignment of two genomes will often be uninformative or uninterpretable. Most of the time whole genome alignments will not even be possible. This does not mean that we will not be able to compare two genomes side-by-side, only that we will first have to break the problem down into smaller pieces and then build it back up. Even larger questions about genome evolution that should not be addressed in a beanbag fashion can benefit from initial multiple single-gene analyses.

Of course the first step in comparing gene sets in two different genomes is to find which genes are present in both. Besides the obvious biological interest of these genes, they can also serve as landmarks in the genome, helping in the identification of homologous regions between two distant sequences. In Chapter 2 we learned the most basic way to find (prokaryotic) genes – find open-reading frames. As we have done before, we can apply our basic ORF-finding program (with a significance threshold of 100 codons) to the genomes of *Chlamydia trachomatis* and *C. pneumoniae*. Our analysis (see below) reveals only slight differences in the number of genes between the two genomes, with *C. pneumoniae* having about 100 more genes:

	Size (nt)	ORFs	GenBank Acc. Num.
C. trachomatis	1 042 519	916	NC_000117
C. pneumoniae	1 229 853	1048	NC_002179

They both have many fewer genes than the model prokaryote, *E. coli* (for which we can find nearly 5000 ORFs), as we expect for intracellular symbionts. In order to see the genes and pathways that have been lost in the *Chlamydia* genomes we first have to identify the genes that are present. We might expect that different biological processes are needed for life in the respiratory and urinary tracts inhabited by these species. In the next section we present methods for comparing the genes that have been lost or gained between *Chlamydia* species.

Similarity on a genomic scale. While comparisons of the total numbers of genes can be informative, we would further like to know the identity of genes in each genome and their similarity to all other genes. Studying nucleotide substitution between orthologous genes (defined in Chapter 3), analyzing changes in the size of gene families, and finding blocks of conserved gene order all require us to have information about the similarity between all pairs of genes.

In order to generate such similarity scores, we take the amino acid sequences of all of the genes found in both genomes and fill out a matrix containing the alignment score between each possible pair of sequences. In the case of the *Chlamydiae* the resulting matrix would be of size 1048 × 916 and we can use the Needleman–Wunsch global alignment algorithm to compute the similarity scores (it is a good idea to normalize the alignment scores by the length of sequences). For larger genomes we may want to use faster but less accurate algorithms such as BLAST. This matrix contains all the information needed to address the questions outlined above.

Identifying orthologous and paralogous genes. With our similarity matrix in hand we can now attempt to distinguish between orthologous and paralogous genes. Remember from Chapter 3 that duplication can generate large gene families of related genes, and that the relationships among these homologous genes can be quite complex. The two main types of relationship are orthology and paralogy. *Orthologous* genes are those that are related not by any duplication event, but merely by speciation. As a result, we rely on orthologous genes to estimate the number of substitutions – and the amount of time – between species in order to reconstruct phylogenetic trees. *Paralogous* genes are those that are related via a duplication event; all of the genes in a gene family from a single genome are paralogous, as are homologous genes between genomes that are not direct orthologs. The complexity of genome evolution means that sometimes there will not be clear one-to-one orthologous relationships. As duplication and deletion events occur in one lineage and not the other, one-to-many, many-to-one, and many-to-many relationships may be created.

There are a number of different ways to identify orthologs between genomes. The most common method is to identify best reciprocal similarity hits or BRHs (for best reciprocal hits). A pair of ORFs is said to be a BRH if the two sequences are each other's best match between two genomes (using alignment-based genetic distances). It is clear from this definition that it is quite possible for an ORF not to belong to any BRH pair, and for an ORF to both have an ortholog in another species as well as highly similar paralogs in the same genome. More importantly, it is clear that these definitions depend on our choice of a similarity measure. For simplicity, in our examples we will use the score produced by a global alignment (which has the drawback of being affected by sequence length). More sophisticated measures can easily be devised and are regularly used.

Example 8.1

Homology in Chlamydia. Given a similarity matrix it is simple to identify orthologs by finding pairs of genes that meet the reciprocal requirement of maximal similarity. With an acceptance threshold of 100 codons we find 1964 total ORFs (916 in *C. trachomatis* [CT] and 1048 in *C. pneumoniae* [CP]). Among these we find 728 pairs that are orthologs. We also find 126 pairs of genes that show high similarity within genomes and can be considered paralogs (56 in CT and 70 in CP). These paralogous pairs were all more similar to each other than to their orthologs, and are therefore likely to be the result of gene duplication events that occurred since the species split. These two categories account for 87% of the ORFs. The remaining 253 ORFs did not have well-defined homologs of any kind and may represent older paralogs or genes whose ortholog was lost from the other genome.

Identifying gene families. Defining what exactly is meant by "gene family" is a tricky thing. At some level, all the genes that exist on Earth are in a gene family: they are homologous sequences that can trace their origin back to a common ancestor (i.e. the first DNA-based genome). However this is not the type of relationship people want to explain with the concept of a gene family. Instead, gene families are intended to represent groups of more closely related genes that likely have similar function (because they share a relatively recent common ancestor). As such, there is no hard and fast rule for how closely related genes must be to put them in the same gene family. Generally people consider genes that are 50% identical and above as being in a gene family; these genes are then considered paralogs or orthologs depending upon which species they are found in.

Just because there is no objective measure to define a gene family does not mean that we cannot be operationally objective when studying these families.

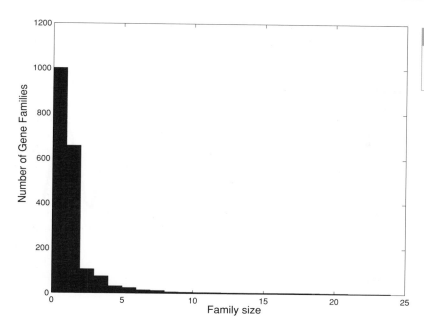

Fig. 8.1 Histogram showing the distribution of gene family size in *Chlamydia*. There are few large families, and many small ones

For instance, consider the case when we want to compare the evolution of some particular gene family between two genomes. If we clustered our genes into families separately for each genome, we might call gene families differently in the two genomes. This is because there is always a certain degree of arbitrariness in clustering methods, as will be discussed in Chapter 9. As a result, the data could look as if there was a difference in gene family size between species that was actually a result of using two sets of criteria.

Because studies of changes in gene family size can tell us a lot about the function and evolution of genes (see Chapter 4 and the odorant receptor family), we need to make sure that we use consistent criteria across genomes. The expansion and contraction of gene families during evolution can be just as important as nucleotide substitutions in determining differences between species.

To ensure the identification of equivalent gene families across genomes, we will cluster all of the genes from both genomes at the same time. Only after defining individual clusters as gene families will we then count the number of genes in each family that come from each genome. The basic algorithm we use takes the similarity matrix generated above and clusters the genes according to a method not unlike UPGMA (see Chapter 7) that is called *hierarchical clustering* and is briefly described in Chapter 9.

The clustering of the data reveals a large number of small gene families and a small number of large families in both *Chlamydia* species, as seen in Figure 8.1. This is of course somewhat arbitrary, since the clustering algorithm has a few tunable parameters, but the general shape of the histogram is rather robust to these settings. (Note that we consider even single genes to be in their own "family.") We can also see that there are differences in the size of a number of gene families between these two genomes The table below compares the sizes

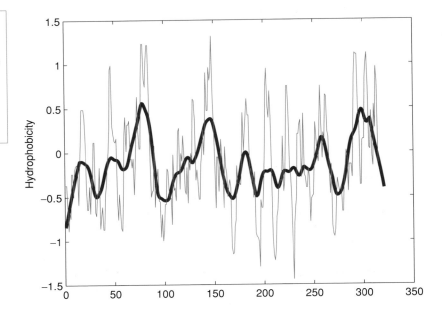

Fig. 8.2 The hydrophobicity profile of ABC transporters, the largest gene family found in *Chlamydia*. Based on the discussion in Chapter 4, we can infer a possible transmembrane function for these proteins. The red line is unsmoothed and the blue one is smoothed

of the largest families, and reports their function according to BLAST:

CT	CP	
12	12	ABC transporters
6	15	G family outer membrane protein
9	10	Function not known
5	7	Function not known

We can identify the function for some of these families, for example the ATP-binding cassette (ABC) transporters. All cells acquire the molecules and ions they need from their surrounding environment through their plasma membrane. ABC transporters are transmembrane proteins that expose a ligand-binding domain at one surface and an ATP-binding domain at the other surface. Much like the proteins discussed in Chapter 4, they cross the membrane. ABC transporters must have evolved early in the history of life, since the ATP-binding domains in Archaea, Eubacteria, and Eukaryotes all share a homologous structure, the ATP-binding cassette; that they must cross the membrane can also be seen by their alternating hydrophobicity profile, shown in Figure 8.2.

Remark 8.1

Alternative approaches to finding orthologs. The clustering of genes into families also suggests another method for identifying orthologous genes between species. If we were to construct a phylogenetic tree for all of the genes in a family from both species, we expect that one-to-one orthologs would appear as sisters to one another on the tips of the tree. This is because these genes are separated only by a speciation event between the two genomes in our comparison. Although tree-building methods are generally considered to be more reliable than the reciprocal similarity method, they can be much less amenable to automated analysis.

8.4 | Synteny

Now that we have identified orthologous genes, we can put them back on to chromosomes in order to examine changes in their physical position over time. The relative ordering of genes on chromosomes is called *synteny*, and we can examine whether syntenic relationships are conserved between species. As we said earlier, inversions and transpositions are the most common mechanisms by which syntenic relationships are reshuffled; insertions, duplications, and deletions can all add noise to the study of synteny. Even with all of these processes going on, it is often quite easy to identify "blocks" of synteny – long stretches where the relative ordering of orthologous genes has been conserved. Finding these blocks will be especially important for annotation of non-coding sequences, as we cover in the next section. It will also allow us to define homologous intergenic regions, which might have little or no similarity, and hence could never be identified by alignment methods.

Visualizing synteny. One convenient, heuristic way to study synteny is by constructing a dot-plot, as in Figure 8.3. To make a dot-plot, we simply line up all the genes in each genome according to their positions and visualize the similarity level between all possible pairs, often by plotting only pairs whose similarity score is above a given threshold (here we have only plotted orthologs).

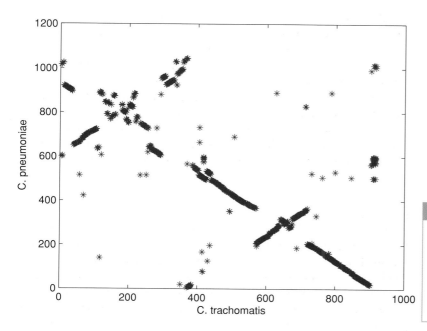

Fig. 8.3 Dot-plot showing homologous genes in *Chlamydia trachomatis* and *Chlamydia pneumoniae*. Synteny blocks are clearly visible, as well as regions where inversions have taken place. Stars represent orthologous gene pairs

In the dot-plot comparing the two pathogenic *Chlamydia* species we see that there is almost complete synteny between the genomes. This is evident because the genes with the highest similarity between the two genomes are also in the same relative positions; hence, we see a strong diagonal line. However, two major inversion events are clearly visible in the off-diagonal stretches. The order of genes has been reversed, resulting in short stretches where the off-diagonal line is strongest. There are also genes that have clearly been transposed to another part of the genome in one or both species.

This high level of conservation in gene position is quite remarkable, but seems to be typical of intracellular symbionts. In a comparison of the genomes of two species of *Buchnera*, obligate intracellular symbionts of pea aphids, there are no rearrangements or horizontal gene transfer events whatsoever after 50 million years. Apparently something about the cloistered lifestyle of these symbiotic organisms shields them from contact with other bacteria or viruses that may otherwise induce rearrangement.

Homologous intergenic regions and phylogenetic footprinting. Detection of synteny blocks also enables us to identify homologous *intergenic* regions. Generally these regions evolve faster than the rest of the genome, and hence are more difficult to align and assign homology to than coding sequences. Using genes as "anchors" to ensure that we are examining homologous intergenic sequences, it is then possible to examine the evolution of these quickly evolving sequences. For instance, we can use intergenic regions to compute the underlying mutation rate in these stretches as we expect there to be little constraint on nucleotide substitution.

Of course we know that there are non-protein-coding regions of the genome that are conserved, possibly because they are RNA-coding genes or because they are regulatory sequences. By anchoring our alignments with syntenic coding regions, it is much easier to find the relatively short sequences that are conserved in non-coding DNA. This procedure is sometimes called *phylogenetic footprinting*, and has been used to find conserved regulatory sequences, as well as coding regions. We have chosen a region of approximately 3500 bp that contains three ORFs preserving synteny between the two *Chlamydia* genomes to examine further. Figure 8.4 was obtained by performing a global alignment and plotting the degree of conservation between the two sequences, using a moving window of size 75 bp for smoothing. The resulting plot shows that intergenic regions are less conserved than regions within ORF.

Sorting by reversals. An interesting algorithmic question is raised by the study of synteny. Since two genomes can be formed by many smaller syntenic blocks that have been rearranged by inversions or transpositions between the two, we would like to have a metric of this syntenic distance. Obviously, simple pairwise alignment will not work, as we are interested in the number of genomic rearrangements that separate the two species and not the number of nucleotide differences. So we are interested in finding the smallest number of inversion events that might have led from one genome to the other; by "inversion event" we mean the inversion of a string of ORFs or

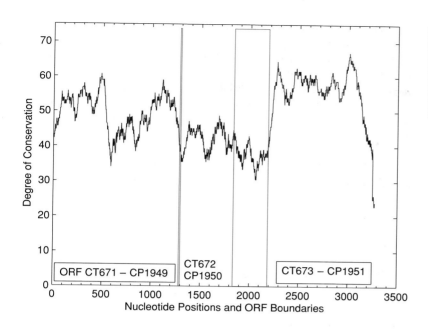

Fig. 8.4 Phylogenetic footprint of three contiguous ORFs in *Chlamydia*. The homologous intergenic regions show higher divergence than the coding regions, as expected

homologous non-coding regions. (It becomes a much more complicated problem to include transposition or translocation events; here we stick to the simplest case where only inversions occur.) This algorithmic problem is called "sorting by reversals." We can informally state the problem as follows: given a permutation of N numbers, find the shortest series of reversals that can sort them back into their original order. A reversal in this case is the inversion of the order of the entries in a given interval of indices, as illustrated in the following table:

3	**2**	**1**	4	8	7	6	5	9
1	2	3	4	**8**	**7**	**6**	**5**	9
1	2	3	4	5	6	7	8	9

Here we see that there have been two reversals relative to the bottom sequence of numbers: the middle sequence has an inversion from 5 to 8, while the top sequence has an inversion from 1 to 3. In practice we do not know the original order of the ORFs, only the relative orders. To deal with this we often designate one of the two genomes as the standard, and try to apply a series of inversion events to the other. We consider the minimum number of reversals as our distance metric (sometimes called the *reversal distance*). Note that there may be multiple series of reversals between two sequences that have the same number of steps (i.e. the same distance) but that solve the problem in a different order or using different specific inversions.

The simplest greedy algorithm for finding the reversal distance between two sequences (the *simple reversal sort* algorithm) is carried out as follows:

Step 1: Designate one of the two sequences as the "standard" (s); reversals will be applied only to the other, non-standard sequence (t).

Step 2: Starting from one end of the standard sequence, move along until there is a position where the two sequences do not match: $s_i \neq t_i$.

Step 3: Perform the necessary reversal so that the symbol in the non-standard sequence matches the standard. If the symbol at position s_i is the same as that in position t_j, then the necessary reversal is from $t_i{:}t_j$.

Step 4: Continue to move down the sequence, applying reversals as necessary until all of the symbols match.

Example 8.2

Simple reversal sort. One such application of the simple reversal sort algorithm is shown below. Given these two sequences:

Standard	1	2	3	4	5	6	7	8	9
Non-standard	1	2	4	3	5	8	7	9	6

we first reverse 3 and 4 in the non-standard sequence:

	1	2	3	4	5	8	7	9	6

then 8, 7, 9, 6:

	1	2	3	4	5	6	9	7	8

then 9 and 7:

	1	2	3	4	5	6	7	9	8

and finally 9 and 8:

	1	2	3	4	5	6	7	8	9.

This has taken us four inversions, for a total reversal distance of 4. In reality, the number of operations performed on the standard sequence to produce the non-standard sequence was three, but our greedy algorithm does not do well when reversals overlap with one another. While this greedy solution may not give the maximally shortest distance, it has the advantage of only requiring linear time. Algorithms do exist that are better estimators of the reversal distance, but they do so at an additional computational cost. We do not discuss these here, but give pointers to the relevant literature in Section 8.6.

8.5 | Exercises

(1) Study the dot-plot for *Mycoplasma genitalium* and *Mycoplasma pneumoniae*, shown in Figure 8.5. Discuss what series of inversions could have led to such a configuration.

(2) Study the distribution of gene family size in *Mycoplasma genitalium* and *Mycoplasma pneumoniae*, by first detecting all ORFs, then computing a pairwise distance matrix, and finally clustering them (using methods discussed in Chapter 9 for clustering).

(3) Align two HIV sequences and produce a phylogenetic footprint of the entire genome. Can you identify ORFs from this footprint?

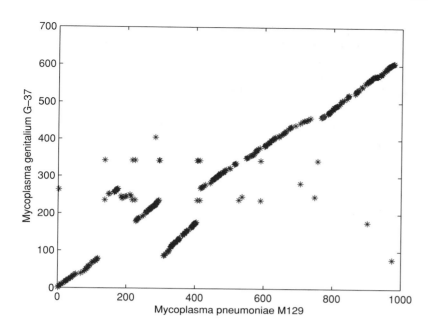

Fig. 8.5 Synteny analysis of *Mycoplasma genitalium* and *Mycoplasma pneumoniae*, using an ORF dot-plot

(4) Figure out the three reversal steps that it takes to go from the standard to the non-standard sequences given in the "Sorting by Reversals" section.

8.6 | Reading list

The genomic sequences of *C. pneumoniae* and *C. trachomatis* were compared in Kalman *et al.* (1999). An interesting discussion of the evolutionary history of *Chlamydiae* can be found in Horn *et al.* (2004), where it is suggested that they might be related to the early history of eukaryotes, and possibly even to the processes by which mitochondria became part of eukaryotic cells.

Rearrangement within organisms that have many chromosomes often involves changes in chromosome number. The genomes of humans and mice share remarkable levels of similarity in ORFs, but these are completely shuffled. An important computational problem is that of identifying the smallest set of moves that can transform a genome into another (where by moves we mean inversions, transpositions, and other major operations). This is related to the important research topic of sorting by reversals, and will not be discussed in this introductory book. A discussion of that problem can be found in the article Bourque *et al.* (2004), comparing human, mouse, and rat, and in the excellent book Jones and Pevzner (2004).

Conserved sequences across multiple species are of great importance as possible functional elements can be detected in this way. The paper Margulies *et al.* (2003). discusses this problem. Statistical analysis and comparison across various whole genomes can be seen also in Karlin *et al.* (1998). A multi-genome comparison of many strains of yeast helped to identify genes and regulatory motifs (see Kellis *et al.*, 2003). A good overall introduction to the field of comparative genomics is Koonin and Galperin (2002).

Free software packages are available for efficient alignment of whole genomes, for example the tool MUMmer, developed by Stephen Salzberg and his colleagues. Pointers to this and other software packages, and to all of the above mentioned papers, datasets, and websites, can be found on the book's website:

www.computational-genomics.net

Chapter 9

The genomics of wine-making
Analysis of gene expression

9.1 | Chateau Hajji Feruz Tepe

- Gene expression data
- Types of DNA microarrays
- Data clustering and visualization
- Expression during the cell cycle

In 1985 the world's most expensive bottle of wine was sold at auction for $160 000. This bottle of 1787 Chateau Lafite came from the cellar of Thomas Jefferson (third president of the United States) and was apparently purchased during his time as ambassador to France. While Jefferson's Bordeaux is undoubtedly an historic artifact (and probably undrinkable), the oldest bottle of wine dates to 5000 BC from the site of Hajji Feruz Tepe in Iran. This 9-liter clay pot did not contain any liquid when found, but still had dried residue from the wine it once held.

The recipe for making wine and other fermented beverages has not changed much in the past 7000 years. A solution rich in sugars (usually fruit juice) is turned into the alcoholic nectar we consume by exploiting a remarkable organism: the yeast, *Saccharomyces cerevisiae*. This unicellular fungus extracts energy from the environment by fermenting sugars, a process which produces alcohol as a by-product. Because *S. cerevisiae* is found naturally on grapevines, wine making is as easy as crushing grapes and putting them into a tightly sealed container for a few months. During this time yeast transforms the sugars contained in grape juice into alcohol, and this is why your wine is so much less sweet (and more alcoholic) than the grape juice it started from.

When the yeast exhausts its supply of sugar, however, it must find a new source of energy. When oxygen is available, the yeast transitions from fermentation to respiration. Respiration allows yeast to use alcohol as a source of energy. As a result, winemakers must keep oxygen out of the containers where fermentation is taking place. (When yeast cannot ferment or respire, it goes into a quiescent phase that allows it to conserve energy.) The switch between fermentation and respiration requires the cell to turn off hundreds of genes involved in fermentation and to turn on hundreds more involved in respiration. This transition has been extensively studied by biologists, and is known as the *diauxic shift*.

In this chapter we will learn how modern genomic techniques allow us to monitor the internal activity of a cell in order to find the genes involved in the diauxic shift and other cellular processes, such as the cell cycle. This is a crucial part of both genome annotation and basic biology, revealing important clues into a gene's function. One technology in particular, known as a *DNA microarray*, lets us simultaneously measure the expression level of every gene in a cell. The expression level essentially tells us the number of mRNA transcripts that each gene is producing at a single point in time. Although the final objective of most experiments is to know the amount of each active protein in a cell – which we assume is an indicator of which processes are active in the cell – censusing proteins is much more difficult to do than censusing RNAs. As a consequence, biologists have turned to microarrays in the hope of better understanding cell function. Before describing the technology of microarrays and their uses we need to review a few salient facts about *Saccharomyces cerevisiae*.

The budding yeast. Saccharomyces cerevisiae is a fungus that goes by many names: "brewer's yeast," "baker's yeast," and "budding yeast" (for its method of replication by budding) are all common names for this unicellular eukaryote. Yeast's connection to baking dates back to around the same time as the discovery of wine making. When mixed with water, sugar, and flour, yeast ferments the sugars in the dough and produces carbon dioxide (CO_2) as a by-product. Trapped bubbles of CO_2 cause the dough to rise. Partly because of its commercial importance, *S. cerevisiae* has become one of the most studied organisms in biology, and is now one of the standard models for genetics and genomics.

 S. cerevisiae is a complex organism, despite the fact that it is unicellular. To start with, it is a eukaryote, so its genome is sequestered inside a nucleus. The genome is organized into 16 linear chromosomes of double-stranded DNA totaling 12.5 Mb (more than twice the size of most bacteria). The genome contains approximately 6400 genes, about 2000 more than are in the bacterium *E. coli*. *S. cerevisiae* was the first eukaryotic genome to be sequenced, in 1996; a simple map of this genome can be seen in Figure 9.1.

 The ability to transition between energy sources is not unique to yeast: many organisms are known to exploit similar mechanisms. *E. coli*, for example, has a well-studied mechanism that allows it to switch from glucose metabolism to lactose metabolism when all of the glucose in the environment has been depleted. Most such mechanisms – in both eukaryotes and prokaryotes – rely on relatively simple switches to control production of the proteins that are necessary in each state. We can imagine that many biochemical changes accompany this transition: entire pathways involved in carbon metabolism, protein synthesis, and carbohydrate storage must be turned on or off. Like an automobile factory that can manufacture either cars or trucks, the raw materials available for production largely dictate which assembly line will be used. While many of the proteins involved in cellular assembly lines are not known, we can begin to implicate genes via their association with the diauxic shift or other cellular changes. In order to do this it is extremely useful to monitor each of the thousands of genes in a yeast cell, following their activity over time. Obtaining this information gene-by-gene is slow and expensive; fortunately, this has now

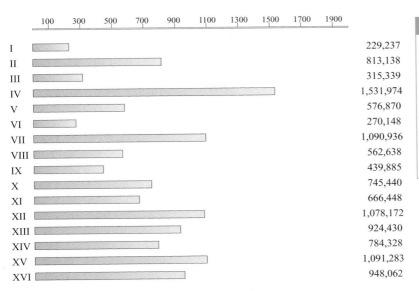

	bp
I	229,237
II	813,138
III	315,339
IV	1,531,974
V	576,870
VI	270,148
VII	1,090,936
VIII	562,638
IX	439,885
X	745,440
XI	666,448
XII	1,078,172
XIII	924,430
XIV	784,328
XV	1,091,283
XVI	948,062

Fig. 9.1 The genome of yeast *S. cerevesiae* is formed by 16 linear chromosomes, for a total length of 12.5 Mb (it also has mtDNA but we neglect it in this map). The length of each chromosome is shown in bp on the right column. This was the first eukaryotic genome to be completely sequenced, in 1996, and it contains approximately 6000 genes

become very efficient with the introduction of high throughput genomic methods such as microarrays.

The type of information obtained about gene function by means of microarrays is of vital importance to computational genomics, but as in the case of sequences, it can only be extracted by means of computational analysis. This chapter discusses various aspects of this process, starting with a description of the uses and technology of microarrays. Following this we will analyze the data from the original whole-genome analysis of yeast undergoing the diauxic shift, as well as of the yeast cell cycle, and present the statistical and computational tools necessary to complete the task.

9.2 | Monitoring cellular communication

In 1995, Pat Brown's lab at Stanford University introduced microarrays to the world. Microarrays allow scientists to monitor the activity of all the genes in a genome in a single experiment. The data produced by microarray experiments – expression levels for every gene – present many computational and statistical challenges, but the potential of this method is so huge that a large effort is under way to develop effective methods to analyze the information it provides. For example, with microarrays we can look at the differences in expression between cancerous and non-cancerous cells, at the effect of drugs on cellular function, as well as how metabolic patterns change when yeast switch from fermentation to respiration. As such, the analysis of gene expression has become one of the fundamental tasks of computational genomics (as well as an economic force in biotechnology), on par with the analysis of DNA sequences.

The purpose of microarrays. Imagine that you could flash-freeze a cell to capture all of the thousands of messenger RNA (mRNA) molecules present at a single point in time. These transcribed RNA sequences, or transcripts, are a record of the proteins the cell intends to produce at this moment in time. If you could count how many molecules of each type are present, you would measure the level of activity of each gene. How would you count all those molecules? The mRNA molecules all have a similar chemical composition and are of relatively comparable length, differing only in the order in which their nucleotides are arranged (which is determined by the gene that produced them).

One way would be to sequence every mRNA transcript in your collection, after reverse transcribing the mRNA to complementary DNA, or cDNA. While this method is rather expensive, it is often done to help in gene annotation since it provides clear evidence that a certain sequence is transcribed. Usually referred to as expressed sequence tag (EST) sequencing, this method can help to identify genes that *ab initio* gene-finding algorithms do not identify. But EST sequencing is not meant to measure the number of transcripts present. In fact, the collection of cDNAs is usually normalized before EST sequencing to remove repeated occurrences of transcripts present in high numbers.

So unless we want to sequence each mRNA one-by-one, we need to exploit some other aspect of DNA sequences to measure expression levels. Luckily there is one such characteristic that can be used to distinguish among different sequences: complementarity. Remember that DNA (or RNA) can be double-stranded because it sticks to its complementary sequence. The important point here is that it does so with high specificity. We can imagine constructing a special probe that is a DNA sequence exactly complementary to an mRNA transcript. If the transcript is present in a cell it will stick or hybridize to our probe; if it is not present we get no hybridization. With hundreds of thousands of identical probes for a single gene, we could in principle quantify the number of transcripts present by measuring the number of probes that have been hybridized (given that we can detect this hybridization).

Now the problem is that there are more than 6000 different genes in yeast, and more than 20 000 in multicellular eukaryotes, such as humans. How can we quantify the expression of all of these genes? This is the problem solved by microarrays. While there are a number of types of microarrays, which we describe in more detail below, the basic idea behind all of them is the same. Complementary DNA sequences for every gene in a genome (the *probes*) are laid down in great quantity on individual spots on a glass slide or silicon chip. This is the microarray itself. Then the mRNAs from a cellular extract are washed over this array to allow them to find and stick to their complements. By counting the number of transcripts that bind to each spot, we can measure at least the relative abundance of each.

This general description begs two further questions: How do we count the number of transcripts bound to each spot, and how do we make an array that contains over 6000 spots in such a small area? The first problem is solved by labeling each transcript with a fluorescent dye; after hybridization a laser is pointed at each spot on the microarray so that the fluorescence level can be measured by a computerized system. The greater the number of mRNA molecules in a cell and therefore hybridizing, the greater the intensity of fluorescence at the spot containing the complementary probe. The second problem of constructing a microarray has a number of solutions, each of which strongly determines experimental design and data analysis. We discuss the most common methods in the next section.

9.3 | Microarray technologies

There are three main technologies for producing and carrying out microarray experiments. These technologies differ in the amount of information about gene sequences needed to construct them, in the accuracy of the data they provide, and in the price of each experiment. The first two of these differences also dictate the analyses that can be done with each platform.

cDNA arrays. The simplest microarrays – and the first arrays to be widely used – are known as cDNA arrays. Simply, cDNA arrays are manufactured by spotting droplets of pre-made complementary DNAs on a glass slide. Pat Brown's lab website has maintained the instructions for making homemade cDNA arrays for more than ten years. Of course, these directions include the use of a robotic arm that can spot hundreds of micro-droplets of cDNA at a time, but most universities have at least one such printer and many labs now have their own.

One of the great advantages of cDNA microarrays is that no prior knowledge of the gene sequences is needed in order to measure expression levels. While this might sound paradoxical, as we explained earlier there are common methods to capture all of the transcripts expressed in a cell. If we make a collection of these mRNA transcripts, regardless of whether we know the sequence of each, we can spot them as cDNAs on the array as our probes. Thereafter, we can hybridize RNA from new cellular extracts to measure expression levels. If there are spots that show interesting patterns (we explain what we mean by "interesting" later), then we can sequence the DNA in that spot to find out what gene it represents.

As we can imagine, there can be huge variation in exactly how much cDNA is printed on each spot of our array. If we cannot be sure that every spot has exactly the same amount of cDNA – and therefore that fluorescence intensities are comparable across spots and across arrays – then we must somehow control for this unevenness. For this reason, cDNA arrays are used by hybridizing two samples to each array. The two samples are labeled with different fluorescent dyes, usually Cy3 (green) and Cy5 (red), that can be read separately by image-processing software.

The data that result from cDNA array experiments are generally represented as the ratio of fluorescent intensities of the two samples (usually as the log of the ratio). As such, these experiments are not meant to measure the absolute level of expression of genes, but rather relative changes in the expression of individual genes between samples. This means that we cannot necessarily distinguish among expression levels of all the genes in a single sample, only the differences within a single gene between samples. This basic microarray was the first to be widely used and was the platform for the 1997 *Science* paper studying yeast sampled at various stages of the diauxic shift that we discuss in our case study. Though it is the most primitive technology in some respects, many of the statistical tools developed for the analysis of cDNA arrays are applicable to all arrays and will be discussed in the case study.

Remark 9.1

Experimental design. One important issue in microarray experiments using two dyes is that the two most common fluorescent dyes, Cy3 and Cy5, differ in their size and rate of decay. For this reason, it is often necessary to include a "dye swap" in experiments. In effect, each sample is run labeled with both Cy3 and Cy5 to accurately measure expression. Generally the average of the two ratios is used as a single value for each spot; alternatively, linear models including dye as a covariate are gaining in popularity.

Remark 9.2

Image processing. A key step in obtaining the data from microarray experiments is neglected in this book: image processing. Every array experiment involves reading the fluorescent intensity of each spot using a scanner or other device, and then transforming this intensity into a numerical value that is used as data. Of course one should be aware of the methods (and potential errors) of this step in the experiment, as it may affect the quality of the data analysis. For simplicity in this introductory text we ignore this aspect of data collection and refer the reader to more advanced books.

Oligonucleotide arrays (two-dye). Soon after the first use of cDNA arrays in measuring gene expression, more advanced methods for constructing arrays were introduced. These methods use chemical or photolithographic technologies to synthesize oligonucleotides (short DNA sequences) on to the array. Each gene can then be represented on the array merely by synthesizing the appropriate sequence. These sequences are usually 25 to 80 bases long, depending on the exact technology used. Of course the synthesis of 6000 or more spots with specific oligonucleotides requires that we know the sequences *a priori* through genome annotation. Oligonucleotide arrays can either use one or two dyes (and therefore one or two samples per array). Two-dye arrays are conceptually similar to cDNA arrays, so we discuss these first.

The most common two-dye oligonucleotide arrays are made by companies such as Agilent, Incyte, and NimbleGen. These companies often have premade arrays for the genomes of many organisms available for purchase. These arrays contain from one to a few probes per gene, each of which is 60 to 100 nucleotides long (there is usually no variation in oligo length within arrays, only between companies and the technologies they use to synthesize probes). While the commercial synthesis of oligonucleotides results in a much more consistent number of probes across spots, two-dye arrays are still generally analyzed as ratios of the two samples.

Though we will not discuss it here, there are quite a number of computational challenges in the design of oligonucleotide arrays. Because we want an array whose probes will complement only a single gene, we need to pick oligonucleotides that are specific to individual genes. While this may sound relatively simple, many recent gene duplicates will be extremely similar to one another (as we saw in Chapter 8). The computational challenge is to design the probes such that they span regions that differ between closely related genes (paralogs). This will be especially important as the length of the oligonucleotide gets bigger, as longer probes will likely complement sequences with one or two mismatches.

Oligonucleotide arrays (one-dye). The most common single-dye oligonucleotide arrays are manufactured by the Affymetrix Corporation, and are sometimes referred to by their commercial trademark name, *GeneChip* microarrays. Affymetrix arrays use from 10 to 20 individual 25 bp oligonucleotides to represent a gene. These probes are intended to provide 10 to 20 independent expression measurements per gene. (Note that the probes are not truly independent as the probe sequences often overlap each other.) In addition, each probe has a paired "mismatch" probe that is exactly the same sequence as the "perfect match" except that the 13th nucleotide is changed. Because of the short probe length (25 bp) on Affymetrix arrays, the mismatch probes are intended to be used as a correction for non-specific hybridization. However, there are many disagreements over the usefulness of the mismatch probes, and they seem to be falling out of use in the majority of studies.

The high accuracy of Affymetrix arrays and the fact that only single samples are used means that absolute levels of expression can be inferred from GeneChip experiments. These expression levels are actually averages of the numerous probes that represent a single gene, but even the average expression level can identify differences within and between samples. On the other hand, multiple studies have shown that the more 3' a probe is, the higher the fluorescence intensity. This is most likely due to the fact that mRNA degrades from 5' to 3'. But the one-chip/one-sample design of Affymetrix arrays means that many of the issues in experimental design are obviated.

9.4 Case study: the diauxic shift and yeast gene expression

In 1997 Joseph DeRisi, Vishwanath Iyer, and Patrick Brown produced the first study that used microarrays to monitor gene expression over time in a single organism. The experimental design used by DeRisi and his collaborators to study expression across the diauxic shift in yeast was relatively simple. Following an initial 9 hours of growth, for 12 hours – approximately six hours before and six hours after the shift – they sampled cultured yeast every two hours and isolated mRNA from each sample. Because they were using cDNA arrays, at each time point they compared the mRNA collected at that time to the mRNA collected at time 0 (the first collection). This experimental set-up is generally referred to as a *reference design* in the microarray literature. The resulting dataset contains just over 43 000 ratios: seven time-points times 6400 genes measured at each point.

Among the main challenges presented by this kind of data is the fact that the number of microarrays used in each experiment is typically much smaller

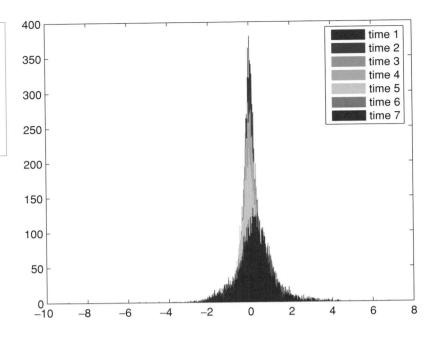

Fig. 9.2 The expression level of most genes remains invariant over time. This histogram shows, for each of the seven time points, the distribution of expression levels (measured as the logarithm of a ratio compared to time 0). Most genes have value close to zero, suggesting no or little activity

than the number of genes screened by each of them, mostly due to the cost of running arrays. This situation creates high-dimensional datasets with low sample sizes (the so-called "large p, small n" problem). Coupled with the relatively high noise levels among arrays, detection of significant patterns becomes a statistically challenging task.

There is no standard routine for all microarray analyses. Sometimes arrays are used as discovery tools, and as such do not require stringent standards for hypothesis testing. At other times arrays are used to explicitly test for the effect of a condition or mutation on gene expression, and more replication may be needed to obtain statistically significant results. Most often microarray experiments provide researchers with a list of candidate genes that deserve closer attention in future experiments. In order to produce such a list, there are a few standard analyses that can be carried out. These analyses can all be categorized as *exploratory data analysis* (a field of statistics unto itself), and in microarray experiments the basic set of analyses consists of data description, data clustering, and data visualization. Additional methods, like classification-learning algorithms, can also be employed. We use the same dataset presented in the study from DeRisi *et al.* to examine and discuss some of these methods.

9.4.1 Data description

The first thing we can explore in this dataset is the relative change in activity of all 6400 genes. Figure 9.2 shows that most genes do not change their activity at all over the 12 hours sampled, and thus are relatively stable in the face of the diauxic shift. In fact, between the first two measurements less than 5% of the genes change more than 1.5 fold. As glucose runs out during the experiment, more genes show many-fold increases, but they are still on the order of hundreds of genes in a set of 6400.

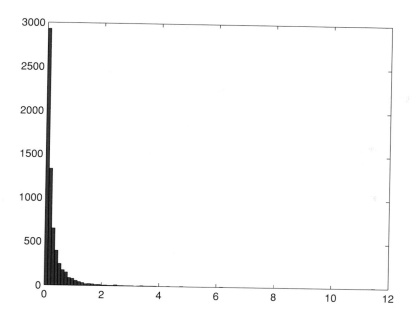

Fig. 9.3 Most yeast genes do not change their expression level during the experiment. We consider here the variance (computed across the seven time points) of each of the 6400 genes. This histogram shows how the variance is distributed.

The remaining genes are either not expressed during this time (many genes are only turned on during specific times or in specific environments), or are so necessary to basic cellular function that they need to be on all the time at constant levels. Remember that 2-dye arrays do not allow us to measure absolute expression levels, just relative changes in concentration.

The maximum change in expression observed above the level at time 0 is a 16-fold increase. Because there was little replication in this early microarray experiment we cannot say whether any of these changes are significant. It may be, in fact, that many of the genes that were increased only 1.5-fold (or 1.0001-fold) were important, replicable changes that the cell made in order to adjust to a changing environment. And it may be that 10-fold changes in other genes affect very little within the cell. Biologists cannot yet generalize the consequences of changes in expression for most genes.

While a simple description of the maximum change in level of expression for any single gene is quite revealing, it neglects the pattern of change over time that occurs in many genes. Most do not simply change in expression at a single time point, but rather either gradually go up or down, or follow a completely different pattern. In addition, as we will see in the next section, many of the genes that do change in level of expression share the same pattern of change over time with one another, and thus appear to be coordinately controlled by the cell. No simple statistic can capture the entirety of this dynamic expression, but measuring the range of expression – the difference between the highest and lowest ratios – does at least help us to find those genes that appear to be very active. Figure 9.3 shows the distribution of the variance and Figure 9.4 that of the range of values assumed by each gene.

In these conditions, with a large set of genes essentially remaining constant, and with few genes showing visible activity, it is essential to focus the analysis on the more promising subset of variable genes. Our next set of analyses

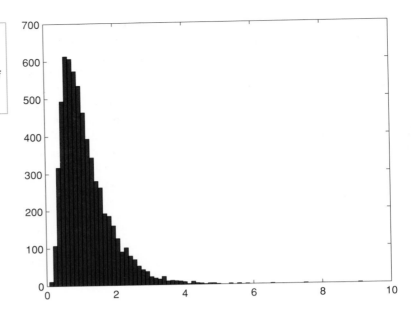

Fig. 9.4 The range of the values assumed by a gene is plotted here for each gene. Note that most genes move within a small range of values, while some of them vary significantly

aim to find those genes that do change in expression over the course of this experiment, and to describe the common patterns (if any) in change among genes. In order to do this, we will narrow down the set of genes considered to include just those whose maximum fold-change is greater than a certain threshold. This leaves us with a much smaller set of genes, focusing our attention on the subset of genes whose expression level changes significantly during this experiment.

We can use various methods to achieve this. The simplest one is to measure the variance of a gene, and to simply keep those genes that have high variance. The goal is to retain just a few hundred "interesting" genes.

Remark 9.3
Missing data. The original 6400×7 matrix used in the experiment has various entries with missing values, possibly due to errors of measurement or in the construction of the array. Statisticians have many ways of dealing with the problem of missing data, but for this study – due largely to the abundance of data – we take the wasteful approach of simply neglecting any gene having at least one missing value.

9.4.2 Data clustering

We will not limit ourselves to the analyses that were performed in the original paper, but rather will apply to this dataset a wider range of techniques that have since become standard, many of them borrowed from the fields of pattern recognition, data mining, and multivariate statistics. These largely overlapping fields deal with different aspects of data analysis and have created a rich toolbox of algorithms that can readily be applied to gene expression data.

One of the most basic tasks in pattern recognition is *clustering*, namely the identification of subsets of data that have high internal similarity, as well as low inter-cluster similarity (similar to finding gene families, as in Chapter 8). Of course the definition of clusters in the data relies on the specific distance measure used between two data points, in this case between two gene expression profiles (similarity and distance are of course two sides of the same coin). After one such distance measure has been defined, we also need to define a criterion by which we partition the dataset into clusters; distances by themselves do not define clusters. The definition of the distance measure, the clustering criterion, and the algorithm needed to find clusters are conceptually separate steps, and various combinations are possible. We go through some of the most common methods below.

Distance measures. Depending on what aspect of the data we want to capture within clusters, we can define different distance measures between data points. For example, we could use some function of the Pearson correlation coefficient:

$$C(x, y) = \frac{\sum_i (x_i - \hat{x})(y_i - \hat{y})}{\sqrt{\sum_i (x_i - \hat{x})^2 \sum_i (y_i - \hat{y})^2}}.$$

This type of correlation captures information about the similarity in relative behavior of two expression profiles, but does not consider similarity in the magnitude of change. A Euclidean distance, on the other hand, includes information on the absolute difference between two expression profiles. More sophisticated measures are possible, depending on what aspect of the data we want to emphasize. Among the most popular choices are: standardized Euclidean distance, Mahalanobis distance, and cosine distance. Here we use the simple similarity metric based on the correlation coefficient: $d(x, y) = 1 - C(x, y)$.

Clustering criterion. A clustering criterion allows us to define which points should be considered as belonging to the same cluster. A simple way to calculate a clustering criterion is to subtract the sum of between-cluster distances from the sum of within-cluster distances (here S is the data sample, $C(S)$ is the "cost" or "quality" of the clustering, and x_i the generic data point i):

$$C(S) = \sum_{i,j \text{ in same cluster}} d(x_i, x_j) - \sum_{i,j \text{ in different clusters}} d(x_i, x_j).$$

Once the distance measure between data points has been established and a clustering criterion has been defined, we still need to search among all possible partitions of the dataset in order to find the one that maximizes the clustering criterion. Unfortunately it turns out that optimizing the clustering of the data over all possible decompositions of it into clusters is computationally intractable. However, various approximation strategies are available. Two classic "greedy" methods are hierarchical clustering and k-means clustering. They are outlined below.

Hierarchical clustering. Hierarchical clustering is the simplest approach to clustering. The basic idea is the same as that of the NJ and UPGMA algorithms for phylogenetic trees mentioned in Chapter 7. It starts with a distance matrix between all pairs of datapoints, then iteratively identifies the closest pairs,

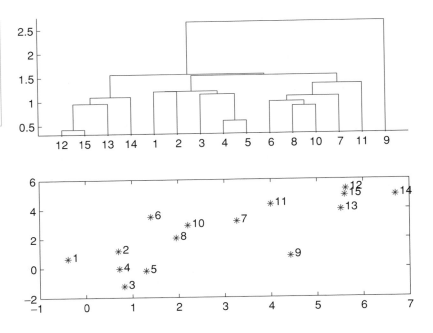

Fig. 9.5 This example shows how clusters can be represented by subtrees, in hierarchical clustering approaches. The leaves in the tree correspond to points in the lower half of the image (representing data points)

merges them into a new cluster, and computes the distance between this new cluster and all the other points or clusters; the cycle is then repeated. When only one element is left in the matrix, the system stops. Notice that in order for the algorithm to be fully specified, we also need to define a distance between sets of points. A popular choice is called single linkage: distances between groups is defined as the distance between the closest pair of objects, where only pairs consisting of one object from each group are considered. Another standard choice is called average linkage: the distance between two clusters is defined as the average of distances between all pairs of objects, where each pair is made up of one object from each group. More sophisticated notions can also be devised.

By keeping track of which points have been merged into which clusters, the algorithm can then produce a tree, though of course this cannot be interpreted in the same manner as a phylogenetic tree. After choosing how many clusters we want, we can cut the tree at the appropriate level. At the root-node level, we have one single cluster containing all the data; at the leaf-nodes level, we have n clusters containing one data-point each; in between, the cluster structure of the dataset can be analyzed. Figure 9.5 demonstrates these concepts on an artificial dataset of 15 points on a multidimensional scaling plane.

Hierarchical clustering thus creates a hierarchy of clusters from small to big, and allows the user to choose the desired number of clusters after seeing the results. Various numbers of clusters can be defined using the same tree, without re-computing the distances each time. In k-means clustering – described below – we need to repeat the entire procedure when a different number of clusters is desired.

We can apply this method to the yeast dataset, arbitrarily choosing to obtain nine clusters. These are displayed in Figure 9.6. Notice that they more or

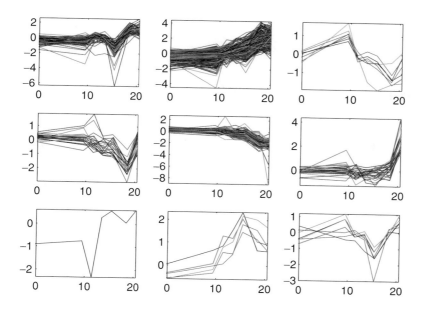

Fig. 9.6 The expression profiles of yeast genes associated with each of the nine clusters in a hierarchical clustering tree

less cover the various behaviors that can be expected: increasing, decreasing, peaking, etc. There appears to be a cluster with only a single representative, so it is possible that forming fewer than nine clusters would have been a better choice. Notice also that a cluster for constant genes is not present, as they have all been eliminated in our earlier pre-processing step. This would have been the largest cluster. One additional important thing to note is that the majority of genes do not simply shut off or turn on at the mid-point of the experiment: it appears as though the diauxic shift is not a single point in time, but rather a gradual switch from one set of internal and external conditions to another.

k-means clustering. This method starts by choosing how many clusters we want to obtain from our dataset. We call this number k. The clusters are implicitly defined by specifying k points called centers or prototypes. Each datapoint belongs to the cluster represented by the nearest center. The iterative strategy known as k-means starts with a random choice of k centers, and then replaces them with the means of the clusters defined by them. The new centers specify new clusters, and hence new means, etc., and the algorithm iterates until it converges. The result is a local minimum of the above clustering criterion. One advantage of this method is that we can also plot the centroids as a way to represent the clusters and to summarize the data.

We applied the k-means algorithm for $k = 9$ to the yeast data, obtaining the results shown in Figure 9.7. Again, it seems that the main types of gene expression behavior have been captured. We also report in Figure 9.8 the nine prototypes that represent the nine clusters.

Gene function and clustering. The earliest studies of microarray data often found that genes with similar expression profiles had related functions. This of

Fig. 9.7 The expression profiles of yeast genes associated with nine clusters obtained by the *K*-means algorithm. See Figure 9.8 for the prototypes associated with each of the clusters

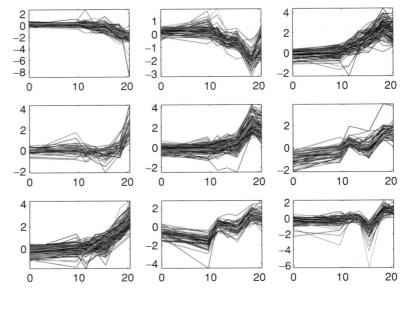

Fig. 9.8 The prototypes representing each of the nine clusters in Figure 9.7

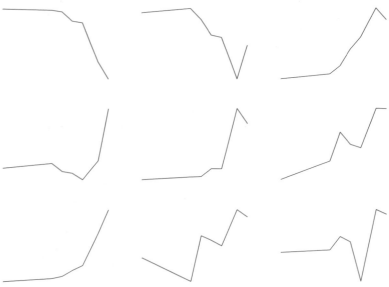

course makes sense, because if genes are involved in the same cellular process (say the diauxic shift), then they should be expressed at the same time. This also immediately suggests a possible strategy for functional annotation of a genome where the function of only a few genes is known. Indeed, one of the main attractions of gene expression analysis is that it can be used to infer gene function information from simple data analysis. Especially when combined with information on gene family relationships and experimental associations using other technologies, many of the functions of unannotated genes can be inferred using microarray data.

9.4.3 Visualization

Detecting patterns in a large matrix of numbers is not easy for most people, but there are various ways to visualize the data so as to make patterns readily visible (though this is not necessarily any better than a statistical analysis). Among the many methods used to sort the data for visualization, ordering the genes according to their position along individual chromosomes might reveal some patterns (it has been shown that neighboring genes are often expressed similarly). Ordering them based on the results of our hierarchical clustering might also reveal interesting patterns.

Of course given a cluster-tree (or dendrogram) there is still significant freedom to the ordering imposed by the tree topology on the list associated with the genes. To be precise, there are $N!$ possible permutations of a list of N elements; when a tree is fixed, for example by hierarchical clustering, there are still 2^N equivalent permutations. So some extra heuristic needs to be invoked to break the ties, often as simple as alphabetic ordering or chromosomal position.

Once an ordering of the list has been chosen, the second step is often to display numbers as colors. The numeric values of each cell can be color coded, resulting in the very popular *heatmaps* that are often associated with microarray experiments. Black represents the experimental mean or a ratio of 1, while green represents increased expression (ratios greater than 1) and red represents decreased expression. Note that though heatmaps are often color-coded red and green, this has nothing to do with the fluorescent dyes used in the experiment: any colors could be used. Figure 9.9 shows one such heatmap of the clustered data.

9.5 | Bonus case study: cell-cycle regulated genes

The diauxic shift is not the only change that occurs during the life of a yeast. In the course of normal existence, in fact, each individual yeast will go through what is known as the cell cycle. From being budded off from its parent cell, to reproducing its own offspring, each yeast goes through a number of typical steps that also involve changes in gene expression, turning whole pathways on and off. In 1998, Paul Spellman and colleagues (again from Stanford University) examined expression of the entire yeast genome through two rounds of the cell cycle over the course of five hours, with samples taken at 24 different time points. (Note: They performed the experiment with a number of different protocols, with differing numbers of time points sampled in each protocol. We discuss only the experiment with the largest number of samples here.) This corresponds to a dataset of about 6000 rows (one for each gene) and 24 columns.

In order to identify genes that vary with the cell cycle, Spellman *et al.* compared the expression of genes over time with sine and cosine functions of a period approximately similar to the length of cell cycle. This is equivalent to looking for genes that go up and down in expression in a regular pattern. One way to find such genes is to first cluster the data via k-means methods, then to compare clusters to cosine or sine functions. When we do this, we find various

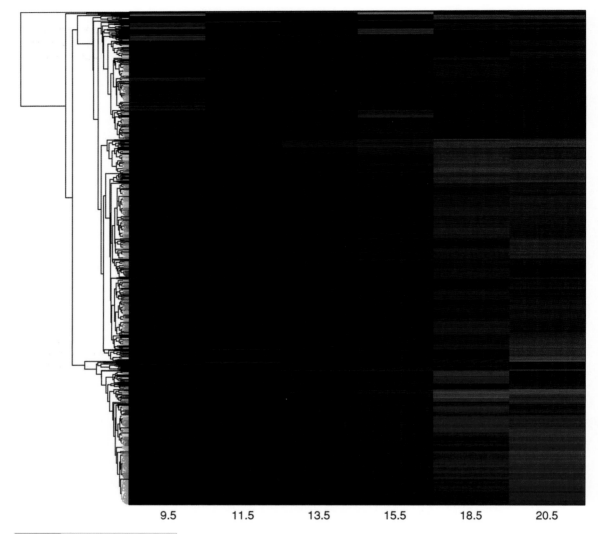

9.5   11.5   13.5   15.5   18.5   20.5

Fig. 9.9 Heatmap of the expression profiles for yeast genes. The genes are clustered by profile similarity, and the activity levels are color coded

sets of genes with clearly periodic behavior, just as Spellman and colleagues did.

For simplicity here we cluster the genes based on the correlation coefficient, as we did before. After a first filtering of the 6400 genes – to remove those with missing values and those with very low variability – we clustered the remaining ones with k-means into 16 clusters (an arbitrary choice), as shown in Figure 9.10. The advantage of using k-means in this context is that it produces, as a by-product, the center of each cluster, shown in Figure 9.11. This can be used to determine if a cluster contains periodic genes, by comparing the center to periodic functions such as cosines of various frequencies and phases. By computing the correlation coefficient between these cluster centers and a cosine function, it is possible to identify as periodic clusters numbers 1, 3, 4, 6, and 15. Of course, different choices of tunable parameters would give different results, but these conclusions are stable and seem reasonable.

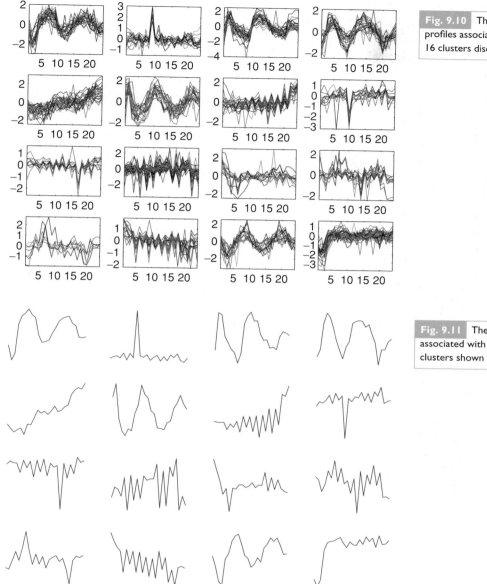

Fig. 9.10 The gene expression profiles associated with each of the 16 clusters discussed in Section 9.5

Fig. 9.11 The prototypes associated with each of the 16 clusters shown in Figure 9.10

It is interesting to note how many genes of yeast are regulated by the cell-cycle, a number much larger than what was previously known. A single set of microarray experiments, followed by careful data analysis, can instantly reveal important clues about the function of hundreds of genes, and greatly help genome annotation.

The paper by Spellman *et al.* went on to analyze the upstream sequences of these genes, looking for DNA elements that might be responsible for this periodic and coordinated control. We will not discuss these methods here, as the next chapter is entirely devoted to this task.

9.6 | Exercises

(1) Download from the book's website the yeast dataset used in the examples above, and cluster it using hierarchical clustering. Try obtaining 2, 3, and 20 clusters. Try different distance measures. Discuss the results.

(2) Visualize the same dataset using one of the many tools available online (accessible via the book's website).

(3) Do a web search to discover the main applications of gene expression data analysis, and the main tools. This is a fast-evolving field, and new technologies are important. Discuss one of the applications.

9.7 | Reading list

The first paper to demonstrate a whole genome analysis over time with cDNA microarrays is that of DeRisi *et al.* (1997). Shortly after that, a paper discussing pattern recognition algorithms for microarrays appeared (Eisen *et al.*, 1998), introducing methods of clustering, visualization, and other techniques. The analysis of the cell cycle with microarrays can be found in Spellman (Spellman *et al.*, 1998), and in Chu (Chu *et al.*, 1998).

A book discussing many of these topics in much greater depth is Baldi and Hatfield (2002). The website of Pat Brown's Lab (link available on the book's website), contains much information about the construction of microarray facilities, as well as about many applications of this technology. Data about the yeast genome can be found at: www.yeastgenome.org.

Machine learning and pattern recognition approaches are routinely used to predict gene function based on microarray data. Brown *et al.* (2000) describes the use of support vector machines for this task.

The tools and methods we have discussed here are only the tip of the iceberg when it comes to microarray analysis. Free software packages for microarray analysis range from the popular tools made available by Mike Eisen on his website, to more sophisticated methods contained in BioConductor, a set of tools written in the statistical language R. All of these packages will lead the reader to more sophisticated methods of analysis. Pointers to all of the above-mentioned papers, datasets, and websites, can be found on the book's website:

www.computational-genomics.net

Chapter 10

A bed-time story

Identification of regulatory sequences

- Regulatory regions and sequence motifs
- Motif finding algorithms
- Combining expression and sequence data

10.1 | The circadian clock

As you step off a trans-oceanic flight into the midday bustle of an airport, your body may be telling you that it's time for bed. This is because our body's sense of time depends as much on an internal clock as it does on external cues. Our internal clock – known as the circadian clock – will eventually synchronize itself with the new day–night cycle, but not before we suffer through the mind-deadening effects of jet lag. Reestablishing a link between the external clock (the sun) and our internal clock is essential for human health. Disruption of circadian rhythms has been linked to mania in people with bipolar disorder, and various health problems manifest themselves more often during the morning (heart attacks) or at night (asthma attacks) depending on our internal clock.

The circadian clock is fundamental to many organisms. Bacteria, insects, fungi, mammals, and many other species maintain an internal clock in order to synchronize their metabolism, activity, and body temperature to the sun. In no other organism is the ability to keep time as important as it is in plants. Much more than in mobile species, plants depend on a steady day–night cycle for energy production: they are able to photosynthesize sunlight during the day to store energy, but must use up these stores at night. Maintaining a circadian clock can confer a significant advantage by allowing the plant to anticipate dawn, dusk, or even seasonal changes.

Plants lead a relatively stressful life, dependent on their environment for many needs, such as nutrients and water, but are unable to move. Unlike mobile organisms, plants often react to external challenges by changing their internal condition. For instance, they may produce chemical insect repellents as soon as they detect an herbivore (nicotine is one such insecticide), or they may produce anti-freeze proteins in reaction to falling temperatures. It is easy to see how the ability of a plant to anticipate such changes can directly translate into a competitive advantage. This is why a circadian clock is so important.

Many of the most important steps in maintaining a circadian clock have been studied in the plant, *Arabidopsis thaliana*. Arabidopsis, whose common name is mouse-ear cress or thale cress, is a small, weedy organism that has become the model genetic and genomic study system for plants. Its genome is approximately 120 Mb long, with five chromosomes and 29 000 genes. (It should be noted that the rice genome has also been sequenced, and appears to also have more genes than humans with at least 36 000.)

Arabidopsis has a cell-autonomous circadian clock, meaning that each cell keeps track of the day–night cycle independently of all other cells. Experiments in tobacco plants have shown that you can keep different sides of the same plant on effectively opposite circadian clocks by alternating the amount and duration of light exposure to each half. If you remove the day–night cycle by keeping *Arabidopsis* in constant light or in constant darkness, it loses the periodicity of the circadian clock over a matter of days. Mice kept in constant light, on the other hand, can maintain the steady rhythm of the circadian clock over a period of months. These experiments demonstrate that the *Arabidopsis* circadian clock is coupled to stimulus from the sun, and that this stimulus is needed to reinforce internal metabolic cycles.

How does *Arabidopsis* tie the external clock set by the sun to cellular activity? It does so largely by controlling the activity of a few key proteins that sit at the top of giant gene cascades. Although all of the steps are not known, it appears that three proteins – LHY, CCA1, and TOC1 – are the key players in an oscillatory loop. These three proteins take part in a negative feedback loop: LHY and CCA1 are activated early in the morning (partly by sunlight) and act to repress the transcription of TOC1. (Remember that gene names are generally italicized and protein names are not.) As the supply of LHY and CCA1 dwindles with diminishing light, TOC1 is produced. During the night the production of TOC1 is at its peak, and TOC1 actually acts to promote the transcription of LHY and CCA1, which in turn act to shut down TOC1 production. Thus a simple negative feedback loop, like those found in many machines, serves to maintain the internal oscillations of the *Arabidopsis* circadian clock.

LHY and CCA1 also affect the expression of many other genes tied to the circadian clock. These two proteins are transcription factors that act to repress or promote the expression of many other genes. By their action, LHY and CCA1 sit at the top of gene cascades that allow the plant to turn on and off large groups of genes needed at different times of day and night. They do so by binding to specific regulatory sequences (called *transcription factor binding sites*, or *TFBS* for short) adjacent to the genes that they regulate.

In this chapter we will learn how to find the regulatory sequences that control gene transcription. This is generally a difficult task because of a number of features of binding sites discussed in the next section. From the perspective of sequence analysis, binding sites appear as sequence *motifs*, that is specific patterns in DNA sequences (see, for example, the discussion in Chapter 4). However, by clustering genes to find those that have similar expression patterns, we will be able to identify the common sequence motifs that contribute to this co-expression. In the previous chapter we covered the basics of the clustering of gene expression profiles, and how to identify sets of expression profiles that cycle together; here we will learn the algorithms that allow us to identify the regulatory sequences key to the cycling of the circadian clock in *Arabidopsis*.

10.2 | Basic mechanisms of gene expression

The goal of this chapter is to present the algorithmic and statistical issues that arise when we search for transcription factor binding sites in DNA sequences. Before we address these issues (generally called *motif finding*), we briefly review the mechanisms by which gene expression is regulated and a few properties of binding sites that may help us in our task of finding them.

The most common way for cells to control the activity of proteins is by controlling the level of transcription of genes. Cells can also regulate protein activity by controlling the number of mRNA transcripts available for translation (through degradation of mRNAs), by post-translational modifications of proteins that determine whether they are in active or inactive states, or by a number of other mechanisms. But to maximize efficiency, the level of proteins is best regulated by controlling gene expression in the first place.

Regulatory DNA: the genetic signposts. A gene embedded in random DNA is inert. Without additional signals that direct the transcriptional machinery, both prokaryotic and eukaryotic cells cannot know where to start transcribing the DNA necessary to construct a protein. In addition, an organism must have a way to control how much of a protein to produce, when to produce it, and in which cells (if it is multi-cellular) to produce it in. All of these tasks are controlled in part by regulatory DNA.

Regulatory DNA (also called *cis*-regulatory DNA, or simply the *promoter*) is the sequence surrounding a gene that specifies proper transcription; it is a mosaic of short sequence motifs (6–12 bases long) and semi-random DNA (see also Figure 2.2). These short motifs, or *binding sites*, are usually found upstream (i.e. 5′) of coding regions, but they can also be found downstream (3′) or even within untranslated parts of the transcribed gene. (The start of transcription is labeled position +1, and anything upstream is numbered −1, −2, etc.) Binding sites direct transcription by binding specific transcription factors; these proteins bind to the regulatory DNA and drive transcription.

One of the most important transcription factor binding sites is the one bound by RNA polymerase – the protein that carries out transcription. In Eubacteria, the binding sites are relatively rigidly defined: there is a "−10" sequence, TATAAT, and a "−35" sequence, TTGACA (where the positions of the sequences are approximately 10 and 35 bases upstream of the start of transcription, respectively). While variants of these sequences appear quite often, these *consensus* sequences represent the most commonly used nucleotides at each position in the binding sites. In Eukaryotes, a different RNA polymerase is used, and hence a different binding site is used. The so-called *TATA-box* consists of the sequence TATAA[A/T] by itself (where the last base can be either A or T with equal frequency), approximately 40 bases upstream of the start of transcription. Of course the start of transcription may itself be many bases upstream of the start of translation (where the start codon, ATG, is found), so identification of the true TATA-box is not a simple task.

Computational challenges in finding binding sites. It is extremely difficult to identify the transcription factor binding sites that control a gene by computational means alone. There are many reasons for this, but three stand out: (1) transcription factor binding site motifs are short and will therefore appear thousands of times in a genome by chance alone, (2) variants on these motifs that are one or a few bases different from each other will often bind the same transcription factor, and (3) we often do not even know the binding site motifs that are recognized by a transcription factor, much less their location.

One strategy to identify TFBSs that has been used to some success involves the methods discussed in Chapter 8: comparison of different genomes to identify conserved elements in intergenic regions. Although some mutations to binding sites will not compromise their function, a majority often result in a lower binding affinity of the transcription factors that must locate and bind them. Therefore, identifying short motifs that appear to be conserved over long periods of time helps to identify functional regulatory sequences. This technique has been applied to organisms ranging from yeast to mammals, with apparent success in identifying otherwise unknown binding sites. A drawback to this approach is that it only produces a list of possible binding sites, but does not give any information about their function or even the transcription factor that binds to them.

Another common method can be used to find binding sites as well as information about their function. This method involves grouping together genes that are co-regulated (by using whole-genome gene expression data) and then looking for motifs that are common to the upstream regions of genes in the same cluster, on the assumption that many of them are directly regulated by the same transcription factors. Hypothesis testing can be used to decide if any motifs identified are likely to be due to biological factors, or if they can be explained by chance. Of course the two methods just described can also be combined.

In this chapter we will discuss the second approach, focusing in particular on motifs that are found upstream of clock-regulated genes. Although scientists believed that LHY and CCA1 controlled the expression of genes involved in day–night oscillations, they did not know what regulatory motifs were bound by these proteins. By finding the motifs bound by LHY and CCA1 we will be able to elucidate the first few interactions that take place at the top of the gene cascades activated or repressed by daylight. The general approach we take to motif finding is to first cluster genes showing a similar day–night oscillatory pattern, and then to look for DNA motifs that occur upstream of all or most of these genes.

10.3 | Motif-finding strategies

The biological problem of finding TFBSs directly translates into the computational problem of finding common sequence motifs. Motifs can generically be defined as patterns in sequences, typically specific sets of words. A number of different biological problems are subsumed under the heading of motif finding and hence various statistical and computational methods are used. In this chapter we focus only on the simplest problems, providing pointers to more detailed literature in Section 10.6. We review here the main design choices to be made by the analyst, before illustrating all of them in Example 10.1.

Given a set of co-regulated genes, the first thing we do is collect the set of DNA sequences surrounding these genes that we believe will contain the relevant binding sites. Generally the sequences collected will be some fixed length sequence upstream of the coding region. The choice of how far upstream to search is always an arbitrary one, and depends on the specific organism being analyzed; one common choice is to use 1000 bases upstream of the ORF. Though regulatory elements can be found hundreds of thousands of bases upstream and downstream of coding regions (at least in the genomes of multicellular organisms), the highest concentration is generally found in the first 1000 bases.

The next choice in our analysis is the type of motif to search for, i.e. the motif model. Is it going to be a gapped or an ungapped motif? Is the gap going to be of fixed or variable length? How long will the motif be? In this chapter we will concentrate on ungapped motifs of fixed length (gapped motifs of variable length were discussed in Chapter 4, in the context of profile HMMs). Ungapped motifs of fixed length can be seen as words of length L that appear somewhere in the upstream regions and that are similar to each other.

As mentioned earlier, binding sites for the same transcription factor are not necessarily identical, only highly similar. One way to summarize any list of fixed-length motifs that differ in their exact sequences is to report the *consensus* sequence: a new sequence formed by the most frequent letter used at each position (the consensus sequence does not necessarily need to appear in the data). When all (equal-length) motifs are aligned, we can easily find the most common nucleotide for each position, and form a consensus motif from these. Thus, from any alignment, we can easily obtain the consensus sequence. This can be a very useful representation of a set of sequences, and is described in Example 10.1.

Another way to summarize motifs (given a multiple alignment) is to report the frequency of each nucleotide used at every position, resulting in a *position specific scoring matrix* (PSSM) or *profile* (these are also sometimes called position specific weight matrices, or PSWMs). The PSSM essentially represents a multinomial model of a sequence of length L, where one of the four bases (or 20 AAs) is chosen independently from a multinomial distribution for each position, and in which parameters are position specific. In other words, a different loaded-die is rolled for each position, its bias represented in the PSSM. The PSSM is a $4 \times L$ (or $20 \times L$) matrix (4 rows, L columns), like the one shown in Example 10.1 . Note that a consensus motif can readily be obtained from a PSSM by taking the most frequent nucleotide in each position.

Example 10.1
Fixed length, ungapped motifs. In this set of eight sequences we find a similar 6-letter motif in each, appearing in various positions. The start positions are

noted with a *, and the motifs are then aligned in the table below:

A	T	G	*C	T	G	A	A	T	G	T	A
*C	T	A	T	A	T	A	G	T	A	A	T
C	T	G	T	*C	A	A	T	A	T	G	T
C	C	T	A	A	A	*G	A	A	T	A	T
A	A	C	*C	T	A	A	T	T	G	T	T
*C	A	G	A	T	T	T	C	C	C	A	C
C	T	C	G	A	*C	A	A	A	T	T	T
A	C	T	*C	A	G	A	T	T	C	T	C

An alignment of these motifs would look like this:

```
C   T   G   A   A   T
C   T   A   T   A   T
C   A   A   T   A   T
G   A   A   T   A   T
C   T   A   A   T   T
C   A   G   A   T   T
C   A   A   A   T   T
C   A   G   A   T   T
```

The consensus sequence and the PSSM for this alignment are shown below. Note that both the PSSM and consensus are completely specified once the set of start positions has been specified. Notice also that the consensus sequence appears once in the dataset:

A	0	5	5	5	4	0
C	7	0	0	0	0	0
G	1	0	3	0	0	0
T	0	3	0	3	4	8
CONSENSUS	C	A	A	A	T	T

Identifying motifs. In the above example we gave the starting positions and lengths of the set of motifs in each sequence, which together define a common motif. The task of motif finding is to identify these starting positions without prior knowledge of motifs that may be similar in all of the sequences. This problem is highly similar to multiple local alignment, where the PSSM can be used as a kind of scoring matrix for each set of starting positions proposed. In order to find the highest scoring set of starting positions (and hence the motif of interest) we will need to define a scoring function.

We also want to know whether the high-scoring motifs we find are significant. This will necessarily depend on our background model to define which motifs we expect to encounter by chance. Rather than using a statistical sequence model, people often select a set of sequences not believed to contain the motif as a background model. This background set should otherwise be similar to the set under investigation, such as using non-coding DNA from different regions of the same genome. Comparing the score of the motifs from the focal dataset with the set of scores from the background dataset will then indicate the significance of the identified motifs.

At this point, we should decide *how* to algorithmically find the motif that maximizes the score. Unfortunately, for most choices of motif representation and scoring function this is a computationally expensive problem to solve exactly, so a number of heuristics have been proposed. Randomized and greedy methods, such as Gibbs sampling, are among the most popular. These procedures iteratively refine the choice of starting positions and will be described briefly below. For situations where there is no variation in the binding site sequence, however, it is still possible to solve the problem exactly and this is the situation that we have selected for our case study on the circadian clock.

We will now go through the algorithmic details of motif finding in some more detail. We focus on finding high-scoring ungapped motifs of fixed length in the form of PSSMs. In other words, we are assuming that the motif can be (approximately) represented in this form:

	1	2	3	4	5	6
A	0	0.625	0.625	0.625	0.5	0
C	0.875	0	0	0	0	0
G	0.125	0	0.375	0	0	0
T	0	0.375	0	0.375	0.5	1

A motif is considered interesting if it is very unlikely under the background distribution. If we assume a uniform distribution for the PSSM, for example, we should prefer motifs with columns that are far from uniform. The matrix above has been made using the data from Example 10.1 , and shows that column 6 is more unbalanced than, say, column 5. Many scoring functions can be defined to embody this imbalance; one of the popular ones is called the *KL divergence* of the motif, which measures how different from the background distribution the motif is

$$\sum_{\text{position } i} \left(\sum_{\text{letter } k} p_{i,k} \log \frac{p_{i,k}}{q_k} \right),$$

where $p_{i,k}$ is the probability of seeing symbol k in position i in the PSSM, and q_k is the probability of symbol k under a multinomial sequence model derived from the background model. Both probabilities are practically obtained by simply counting the frequencies of symbols at each position in a multiple alignment. Note that for statistical and computational reasons, it is often a good idea to add *pseudocounts* to the entries of the matrix (increasing their value by a fixed amount before normalizing) so that we never have to deal with zero entries. The reason behind this step is that we are estimating a probability based on a small sample, and it is quite possible that we never observe symbols that have small – but positive – probability. Having zeros in the PSSM would automatically prevent the motif from matching certain patterns, whereas we would prefer to just make this unlikely. After adding pseudocounts to the above matrix (in this case we added 1 to each entry of the matrix from Example 10.1) we would obtain the following new PSSM:

	1	2	3	4	5	6
A	0.083	0.5	0.5	0.5	0.416	0.083
C	0.666	0.083	0.083	0.083	0.083	0.083
G	0.167	0.083	0.333	0.083	0.083	0.083
T	0.083	0.333	0.083	0.333	0.416	0.75

Finding high-scoring motifs. The problem now is to find a PSSM from a set of sequences that maximizes the score of choices of starting positions, and thus gives us our motif of interest. This is a problem of pattern discovery; the related problem of pattern matching is quite simple. It involves finding the starting position in the sequence, s, that best matches a previously defined PSSM. We will use pattern matching as one step in our goal of pattern discovery.

Given a single sequence, $\mathbf{s}$, of length n (longer than the length, L, of the PSSM), we can easily slide a defined PSSM along, computing the likelihood of the match at each position. For each starting position, j, in the sequence, $\mathbf{s}$, we calculate the likelihood of the motif as follows:

$$\mathcal{L}(j) = \prod_{j=1}^{n} p_{i,k},$$

where again $p_{i,k}$ is the probability of seeing symbol k in position i in the PSSM. (This is more commonly reported as the log of the likelihood.) This likelihood represents how well the PSSM fits the segment of the sequence $\mathbf{s}(j : j + L - 1)$. The starting position j where $\mathcal{L}(j)$ is maximal represents the best match of the PSSM to the sequence. For the purposes of demonstration we compute the log-likelihood score of the PSSM given above on an artificial sequence obtained concatenating together all eight sequences from Example 10.1 . Since each of them contained one instance of the common motif, it is not surprising to see (approximately) eight high peaks in Figure 10.1.

So we are left with the following situation: given a set of sequences, and a PSSM, we can easily find the best-matched positions (the ones with the highest likelihoods) for the PSSM in each sequence. And at the same time, given a set of starting positions, we can readily find the corresponding PSSM, as was shown previously. This suggests an iterative process, starting with random positions – and a random PSSM – and gradually improving them both. Although this is not guaranteed to find the highest scoring motif, it is guaranteed to converge to a local optimum and stop. This is one of the many variations of the expectation-maximization (EM) algorithm that was encountered in Chapter 4.

Instead of selecting as matches of the motif the positions with maximum score, we could alternatively introduce some randomization into the iterative process, randomly choosing these positions from a distribution that is proportional to the resulting score. This, and other tricks, can reduce the risk of getting stuck in local minima during our search, and generally have been observed to lead to better scoring PSSMs. The implementation of this and other randomization steps leads to a method known as *Gibbs sampling*.

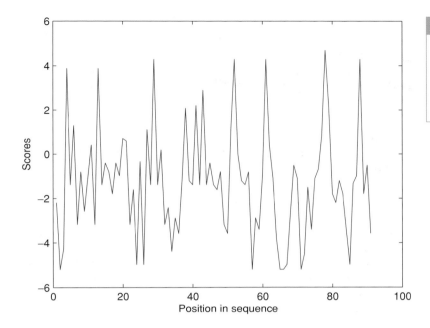

Fig. 10.1 The log likelihood score resulting from sliding the PSSM defined above on a sequence obtained by concatenating the eight sequences of Example 10.1 . Note that as expected we can see at least eight peaks

These computational complications are necessary because the set of all possible start positions for a motif-match is very large, and there are as many possible solutions as there are motif position vectors in the dataset. However, if we make an extra simplifying assumption, one that is rarely realistic, we can greatly accelerate the search process. The assumption is that the motif appears every time with the same spelling. In this case, the search space is restricted to all exact words of length L appearing in the dataset, and this grows only linearly with the number of sequences. Exhaustive search is now possible. In our case study below, we analyze one such example. We find a motif that is identical in every instance where it is found, the motif controlling a group of clock-regulated genes in *Arabidopsis*. The scoring function we use here to find the motif is given by the difference in frequency of the motif between two sets of sequences (the target set and a background set). We will call this quantity the *margin*.

10.4 Case study: the clock again

We illustrate the problem of motif finding by studying a simple case in detail, the discovery of regulatory motifs for clock-regulated genes in *Arabidopsis* activated in the evening. The discovery of a specific motif for evening genes was originally carried out by Stacey Harmer and colleagues in 2000; they found an identical word of nine bases found upstream of genes turned on in the evening, aptly named the *evening element* (EE). The study of this discovery is important because it contains all the elements of a standard motif discovery problem, but having a completely identical motif frees us from many algorithmic details. This in turn allows us to use a number of simpler strategies. This type of motif does not need to be represented by a PSSM or a consensus sequence, and can be found by simply comparing the frequency of all words of a given length between two sets of sequences. Nevertheless, even this simple task requires us to deal with all of the classical problems: comparing a set of sequences with a background set; filtering out repeats and other uninformative signals; focusing only on significant patterns. The evening element motif is

    AAAATATCT,

and it appears upstream of many of the genes that are activated in the evening.

Experimental design. Harmer and coworkers were interested in finding genes that are regulated by the circadian clock and in discovering how exactly the clock controls them. The experiment they designed was able to deliver both a list of hundreds of clock-regulated genes, and a specific regulatory element that controls genes activated in a specific time phase, the evening. The key to identifying this binding site was in combining the gene expression and sequence data, and analyzing them jointly.

Harmer *et al.* used DNA microarrays to determine mRNA levels in *Arabidopsis* at six 4-hour intervals during the subjective day and night. Before the start of the experiment, the plants lived in controlled growth chambers, with day length set by the experimenters as cycles of 24 hours (12 light and 12 dark). During the experiment itself, the lighting conditions were kept constant, but the internal clock of the plant kept ticking. In order to identify which ones of the thousands of genes are regulated by the clock, tissue (and mRNA) was extracted and hybridized on microarrays at four-hour intervals. (The microarrays used contained probes for only 8 200 genes, but remember that *Arabidopsis* has more than 28 000 genes.) The resulting dataset contained expression levels of each of the genes through the 24 hour day/night cycle. Because the experiment was started at the equivalent of 8 AM, the different time intervals are labeled circadian time (CT) 0, 4, 8, 12, 16, and 20, with CT $= 0$ at 8 AM and CT$=8$ at 4 PM. These are the data we use in our analysis, although we use slightly simpler analysis methods.

Expression data analysis. To determine which of the 8 200 genes exhibited a circadian pattern of expression, the gene expression profiles were compared with various cosine functions of different periods and phases. Genes that showed a high correlation with a cosine wave that had a period between 20 and 28 hours (independent of amplitude) were considered to be clock regulated. We then clustered these clock-regulated genes into three main phases: cluster 1, corresponding to genes whose expression peaked in phases 0 and 4, cluster 2 for phases 8 and 12, and cluster 3 for phases 16 and 20. The computational tools used for this part of the experiment are the same as those discussed in Chapter 9, and thus will not be described in detail here.

According to this criterion for identifying clock-regulated genes, 437 genes, or 6% of the genes on the chip, were classified as cycling. Of these, 191 were highly expressed in cluster 2, the evening (corresponding to genes peaking at 4 PM and 8 PM). These will be the genes among which we look for common binding sites. The others will be used to provide a background against which to contrast the patterns found in cluster 2.

Table 10.1 The 9-mers with the largest difference in frequency between cluster 2 and the rest of the data. The difference in frequency is called here "margin." Note the presence of repeats and other motifs without biological relevance

Motif (and reverse complement)		Margin	Frequency 2	Frequency 1 and 3
AAAAAAAAA	TTTTTTTTT	−0.00022218	0.001191099	0.001413279
AAAATATCT	AGATATTTT	0.000147462	0.000198953	5.14905E-05
CTCTCTCTC	GAGAGAGAG	0.00012498	0.000183246	5.82656E-05
AGAGAGAGA	TCTCTCTCT	0.000121717	0.000198953	7.72358E-05
AAAAAAAAC	GTTTTTTTT	−8.07687E-05	0.000138743	0.000219512
ATATATATA	TATATATAT	7.58808E-05	0.0005	0.000424119
AAATATCTT	AAGATATTT	7.47173E-05	0.000109948	3.52304E-05
AAAAATATC	GATATTTTT	6.62183E-05	0.000120419	5.42005E-05
AAATAAAAT	ATTTTATTT	6.57004E-05	0.000212042	0.000146341
TAAAAAAAA	TTTTTTTTA	−6.07486E-05	0.000185864	0.000246612

Motif-finding results. If we decide to look just for motifs that are formed by exact words of length L, many of the computational problems mentioned previously disappear, while all of the statistical and biological ones remain. An easy way to discover the evening element is to consider all words of length L whose frequency in the evening cluster is very different from its frequency in the rest of the data. This can be achieved by a program that simply counts the frequency of each word in both sequence sets. The frequency needs to be counted in all available sequences and in their reverse complement, meaning that the motif could be present on the complementary DNA strand.

We will score every candidate motif (that is every length L word) by computing the difference between its frequency in cluster 2 and its frequency in the rest of the data, a quantity we call the margin. This score can also be directly used to assess the significance of the motif. Over-represented motifs are those that appear very frequently in the 1000 bp upstream regions of cluster 2 genes, and much less frequently in the corresponding regions of the other genes.

The top 10 9-mers with largest frequency difference between cluster 2 and the rest of the data are given in Table 10.1.

Here we note a phenomenon that is very typical in motif finding: the presence of repeats (or near repeats) in the set. Repeats (either of single letters or of 2-mers) are highly common and generally non-functional components of the genome, and likely have no biological significance in this context. So it is customary to filter them out during the analysis, though there are definitely some repeats that do actually have a function as binding sites in many organisms. Similarly, this filtering is often done with near-repeats, patterns such as AAAAAAAAAT. Once the filtering is complete, large differences in frequency between motifs in different clusters can reveal functionally important elements, or at least restrict the attention of researchers to examining just a few interesting candidates.

Excluding motifs formed by repeats, the top four 9-mers with the largest difference in frequency between clusters are given in Table 10.2. After removing the repeated elements, we now see that the evening element emerges as

Table 10.2 The 9-mers with the largest difference in frequency between cluster 2 and the rest of the data, excluding repeats and partial repeats. Note the evening element in top position, followed by related motifs

Motif (and its reverse complement)		Margin	Frequency 2	Frequency 1 and 3
AAAATATCT	AGATATTTT	0.000147462	0.000198953	5.14905E-05
AAATATCTT	AAGATATTT	7.47173E-05	0.000109948	3.52304E-05
AAAAATATC	GATATTTTT	6.62183E-05	0.000120419	5.42005E-05
AAATAAAAT	ATTTTATTT	6.57004E-05	0.000212042	0.000146341

the strongest signal distinguishing the two clusters; note that two of the other top three motifs in the table are simply variants of the evening element that include extra A nucleotides (AAATATCTT and AAAAATATC). The margin of the evening element (the difference in frequency between cluster 2 and clusters 1 and 3) is 0.000 147 462. In order to decide if such a margin could occur by chance (and hence to assess its significance) we performed many random splits of the data and for each of them we measured the margin of the highest-scoring element. This is the score we could expect to see as the result of chance. In 100 trials, we never observed a larger margin, giving us a p-value estimate of < 0.01.

Now that we have identified the putative evening element, we can look in more detail at its frequency among all of the clock-regulated genes. Below we show the number of times the EE is present in the upstream regions (on both strands) of the genes peaking in each of the six time points sampled by Harmer and colleagues (starting at 8 AM):

Circadian Time	0	4	8	12	16	20
Number of genes	78	45	124	67	30	93
EE Count	5	6	49	27	8	8

It appears as though not all genes in the second cluster have the evening element, nor is this motif limited only to these genes. However, it is definitely enriched in cluster 2.

Selecting motif length (why $L = 9$). If we look for the largest-margin (non-repeat) words of length L distinguishing cluster 2 from the rest, we have a clear result: for all values of $L < 9$ they are simply substrings of the evening element, and for $L = 10$ it is a superstring of it (with an extra A on the left). So how do we know which one of these motifs is the evening element, and how do we know that we were looking at the correct motif length to begin with? One way to decide on the optimal motif length is to compare the margins of the motifs of different lengths to find the one that has the maximum. This can then be used as a guide to the motif length that has the most biological significance.

In order to compare the margins among motifs of different lengths we need to consider the fact that longer words naturally have lower frequency, and hence we can expect a lower margin for longer motifs. In order to avoid this artifact, we use the ratio between the maximal margin obtained for each motif length and what we would expect to obtain in a background model. In other words, we should divide the score obtained for each motif length by the score obtained on

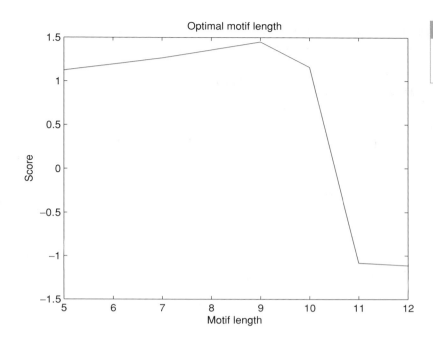

random sequences with the same parameters. As an estimate of this quantity we use the score obtained by averaging the scores in the two other clusters.

If we carry out this procedure, we find that motifs of length 9 are maximally informative in discriminating cluster 2 from the others (see Figure 10.2).

Biological validation. A motif-finding task is only truly complete after it has received biological validation. After detecting one or a few promising motifs, one typically searches TFBS databases to see if that motif is already known to be a regulatory element, and which factors bind to it if any are known. More direct experimental validation is eventually required to confirm the motif and its function.

In this case, Harmer and colleagues experimentally validated the newly discovered regulatory element by directly attaching it to a gene whose fluorescent product can be viewed under a microscope. The resulting experiment showed that the fluorescence was only detected during the plant's evening, indicating that the evening element directly drove transcription during the evening. In this case, computational analysis found a new putative transcription factor binding site, and biological experiment validated it.

Now that researchers have the evening element sequence, they can simply go to the *Arabidopsis* genome sequence to find other genes (not represented on the original array) that may be regulated by the genes at the top of the circadian clock regulatory cascade. In addition, not all of the genes that showed peak expression during the evening necessarily had an EE sequence in their regulatory regions. Because not all genes are directly regulated by the first few transcription factors in the circadian regulatory cascade, the presence or absence of the EE motif can begin to reveal the exact sequence of events that occur during circadian control.

10.5 | Exercises

(1) Use the free package AlignACE to analyze the same set of sequences discussed in this chapter (data available online). Compare the results with those in the book.

(2) Practice obtaining upstream regions of yeast genes, using the resources provided in book website.

(3) Detect cell-cycle genes in yeast, using the methods and the data discussed in Chapter 9. Can you find any motifs in the upstream regions of those genes?

10.6 | Reading list

The paper by Stacey Harmer and co-workers on the circadian clock in *Arabidopsis* is Harmer *et al.* (2000). An interesting paper on the computational identification of regulatory elements in *Saccharomyces cerevisiae* makes uses of similar techniques, and can be found in Hughes *et al.* (2000).

The Gibbs sampling approach is presented in Lawrence *et al.* (1993). The paper Brazma *et al.* (1998) discusses various aspects of the computational discovery of regulatory motifs. The paper Guhathakurta *et al.* (2002) presents similar approaches, this time to discover regulatory motifs controlling heat shock proteins in *Caenorhabditis elegans*. Motifs of course can be found in many other ways, for example by phylogenetic comparisons of the type discussed in Chapter 8: the papers Kellis *et al.* (2003) and McCue *et al.* (2001) present and use this approach.

The software packages MEME and AlignACE are the most commonly used free tools for motif finding. They use EM and Gibbs strategies, respectively. They can be found, as all papers, websites and software tools referred to in this book, by following links contained on the book's website:

www.computational-genomics.net

Bibliography

Altschul, S. F., W. Gish, W. Miller, E. W. Myers, and D. J. Lipman. Basic local alignment search tool. *Journal of Molecular Biology*, **215**, 1990.

Anderson, S., A. Bankier, B. G. Barrell, M. H. de Bruijn, A. R. Coulson, J. Drouin, I. C. Eperon, D. P. Nierlich, B. A. Roe, F. Sanger, P. H. Schreier, A. J. Smith, R. Staden, and I. G. Young. Sequence and organization of the human mitochondrial genome. *Nature*, **290**(5806), 1981.

Axel, Richard. The molecular logic of smell. *Scientific American Magazine* (October), 1995.

Baldi, Pierre, and G. Wesley Hatfield. *DNA Microarrays and Gene Expression: From Experiments to Data Analysis and Modeling*. Cambridge University Press, 2002.

Baldi, P., Y. Chauvin, T. Hunkapillar, and M. McClure. Hidden Markov models of biological primary sequence information. *Proceedings of the National Academy of Sciences*, **91**, 1994.

Barnett, R., I. Barnes, M. J. Phillips, L. D. Martin, C. R. Harington, J. A. Leonard, and A. Cooper. Evolution of the extinct sabretooths and the American cheetah-like cat. *Current Biology*, **15**(15), 2005.

Benson, D. A., I. Karsch-Mizrachi, D. J. Lipman, J. Ostell, and D. L. Wheeler. GenBank: update. *Nucleic Acids Research*, **32**(1), 2004.

Bibb, M. J., R. A. Van Etten, C. T. Wright, M. W. Walberg, and D. A. Clayton. Sequence and gene organization of mouse mitochondrial DNA. *Cell*, **26**(2), 1981.

Blattner, F. R., G. III Plunkett, C. A. Bloch, N. T. Perna, V. Burland, M. Riley, J. Collado-Vides, J. D. Glasner, C. K. Rode, G. F. Mayhew, J. Gregor, N. W. Davis, H. A. Kirkpatrick, M. A. Goeden, D. J. Rose, B. Mau, and Y. Shao. The complete genome sequence of *Escherichia coli* K-12. *Science*, **277**(5331), 1997.

Bourque, G., P. A. Pevzner, and G. Tesler. Reconstructing the genomic architecture of ancestral mammals: lessons from human, mouse, and rat genomes. *Genome Research*, **14**(4), 2004.

Brazma, A., I. Jonassen, J. Vilo, and E. Ukkonen. Predicting gene regulatory elements in silico on a genomic scale. *Genome Research*, **8**, 1998.

Brown, M. P. S., W. N. Grundy, D. Lin, N. Cristianini, C. W. Sugnet, T. S. Furey, M. Ares. Jr, and D. Haussler. Knowledge-based analysis of microarray gene expression data by using support vector machines. *Proceedings of the National Academy of Sciences*, **97**, 2000.

Brown, T. *Genomes*. John Wiley & Sons, 1999.

Burge, C., and S. Karlin. Prediction of complete gene structures in human genomic DNA. *Journal of Molecular Biology*, **268**, 1997.

Burge, C., and S. Karlin. Finding the genes in genomic DNA. *Curr. Opin. Struct. Biol* (8), 1998.

Cann, R., and A. Wilson. The recent African genesis of humans. *Scientific American*, 2003.

Cavalli-Sforza, L. L. The DNA revolution in population genetics. *Trends in Genetics*, **14**, 1998.

Cavalli-Sforza, L. L. P. Menozzi, and A. Piazza. *The History and Geography of Human Genes*. Princeton University Press, 1996.

Cavalli-Sforza, L. L. *Genes, Peoples, and Languages*. University of California Press, 2001.

Chu, S., J. DeRisi, M. Eisen, J. Mulholland, D. Botstein, P. O. Brown, and I. Herskowitz. The transcriptional program of sporulation in budding yeast. *Science*, **282**, 1998.

Churchill, G. Stochastic models for heterogeneous DNA sequences. *Bull Math Biol.*, **51**(1), 1989.

Churchill, G. Hidden Markov chains and the analysis of genome structure. *Computers and Chemistry*, **16**(2), 1992.

Crick, F. H. On the genetic code. *Nobel Lectures, Physiology or Medicine 1942–1962*. Elsevier Publishing Company, 1964.

Crick, F. H., L. Barnett, S. Brenner, and R. J. Watta-Tobin. General nature of the genetic code for proteins. *Nature*, **192**, 1961.

DeRisi, J. L., V. R., Iyer, and P. O. Brown. Exploring the metabolic and genetic control of gene expression on a genomic scale. *Science*, **278**, 1997.

Doolittle, R. F. *Of URFs and ORFs*. University Science Books, 1986.

Doolittle, W. F. Uprooting the tree of life. *Scientific American*, February, 2000.

Durbin, R., S. Eddy, A. Krogh, and G. Mitchison. *Biological Sequence Analysis: Probabilistic Models of Proteins and Nucleic Acids*. Cambridge University Press, 1998.

Eddy, S., G. Mitchison, and R. Durbin. Maximum discrimination hidden Markov models of sequence consensus. *J. Comput. Biol.*, **2**, 1995.

Efron, B., and G. Gong. A leisurely look at the bootstrap, the jackknife, and cross-validation. *The American Statistician*, **37**(1), 1983.

Eickmann, M., S. Becker, H. D. Klenk, H. W. Doerr, K. Stadler, S. Censini, S. Guidotti, V. Masignani, M. Scarselli, M. Mora, C. Donati, J. H. Han, H. C. Song, S. Abrignani, A. Covacci, and R. Rappuoli. Phylogeny of the SARS coronavirus. *Science*, **302**, 2003.

Eisen, M. B., P. T. Spellman, P. O. Brown, and D. Botstein. Cluster analysis and display of genome-wide expression patterns. *Proceedings of the National Academy of Sciences USA*, **95**, 1998.

Ewens, W. J. and G. Grant. *Statistical Methods in Bioinformatics – An Introduction*. Springer, 2006.

Felsenstein, J. *Inferring Phylogenies*. Sinauer Associates, 2004.

Feynman, R. P. There's plenty of room at the bottom: an invitation to enter a new world of physics. *Engineering and Science*, **23**(5), 1960.

Fitch, W. M., and E. Margoliash. Construction of phylogenetic trees. *Science*, **155**, 1967.

Fleischmann, R. D. *et al*. Whole-genome random sequencing and assembly of *Haemophilus influenzae* rd. *Science*, **269**, 1995.

Fraser, C. M., J. D. Gocayne, O. White, M. D. Adams, R. A. Clayton, R. D. Fleischmann, C. J. Bult, A. R. Kerlavage, G. Sutton, J. M. Kelley, R. D. Fritchman, J. F. Weidman, K. V. Small, M. Sandusky, J. Fuhrmann, D. Nguyen, T. R. Utterback, D. M. Saudek, C. A. Phillips, J. M. Merrick, J. F. Tomb, B. A. Dougherty, K. F. Bott, P. C. Hu, T. S. Lucier, S. N. Peterson, H. O. Smith, C. A. Hutchison 3rd, and J. C. Venter. The minimal gene complement of *Mycoplasma genitalium*. *Science*, **270**(5235), 1995.

Gibson, G., and S. V. Muse. *A Primer of Genome Science*. Sinauer, 2004.

Goffeau, A., B. G. Barrell, H. Bussey, R. W. Davis, B. Dujon, H. Feldmann, F. Galibert, J. D. Hoheisel, C. Jacq, M. Johnston, E. J. Louis, H. W. Mewes, Y. Murakami, P. Philippsen, H. Tettelin H., and S. G. Oliver. Life with 6000 genes. *Science*, **274**, 1996.

Greene, W. AIDS and the immune system. *Scientific American*, September 1993.

Gribskov M., A. D. McLachlan, and D. Eisenberg. Profile analysis: detection of distantly related proteins. *Proceedings of the National Academy of Sciences*, **84**, 1987.

Gribskov, M. and D. Eisenberg. Profile analysis: detection of distantly related proteins. *Proceedings of the National Academy of Sciences USA*, **84**, 1987.

Guan, Y., B. J. Zheng, Y. Q. He, X. L. Liu, Z. X. Zhuang, C. L. Cheung, S. W. Luo, P. H. Li, L. J. Zhang, Y. J. Guan, K. M. Butt, K. L. Wong, K. W. Chan, W. Lim, K. F. Shortridge, K. Y. Yuen, J. S. M. Peiris, and L. L. M. Poon. Isolation and characterization of viruses related to the SARS coronavirus from animals in southern china. *Science*, **302**, 2003.

Guhathakurta, G., L. Palomar, G. D. Stormo, P. Tedesco, T. E. Johnson, D. W. Walker, G. Lithgow, S. Kim, and C. D. Link. Identification of a novel *cis*-regulatory element involved in the heat shock response in *Caenorhabditis elegans* using microarray gene expression and computational methods. *Genome Research*, **12**(5), 2002.

Handt, O., S. Meyer, and A. von Haeseler. Compilation of human mtDNA control region sequences. *Nucleic Acids Research*, **26**, 1998.

Harmer, S. L., J. B. Hogenesch, M. Straume, H.-S. Chang, B. Han, T. Zhu, X. Wang, J. A. Kreps, and S. A. Kay. Orchestrated transcription of key pathways in Arabidopsis by the circadian clock. *Science*, **290**, 2000.

Haussler, D., A. Krogh, K. Mian, and I. S. Sjölander. Protein modeling using hidden Markov models: analysis of globins. *Proceedings of the Hawaii International Conference on System Sciences*, volume 1. IEEE Computer Society Press, 1993.

Haussler, D., A. Krogh, and I. Mian. A hidden Markov model that finds genes in *E. coli* DNA. *Nucleic Acids Research*, **22**(22), 1994.

Haussler, D., E. D. Green, E. H. Margulies, and M. Blanchette. Identification and characterization of multi-species conserved sequences. *Genome Research*, **13**(12), 2003.

Higgins, D. G., J. D. Thompson, and T. J. Gibson. Using CLUSTAL for multiple sequence alignments. *Methods Enzymol*, **266**, 1996.

Hongchao, L., Y. Zhao, J. Zhang, Y. Wang, W. Li, X. Zhu, S. Sun, J. Xu, L. Ling, L. Cai, D. Bu, and R. Chen. Date of origin of the SARS coronavirus strains. *BMC Infectious Diseases*, **4**(3), 2004.

Holmes, E. C., and A. Rambaut. Viral evolution and the emergence of SARS coronavirus. *Phil. Trans. R. Soc. Lond. B*, **359**, 2004.

Horn, M., A. Collingro, S. Schmitz-Esser, C. L. Beier, U. Purkhold, B. Fartmann, P. Brandt, G. J. Nyakatura, M. Droege, D. Frishman, T. Rattei, H. W. Mewes, and M. Wagner. Illuminating the evolutionary history of Chlamydiae. *Science*, **304**(5671), 2004.

Hughes, J. D., P. W. Estep, S. Tavazoie, and G. M. Church. Computational identification of *cis*-regulatory elements associated with groups of functionally related genes in *Saccharomyces cerevisiae*. *Journal of Molecular Biology*, **296**, 2000.

Hurst, L. D. The Ka/Ks ratio: diagnosing the form of sequence evolution. *Trends in Genetics*, **18**(9), 2002.

Ingman, M., H. Kaessmann, S. Pääbo, and U. Gyllensten. Mitochondrial genome variation and the origin of modern humans. *Nature*, **408**, 2000.

Int'l. Human Genome Sequencing Consortium. Initial sequencing and analysis of the human genome. *Nature*, **409**(6822), 2001.

Jones, N. C., and P. A. Pevzner. *An Introduction to Bioinformatics Algorithms*. MIT Press, 2004.

Jukes, T. H., and C. R. Cantor. Evolution of protein molecules. In H. N. Munro, editor, *Mammalian Protein Metabolism*, pp. 21–32. Academic Press, 1969.

Kalman, S., W. Mitchell, R. Marathe, C. Lammel, J. Fan, R. W. Hyman, L. Olinger, J. Grimwood, R. W. Davis, and R. S. Stephens. Comparative genomes of *Chlamydia pneumoniae* and *Chlamydia trachomatis*. *Nat Genet.*, **21**(4), 1999.

Karlin, S., A. M. Campbell, and J. Mrazek. Comparative DNA analysis across diverse genomes. *Annu Rev Genet.*, **32**, 1998.

Kellis, M., N. Patterson, M. Endrizzi, B. Birren, and E. Lander. Sequencing and comparison of yeast species to identify genes and regulatory motifs. *Nature*, May 15, 2003.

Khorana, H. G., H. Buchi, H. Ghosh, N. Gupta, T. M. Jacob, H. Kossel, R. Morgan, S. A. Narang, E. Ohtsuka, and R. D. Wells. Polynucleotide synthesis and the genetic code. *Cold Spring Harb. Symp. Quant. Biol*, 1966.

Kimura, M. Evolutionary rate at the molecular level. *Nature*, **217**, 1968.

Kimura, M. A simple method for estimating evolutionary rates of base substitutions through comparative studies of nucleotide sequences. *Journal of Molecular Evolution*, **16**, 1980.

Kimura, M., and T. Ohta. On the stochastic model for estimation of mutational distance between homologous proteins. *Journal of Molecular Evolution*, **2**(1), 1972.

Koonin, E. V., and M. Y. Galperin. *Sequence – Evolution – Function: Computational Approaches in Comparative Genomics*. Springer Verlag, 2002.

Krings, M., A. Stone, R. W. Schmitz, H. Krainitzki, M. Stoneking, and S. Paabo. Neandertal DNA sequences and the origin of modern humans. *Cell*, **90**(1), 1997.

Krings, M., C. Capelli, F. Tschentscher, H. Geisert, S. Meyer, A. von Haeseler, K. Grossschmidt, G. Possnert, M. Paunovic, and S. Paabo. A view of Neandertal genetic diversity. *Nat. Genet.*, **26**(2), 2000.

Krogh, A., M. Brown, I. S. Mian, K. Sjlander, and D. Haussler. Hidden Markov models in computational biology: applications to protein modeling. *Journal of Molecular Biology*, **235**, 1994.

Kulp, D., D. Haussler, M. G. Reese, and F. H. Eeckman. A generalized hidden Markov model for the recognition of human genes in DNA. *Proceedings of the Fourth International Conference on Intelligent Systems for Molecular Biology*, pp. 134–142. AAAI Press, 1996.

Kumar, S. Patterns of nucleotide substitution in mitochondrial protein coding genes of vertebrates. *Genetics*, **1**(143), 1996.

Lawrence, C. E., S. Altschul, M. Boguski, J. Liu, A. Neuwald, and J. Wootton. Detecting subtle sequence signals: a Gibbs sampling strategy for multiple alignment. *Science*, **262**, 1993.

Lei, G., Q. Ji, W. Haibin, S. Yigang, and H. Bailin. Molecular phylogeny of coronaviruses including human SARS-cov. *Chinese Science Bulletin*, **48**(12), 2003.

Lu, Hongchao, Y. Zhao, J. Zhang, Y. Wang, W. Li, X. Zhu, S. Sun, J. Xu, L. Ling, L. Cai, D. Bu, and R. Chen. Date of origin of the SARS coronavirus strains. *BMC Infectious Diseases*, **4**(3), 2004.

Margulies, E. H., M. Blanchett, D. Haussler, and E. D. Green. Identification and characterization of multi-species conserved sequences. *Genome Research*, **13**(12), 2003.

Marra, M. A., S. J. Jones, C. R. Astell, R. A. Holt, A. Brooks-Wilson, Y. S. Butterfield, J. Khattra, J. K. Asano, S. A. Barber, S. Y. Chan, A. Cloutier, S. M. Coughlin, D. Freeman, N. Girn, O. L. Griffith, S. R. Leach, M. Mayo, H. McDonald, S. B. Montgomery, P. K. Pandoh, A. S. Petrescu, and A. G. Robertson. The genome sequence of the SARS-associated coronavirus. *Science*, **300**, 2003.

McCue, L. A., W. Thompson, C. S. Carmack, M. P. Ryan, J. S. Liu, V. Derbyshire, and C. E. Lawrence. Phylogenetic footprinting of transcription factor binding sites in proteobacterial genomes. *Nucleic Acids Research,* **29**, 2001.

Miyata, T., and T. Yasunaga. Molecular evolution of mRNA: a method for estimating evolutionary rates of synonymous and amino acid subtitutions from homologous nucleotide sequences and its applications. *Journal of Molecular Evolution*, **16**, 1980.

Muse, S. V. Estimating synonymous and nonsynonymous substitution rates. *Molecular Biology and Evolution*, **13**, 1996.

Needleman, S. B., and C. D. Wunsch. A general method applicable to the search for similarities in the amino acid sequence of two proteins. *Journal of Molecular Biology*, **48**, 1970.

Nei, M., and T. Gojobori. Simple methods for estimating the numbers of synonymous and nonsynonymous nucleotide substitutions. *Molecular Biology and Evolution*, **5**(3), 1986.

Nirenberg, M. W. The genetic code. In *Nobel Lectures, Physiology or Medicine 1963–1970*. Elsevier Publishing Company, 1972.

Ota, T., and M Nei. Variance and covariances of the numbers of synonymous and nonsynonymous substitutions per site. *Molecular Biology and Evolution*, **4**(11), 1994.

Ovchinnikov, I. V., A. Gotherstrom, G. P. Romanova, V. M. Kharitonov, K. Liden, and W. Goodwin. Molecular analysis of Neanderthal DNA from the northern caucasus. *Nature*, **404**, 2000.

Pennisi, E. Human genome: a low number wins the genesweep pool. *Science*, **300**(1484), 2003.

Rabiner, L. R. A tutorial on hidden Markov models and selected applications in speech recognition. *Proc. IEEE,* **77**, 1989.

Reilley, B., M. Van Herp, D. Sermand, and N. Dentico: SARS and Carlo Urbani. *New England Journal of Medicine*, **348**(20), 2003.

Rota, P. A., M. S. Oberste, S. S. Monroe, W. A. Nix, R. Campagnoli, J. P. Icenogle, S. Penaranda, B. Bankamp, K. Maher, M. H. Chen, S. Tong, A. Tamin, L. Lowe, M. Frace, J. L. DeRisi, Q. Chen, D. Wang, D. D. Erdman, T. C. Peret, C. Burns, T. G. Ksiazek, P. E. Rollin, A. Sanchez, S. Liffick, and B. Holloway. Characterization of a novel coronavirus associated with severe acute respiratory syndrome. *Science*, **300**, 2003.

Saitou, N., and M. Nei. The neighbor-joining method: a new method for reconstructing phylogenetic trees. *Molecular Biology and Evolution*, **4**, 1987.

Sanger, F., A. R. Coulson, T. Friedmann, G. M. Air, B. G. Barrell, N. L. Brown, J. C. Fiddes, C. A. Hutchison 3rd, P. M. Slocombe, and M. Smith. The nucleotide sequence of bacteriophage phix174. *Journal of Molecular Biology*, **125**(2), 1978.

Sanger, F., Coulson A. R., Hong G. F., D. F. Hill, and G. B. Petersen. Nucleotide sequence of bacteriophage lambda DNA. *Journal of Molecular Biology*, **162**, 1982.

Schmitz, R. W., D. Serre, G. Bonani, S. Feine, F. Hillgruber, H. Krainitzki, S. Paabo, and F. H. Smith. The Neandertal type site revisited: interdisciplinary investigations of skeletal remains from the Neander Valley, Germany. *Proceedings of the National Academy of Sciences USA*, **99**(20), 2002.

Smith, T. F., and M. S. Waterman. Comparison in biosequences. *Advances in Applied Mathematics*, **2**, 1981.

Spellman, P. T., G. Sherlock, M. Q. Zhang, V. R. Iyer, K. Anders, M. B. Eisen, P. O. Brown, D. Botstein, and B. Futcher. Comprehensive identification of cell cycle-regulated genes of the yeast *Saccharomyces cerevisiae* by microarray hybridization. *Mol Biol Cell*, **9**, 1998.

Suzuki, Y., and T Gojobori. A method for detecting positive selection at single amino acid sites. *Molecular Biology and Evolution*, **10**(16), 1999.

Sykes, B. *The Seven Daughters of Eve*. W. W. Norton & Company, 2002.

The Chinese SARS Molecular Epidemiology Consortium. Molecular evolution of the SARS coronavirus during the course of the SARS epidemic in China. *Science*, **303**, 2003.

Thompson, J. D., D. G. Higgins, and T. J. Gibson. CLUSTAL W: improving the sensitivity of progressive multiple sequence alignment through sequence weighting, position-specific gap penalties and weight matrix choice. *Nucleic Acids Research*, **22**, 1994.

Thorne, J. L., H. Kishino, and J. Felsenstein. An evolutionary model for maximum likelihood alignment of DNA sequences. *Molecular Biology and Evolution*, **2**(33), 1991.

Tzeng, Y. H., R. Pan, and W. H. Li. Comparison of three methods for estimating rates of synonymous and non-synonymous nucleotide substitutions. *Molecular Biology and Evolution*, **21**(12), 2004.

Venter, J. C., *et al*. The sequence of the human genome. *Science*, **291**(5507), 2001.

Wain-Hobson, S., P. Sonigo, O. Danos, S. Cole, and M. Alizon. Nucleotide sequence of the AIDS virus, LAV. *Cell*, **40**(1), 1985.

Watson, J., The involvement of RNA in the synthesis of proteins. In *Nobel Lectures, Physiology or Medicine 1942–1962*. Elsevier Publishing Company, 1964.

Watson, J., and F. Crick. A structure for deoxyribose nucleic acid. *Nature*, **171**(4356), 1953.

Yang, Z., and J. Bielawski. Statistical methods for detecting molecular adaptation. *Trends Ecol Evol.*, **15**, 2000.

Zeng, F., K. Y. C. Chow, and F. C. Leung. Estimated timing of the last common ancestor of the SARS coronavirus. *New England Journal of Medicine*, **349**, 25, 2003.

Zhang, Y., and N. Zheng. Genomic phylogeny of SARS coronavirus suggested that Guangdong province is the origin area. Unpublished Manuscript, 2003.

Zozulya, S., F. Echeverri, and T. Nguyen. The human olfactory receptor repertoire. *Genome Biology* **2**, 2001.

Index

3-point formula, 118
4-point condition, 119

ab initio methods, 29, 40
accession number, 18, 19
additive distance, 117
additive tree, 117
Affymetrix, 147
AIDS, 96
Alanine, 24
AlignACE, 172
alignment, 39, 48
    approximate, 51
    global, 42, 43, 48
    local, 47, 51
    multiple, 53, 62, 71
    optimal global, 45
    optimal local, 46
    pairwise, 42
alignment score, 48
alignment scoring function, 43
allele, 80
alternative hypothesis, 32
Altschul, Stephen, 42, 51
amino acid, xiii, 44
amino acid alphabet, 24
amino acid sequence, 7
amino acid substitution matrix, 82
amino acids, 23
aniridia, 38, 60
Anopheles gambiae, 5
approximate alignment, 51
Arabidopsis thaliana, 2, *159*, *160*, *167*
Arber, Werner, 16
Archaea, 4
Arginine, 24
Asparagine, 24
Aspartic acid, 24
Avery, Oswald, xiv
Axel, Richard, 61
AZT, 97

baker's yeast, 1
base, 3, 4
best reciprocal hit, 132
binding site, 16, 160, 161
bioinformatics, xii
biological validation, 171
Birney, Ewan, 22
BLAST, xv, 40, 51, 60

BLOSUM matrix, 45, 83
blue whale, 95
bonobo, 78, 85, 93
bootstrap, 35
branch length, 115
branches, 113
BRH, *see* best reciprocal hit
Brown, Pat, 3, 143
buchnera, *136*
Buck Linda, 61

Caenorhabditis elegans, 5, *21*, *22*
cancer, 80
Cantor, Charles, 88, 95
Cavalli-Sforza Luigi Luca, 95
CCA1, 160
CCR5, 107
cDNA, 144
cDNA microarray, 145
central dogma, 25
change point analysis, 13, 62
chaos game representation, 15
chimpanzee, 78, 85, 93, 108
Chlamydia, xvi, *4*
Chlamydia pneumoniae, *129*, *131*
Chlamydia trachomatis, *2*, *129*, *131*
chloroplast, 5, 129
chromosome, 3, 30
Churchill, Gary, 63
circadian clock, xvii, 159
CLUSTALW, 54, 60
clustering, 151
    k-means, 151
    hierarchical, 151
codon, 26, 81
    start, 29, 33
    stop, 26, 28, 33
codon bias, 34, 100
codon distribution
    non-uniform, 34
    uniform, 34
codon sequence, 7
codon structure, 69
comparative genomics, 130
comparison-based methods, 29
complementarity, 3, 30
consensus sequence, 163
coronavirus, 111
correlation coefficient, 151

cow, 95
Crick, Francis, xiv, 21, 27, 37
CRS, 84
Cysteine, 24

D-loop, 84
Danio rerio, *5*
database searching, 40
Dayhoff, Margaret, 82
DDBJ database, 18
degradase, 23
delta method, 90
dendrogram, 155
diauxic shift, 141, 145, 147, 153
dimer, 14
dinucleotide, 14
diploid, 79
directed tree, 115
distance matrix, 117
distance measures, 151
distance-based methods, 117
DNA, xiii, xiv, 3, 26
    regulatory, 161
DNA alignment, 44
DNA fingerprinting, 81
DNA microarray, 142
DNA sequence, xiv, 3, 6, 7, 79
Drosophila melanogaster, *5*, *38*, *53*
drug resistance, xvi
duplications, 81
dynamic programming, 46, 56, 62, 75

E-value, 52
E. coli K12, *2*, *13*, *128*
elephant, 94
EM algorithm, *see*
    expectation-maximization algorithm
EMBL database, 18
emission matrix, 65, 66
emission probability, 63
ENV, 107, 121, 127
enzyme, xiii
epitopes, 98
EST, 144
Eubacteria, 4, 161
Eukaryote, xiii, 69
evening element, 167
evolution, 97, 98
exceptions, xii, 26
exon, 29, 70

expectation-maximization algorithm, 66, 76, 166
exploratory data analysis, 148
external node, 113
eyeless gene, 38, 41, 46, 49, 60

false negative, *see* Type II error
false positive, *see* Type I error
fast heuristic methods, 42
FASTA, 18, 51
FASTA format, 19
footprinting, 136
forward algorithm, 66, 76
frame shift mutation, 29
function
    prediction, 40, 62

GAG, 108
GC content, 12
Gehring, Walter, 38
GenBank, 18
gene, xiv, 3
gene duplication, 41, 130
gene expression, xv
gene family, 41, 132, 133
gene finding, 29, *see* gene prediction, 48, 62, 69
    prokaryotic, 22
gene function, 154
gene-finding, 28, 40
    prokaryotic, 29
GeneChip, 147
genetic algorithms, 98
genetic code, 26
    mitochondrial, 37
genetic distance, 86, 87, 88, 89, 91
genome, 3, 6
    annotation, 1
    eukaryotic, 4
    organelle, 5
    prokaryotic, 4
    viral, 4
genome signature, 15
germline mutation, 80
gibbon, 93
Gibbs sampling, 165, 166
Gibson, Toby, 54
Gish, Warren, 42
global alignment, 42, 43, 49
    optimal, 45
Glutamic acid, 24
Glutamine, 24

Glycine, 24
Gojobori, Takashi, 102
gorilla, 85, 93
gp120, 107
gp160, 107
gp41, 107
graph
    cyclic, 67
GTR model, 92

Haemophilus influenzae, xv, 1, 2, 4, 10, 12, 14, 16, 18, 21, 25, 31, 35, 36
haplotype, 85
Harmer, Stacey, 167
Haussler, David, 63
heat maps, 155
helix, double, 3
hemoglobin, 23
hidden Markov model, xv, 13, 62, 63, 65, 67, 69
hierarchical clustering, 133
Higgins, Desmond, 54
Histidine, 24
HIV, 96, 127
HIV genome, 105
Holley, Robert, 26
homeobox domain, 38, 41
Homeobox, 52
Homo erectus, 78, 79, 93
Homo habilis, 78
Homo neanderthalis, 78, 85
Homo sapiens, xv, 2, 5, 79, 85, 92
Homo sapiens mitochondrion, 18
homolog, 38, 40
homologous sequence, 67
homology, 40, 48, 51, 53
    multiple levels of, 39
homology-based methods, 29
horizontal gene transfer, 12
Hotel Metropole, 111, 121, 122
hotspot, 52
HOX, 38
HOX domain, 49
HOX gene, 49
human genome sequence, 2
human mtDNA, 2
HVR, *see* hypervariable region
hybridization, 144
hydrophilic, 72
hydrophobic, 72
hydrophobicity, 82
hypervariable region, 18, 84, 92, 100
Hypothesis Testing, 31

i.i.d, 7, 12
image processing, 146
immune system, 97, 98
indel, 41, 81
insulin, 23
intergenic region, 136
internal node, 113
intron, 29, 63, 69, 70
inversions, 81
Isoleucine, 24

Java Man, 78
Jukes, Thomas, 88, 95
Jukes–Cantor formula, 88, 90, 91

k-mers, 14
Ka/Ks Ratio, 100
Khorana, Gobind, 26, 37
Kimura Model, 91
Kimura, Motoo, 91, 95, 100
kinking, 16
KL divergence, 165

Leakey, Louis, 78
leaves, 113
length of a tree, 118
Leucine, 24
LHY, 160
ligase, 23
likelihood, 8
Lipman, David, 42
loaded dice, 64
local alignment, 42, 47, 51
    optimal, 46
locus, 19
Lysine, 24

mad cow disease, 25
malaria, 96
mammoth, 94
manganese-dependent superoxide dismutase, 25
Markov chain, 8, 9, 88
Markov DNA sequence, 9
Markov model, 7, 9, 48
master regularity gene, 38
matrix
    substitution, 82
maximal segment pair, 51
MEGA, 109
MEME, 172
Mendel, Gregor, xiv
metabolism, xiii
methionine, 24, 28

microarray, xv, 144
  one-dye, 147
  two-dye, 146
  cDNA, 145
microsatellites, 81
midpoint rooting, 120
Miller, Webb, 42
missing data, 150
mitochondria, 5, 26, 129
motif, 15, 16, 54, 161
  ungapped, 163
motif bias, 14
motif finding, 160, 164
mouse, 108, 160
mRNA, 26, 28, 70
mtDNA, 5, 82, 83, 85, 95
multidimensional scaling, 92, 124
multinomial model, 7, 9, 16, 48
multiple alignment, 53, 62, 71
multiple testing, 36
MUMmer, 140
Mus musculus, *5*, *53*
mutation, 79, 80, 81, 82, 86, 97
  fixed, 86
  germline, 80
  neutral, 86
  point, 80
Mycoplasma genitalium, *1*, *2*, *4*, *18*, *21*, *22*, *31*, *35*, *36*, *129*, *138*
Mycoplasma pneumoniae, *138*
Myers, Gene, 42

Nathans, Dan, 16
natural selection, 97
Neanderthal, xv, 19, 78, 85, 92, 93, 95, 127
Needleman, Saul, 42
Needleman–Wunsch algorithm, 45, 47, 51, 54, 55, 58, 60
Nei, Masatoshi, 102, 118
Nei–Gojobori Algorithm, 102, 105
neighbor-joining algorithm, 117, 118, 119, 120
neighborliness, 119
network
  phylogenetic, 112
neurogenesis, 49
neutral mutation, 86
Neutral Theory of Evolution, 100
Newick format, 115, 126
Nirenberg, Marshall, 26, 37
NJ algorithm, *see* neighbor-joining algorithm

non-synonymous substitution, 99, 101
nucleotides, 3, 4, 6, 8
null hypothesis, 32

odds ratio, 16
odorant receptors, 61, 69, 71, 72, 127
olfactory system, 61
open reading frame, 29, 30
optimal global alignment, 45
optimal local alignment, 46
orangutan, 85, 93
ORF, *see* open reading frame, *see* Open Reading Frame, 132
ORF finding, 69, 106
ortholog, 41
orthologous genes, 41
orthology, 41, 131
Oryza sativa, 5
out of africa, 93
outgroup, 113
oxidative phosphorylation, 83

p-value, 32
paired-box domain, 38, 42
pairwise alignment, 42
palindrome, 17
palm civet, 111, 121
PAM matrix, 45, 83
paralogous genes, 41
paralogy, 41, 131
parasite, 129
pathway, xiv
pattern detection, 62
pattern discovery, 18, 166
pattern matching, 18, 166
PAX, 38
PAX domain, 49
PAX gene, 49, 50
Peking Man, 78
permutaton test, 35
phage, 1, 2, 13, 18, 20, 66, 77
Phenylalanine, 24
pheromone, 61
pHMM, *see* profile HMM, 68, 71
Phylip, 127
phylogenetic analysis, 114
phylogenetic footprinting, 136
phylogenetic network, 112
phylogenetic tree, xvi, 93, 112, 116
phylogenetics, 112
polymerase, 108, 161
polymorphism, 80,
polypeptides, 24

polyploid, 130
prediction of function, 40, 62
primate evolution, 93
prion, 25
probabilistic model, 6
probability, 8
  conditional, 9
  joint, 9
  transition, 8
probes, 144
profile, 68
profile HMM, 68
Prokaryote, xiii, 4
Proline, 24
promoter, 30, 163
protein, xiii, 23, 26
  domains, 41
protein coding, 60
protein fold prediction, 24
protein folding, 24
protozoa, 128
Prusiner, Stanley, 25
pseudocount, 165
pseudogenes, 61
PSSM, 68, 163, 166
PSWM, *see* PSSM
purines, 81
pyrimidines, 81

randomization test, 34
reading frame, 28
recombination, 116
reference design, 147
regulatory DNA, 161
repeats, 169
replicase, 121
reversal distance, 137
reversal sort algorithm, 138
rhodopsin, 71
ribosome, 26, 28
RNA, 26
RNA sequence, 7
RNA-coding genes, 69
rooted tree, 113

sabre-tooth tiger, 95
Saccharomyces cerevisiae, *1*, *2*, *5*, *21*, *141*, 142
Saitou, Naruya, 118
Sanger, Fred, 1, 21
SARS, xvi, 2, 108, 110, 115
saturation, 87

scoring function, 44, 164
    alignment, 43
segment pair, 51
    maximal, 51
segmentation, 62, 64
selection
    negative, 97
    positive, 97
    purifying, 97
sequence alignment, xv, 3, 39
sequence assembly, 40
sequence divergence, 40
sequence evolution, 88
sequence polymorphism, 80
sequence similarity, xv, 40
Serine, 24
Sharp, Paul, 54
significance level, 32
significant, 32
similarity, 51
Single Nucleotide Polymorphism, *see*
    SNP
single nucleotide polymorphisms, xvi
SIV, 127
sliding window, 107
Smith, Hamilton, 16
Smith, Temple, 42
Smith–Waterman algorithm, 47, 49, 50,
    54, 58, 59, 60
SNP, 80, 81
sorting by reversals, 136
speciation, 41, 131
Spike gene, 121
splice sites, 70
standard nucleotide alphabet, 20
start codon, 29, 33
stop codon, 26, 28, 33, 34, 103

STR, 81
string, 7
subsequence, 7
substitution, 82, 86
    matrix, 44
    multiple, 87
    non-synonymous, 99
    synonymous, 99
substitution matrix, 82
substitution rate, 86
substring, 7
symbiont, 128
synonymous substitution, 99, 101
synteny, 135, 136

T Cells, 98
tabular computation, 56
tandem repeats, 81
TATA-box, 161
taxa, 112
test statistic, 32
theorem of total probability, 66
Thompson, Julie, 54
Threonine, 24, 27
tobacco, 160
TOC1, 160
topology, 113
trace-back, 57
transcription, 26
transcription factors, 160
transition matrix, 9, 65, 66
transition probability, 63
transitions, 81
translation, 26
transmembrane domain, 61
tranversions, 81
tree, 116

additive, 117
bifurcating, 113
directed, 115
oriented, 114
phylogenetic, 112
rooted, 113
unrooted, 113
Tryptophan, 24
Type I error, 32, 33
Type II error, 33
Tyrosine, 24

ultrametricity, 120
ungapped motif, 163
unrooted tree, 113
untranslated regions, 28
UPGMA, 120
upstream region, 163
Urbani strain, 122
Urbani, Carlo, 110

Valine, 24
variation between species, 86
Venter, Craig, 1
visualization, 155
Viterbi algorithm, 66, 75

Waterman, Michael, 42
Watson, James, xiv, 21, 37
whole-genome analysis, xvi,
    5
wine, 141
Wunsch, Christian, 42

yeast, 141, 142, 143, 172

zebrafish, 5